SMILE
BECAUSE
IT
HAPPENED

A Memoir

By
Margaret Jean Baptist

FriesenPress

One Printers Way
Altona, MB R0G 0B0
Canada

www.friesenpress.com

Copyright © 2022 by Margaret Jean Baptist
First Edition — 2022

Photos from family albums unless noted otherwise.

All rights reserved.

ISBN
978-1-03-911240-7 (Hardcover)
978-1-03-911239-1 (Paperback)
978-1-03-911241-4 (eBook)

1. BIOGRAPHY & AUTOBIOGRAPHY, PERSONAL MEMOIRS

Distributed to the trade by The Ingram Book Company

TABLE OF CONTENTS

This book is dedicated to my family, who bring joy to my life:

-my children–Darryl, Lloyd, and Lynn,
-my grandchildren–Laura, Jason, Kim, Kyle, and Marlo,
-my great-grandchildren–Connor, Zachery, Emilee, Rowyn, Sawyer, Huxley, Forrest, Audrey and Eamon,

-my great-great-grandson, Xavier,

and all the greats and great-greats to come,

and in loving memory of my husband John, and great-grandson Jordan.

Family is not an important thing,

it's everything.

Michael J. Fox

INTRODUCTION

When I retired in 1992, I told my grandchildren I was going to write a memoir describing my childhood growing up during the depression of the 1930s, so they could see how different life was back then.

I did make a start. I have 21 hand-written pages that I produced over the next few years. And then the project sat, though it continued to niggle at the back of my mind. However, like a New Year's resolution, it was easy to leave it merely niggling–for years. Finally, in 2011, when I learned the University of Winnipeg was offering an adult education course on *Writing Your Memoir,* with instructor Diane Kristjansson, I decided the time had come to translate my goal into action.

While taking three courses with Diane in 2011 and 2012, I began writing again. This book has been nine years in the making, writing during winter months only, as summer weather in Winnipeg is too precious to spend indoors at a computer. Also, current life events frequently intervened, taking precedence over any mining of memories–Christmas holidays, family visits, caring for my husband who developed dementia, dealing with his death as well as the loss of five other family members, and lastly, recovering from my knee-replacement surgery. But at last, here it is.

This is not a straightforward, linear reflection on my life. I realized most of the first pieces I was writing dealt with my childhood bout with osteo-myelitis. It was clearly a defining event in my life, so those memories form the first section of the book. Then I flip back in time to stories about my parents and grandparents, before progressing to my childhood, followed by my marriage and our family stories. The articles in the next section are not truly memoir, as most were written shortly after the events occurred, though sometimes they evoked childhood memories. In fact, in every section, stories may span many years, starting in the past and ending with a modern perspective, or conversely, starting today and going back in time. Letters to my mother, father, two sisters, two brothers, a great-grandson, and my husband are in an "In Memory" section. I have chosen to end with a look to the future in a letter to my great-great-great-grandchildren.

Reliving some memories was painful. I could feel the agony of tape being pulled off tender flesh in "I Still Hate Adhesive Tape." And even worse, while writing "My Conductor" I was overcome by the depth of loneliness I experienced during those months in the hospital and began to weep. It was the first time I cried while I wrote, but not the last. Exploring my complicated relationship with my father was an emotionally difficult process that led to tears. All the letters in the "In Memory" section were heart-wrenching to write, but also reminded me of many happy family times. In "Reading, Writing, and 'Rithmetic," I experienced anew the hurt caused by a teacher's unthinking comments. In that same piece I recalled the loneliness of my first year away from home, but also my happiness when my sisters joined me in my final year of high school.

One of the joys of the writing has been reliving so many happy times and events in my life—the freedom of childhood on the farm, the sharing of life with my new husband, the arrival of our babies, and all the family fun and love that has enriched my life. Recently, in a discussion about aging parents, my son Lloyd said, "My mother is 88—and she's getting younger." Could it be all the "time-travelling" I have been doing?

As I was writing, I frequently found recalling one memory would wake another to float up from the depths of my unconscious. For example, when describing our goofy, springtime wading game in "Fun for Free," the memory of "My Magic Slough" resurfaced—just like magic.

Indeed, the process of writing is a bit like mining. You dig up memories, and then as you dig deeper, you gain new understandings and perspectives. For example, my mother appears in many stories, and as I was writing I gained an increasing understanding and appreciation of her wisdom and strength of character. The writing has also been a process in self-discovery, which I explore in "Osteomyelitis and Me", but is implicit in many later pieces.

I realize I am, inherently, a very private person, and outside of my family, do not express feelings easily. In my writing I have learned to "loosen up"–to share my life and my innermost emotions, thoughts, and beliefs. It has been an interesting journey and one I am glad I began.

However, I discovered how fallible memory is after I wrote "My Conductor," as explained in the addendum to that story. As another example, Auntie Violet, in the forward to the *Bainbridge/Putland Centennial History Book*, says their cooler was a dugout, lined with stones, in the hill near the house. In the piece I wrote about my grandparents' log home, I describe the cold room behind the kitchen. Is my memory correct? Was the dugout in the hill no longer being used? I don't know. I just know I described it as it is in my memory.

Many years ago, our sister Lorna wrote a 10-page story of her life and then asked each of her siblings to write a short piece on their lives. When we three oldest compared our stories, we found the others remembered events we had completely forgotten, or our memories of the same event often varied in the details. For example, Mary remembered Auntie Lucille having a costume malfunction on one of our annual trips to the lake–"her boobies didn't get tucked in properly and were shamelessly poking out the bottom of the bra of her two-piece bathing suit." I have no memory of that momentous event, so it does not appear in my story about those lake days. Another example is when Lorna wrote about our mother losing a bandage on her finger, but in her story, it ended up in a sealer of pork and beans, not a sausage, as I remember it in my story "An Unexpected Ingredient."

The stories in this book are the truth as I remember them. That is the best I can do.

FAMILY TREES

My Putland Great- Grandparents

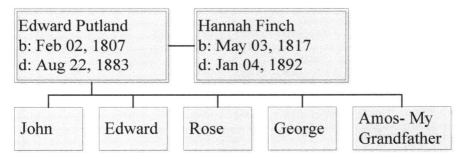

My Baimbridge Great- Grandparents

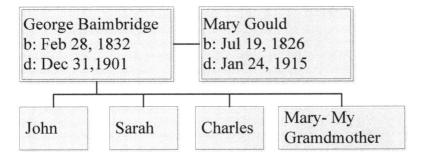

My Putland Grandparents

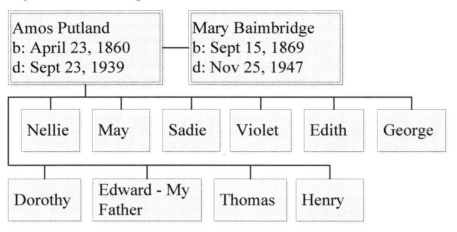

Amos Putland
b: April 23, 1860
d: Sept 23, 1939

Mary Baimbridge
b: Sept 15, 1869
d: Nov 25, 1947

Nellie | May | Sadie | Violet | Edith | George

Dorothy | Edward - My Father | Thomas | Henry

My Fraser Great-Grandparents

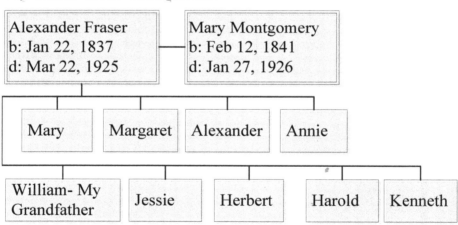

Alexander Fraser
b: Jan 22, 1837
d: Mar 22, 1925

Mary Montgomery
b: Feb 12, 1841
d: Jan 27, 1926

Mary | Margaret | Alexander | Annie

William- My Grandfather | Jessie | Herbert | Harold | Kenneth

My Burton Great-Grandparents

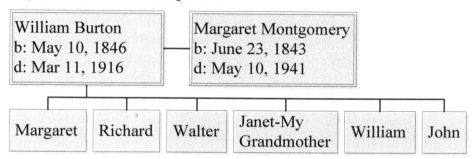

William Burton	Margaret Montgomery
b: May 10, 1846	b: June 23, 1843
d: Mar 11, 1916	d: May 10, 1941

Margaret	Richard	Walter	Janet-My Grandmother	William	John

My Fraser Grandparents

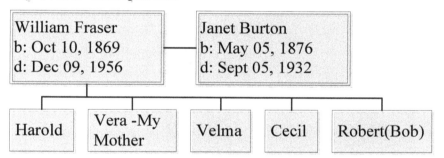

William Fraser	Janet Burton
b: Oct 10, 1869	b: May 05, 1876
d: Dec 09, 1956	d: Sept 05, 1932

Harold	Vera -My Mother	Velma	Cecil	Robert(Bob)

My Parents

Edward John Putland
b: July 09, 1907
d: Aug 07,1999

Vera Margaret Fraser
b: April 03,1902
d: Feb 12, 1971

Margaret Jean
b: Nov 08, 1932

Mary Elizabeth
b: Dec 08, 1933
d: Jan 28, 2008

Lorna Velma May
b: May 08, 1935
d: Jan 15, 2017

William Edward
b: June 01, 1937
d: Aug 15, 2019

Denis Gordon
b: Dec 27, 1939
d: June 16 2015

Leila
b: 1941

Leslie
b: 1945

PART 1
Osteomyelitis and Me

The Day That Changed My Life

Sunday, January 19th, 1941. When I opened my eyes that morning, I did not know that this day would change my eight-year-old life forever.

Feeling the winter chill in my bedroom, I wrap myself tighter in my cocoon of cozy bedcovers till I hear my mother's voice calling up the stairs, "Time to get up." Reluctantly, I throw back the blankets and swing my legs over the side of the bed to sit up. To my surprise I feel a sharp stab of pain. My leg has been sore since I fell on a patch of ice several days ago, but nothing like this.

It takes me longer than usual to get dressed as I move cautiously, trying to avoid hurting my leg. At a second call from Mama, I yell, "Coming." One step on my left leg and the pain makes me gasp. I hop on my right foot to the top of the stairs. Holding onto the handrail, I carefully lower myself to the top step and slide down the stairs on my bum, one step at a time. Setting the breakfast table is my job. I hop into the kitchen and hop around the table as I put cereal bowls, cutlery, and glasses in place.

"Don't be so silly, Jean," Mama says.

"My leg hurts."

"Can't be that bad."

"It is. I can't stand on it."

My mother looks up sharply from the oatmeal porridge she is stirring. "Where's it hurt?"

"Up here." I point to my hip.

Pausing for a moment in her stirring, Mama lifts my skirt. "Hmm...is swollen." I feel her cool hand on my forehead. "Go lie on the couch. I'll finish the table."

I hop to the little room we call a parlour and carefully lower myself onto the "couch," a narrow cot covered with one of my mother's colourful patchwork quilts. "Mama," I call. "I can't get my leg up on the couch."

My mother is there in an instant. She is careful as she lifts my leg, but I still go, "Ow! Ow!" a few times before I am lying down. "I'll bring your breakfast," Mama says and hurries back to her porridge.

I remember little about the next two days. I do recall crying out in pain whenever my one-year-old brother, Denis, toddled over to investigate and bumped into my bed, till my mother used chairs to barricade the archway between the living room and the parlour.

By the time I was taken to see Dr. Mackenzie in Langenburg I had a temperature of 104° and was drifting in and out of consciousness. The diagnosis was osteomyelitis, an infection of the bone, and my parents were informed that I would have to go to a hospital in Winnipeg. All I understood, in a hazy kind of way, was that my mother and I were going on the train.

I do have one short, clear memory fragment. I am lying against my mother. We are in an open cutter and wrapped in a heavy buffalo skin blanket. The bite of frosty air feels wonderful on my face. That is probably what roused me to consciousness. I am surprised to see the cutter is not being pulled by a horse. The doctor and his wife each have a grip on one of the shafts and are pulling my mother and me down the snow-packed street to the train.

Many months, maybe years later, when I asked my mother if this really happened, she said it did. I never asked, "Why?" So all I can do now is surmise. By 1941, the doctor would certainly have had a car for making house calls. Although he would have sold the horses he no longer needed, the cutter he once used for winter travel was probably still sitting in his backyard. I imagine he decided it would cause less pain to get me into an open cutter than into a car, so he and his wife used a little small-town ingenuity to make me more comfortable on what was to become a long journey back to the life I had before, but forever changed.

That was it–one crystal clear memory before, thankfully, the mind fog returned, making me oblivious to the pain of being transferred to the train. Most of that night-time trip–my first train ride–was a semi-conscious blur.

My Conductor

The need to pee rouses me from my stupor.

I look at my mother sitting on the seat across from me. She is sound asleep, eyes shut, head tilted against the seat back, mouth gaping slightly open.

I try to move. I can't. It hurts too much. "Mama," I say. My mother's eyes fly open. "I have to pee."

Mama rises quickly. "I need the conductor's help–be right back," she says and hurries away.

I cry out in pain as two strong arms pick me up and carry me. It hurts even more and my crying becomes a wail as Mama gently pulls down my panties while I am still held in those strong arms.

As the arms begin to slowly tighten, attempting to move me into a sitting position, my wail becomes an agonized howl.

"Impossible. She can't sit on the toilet." I hear a man's voice.

"She has to go." Mama sounds desperate.

The man is holding me over the wash basin. "All right," he says gently. "You can go now." I pee in the wash basin even though I know that is not what you are supposed to do. I wonder if the man will get in trouble for letting me go there.

This is how the conductor came into my life.

§

I open my eyes groggily. I must be lying in a high bed because Mama is sitting beside me, and I can see only the top part of her. I am confused. "Where am I?"

"You're in St. Boniface hospital in Winnipeg," Mama says. "The doctors say you have osteomyelitis."

"What's......?" I stop. I don't know how to say the word.

"Osteomyelitis," Mama says slowly. "It's from the Latin word "osteo," for bone. You've got an infection in your hip bone."

"I can't move," I complain.

"That's because you've got weights fastened to your legs. They'll keep your legs straight till your hip heals." Mama shows me the pulleys attached to the foot of the bed and explains how the weights are suspended over the pulleys. "It's called traction," she says. That is another new word for me to remember.

§

Mama comes to see me every day, bringing a surprise. There is always a book, which she reads to me. After she leaves, I read it by myself. If I don't remember a word, I sound it out. Sometimes there is another surprise. In the drawer of my bedside table, there is a fairy-tale colouring book, a box of rainbow-coloured crayons, a book of cut-out dolls, and a pair of scissors. The scissors have round ends so I can't accidentally poke myself. Yesterday, the book was *Goldilocks and the Three Bears*. After she read the story to me, Mama gave me a little box. Inside were four tiny, pink celluloid dolls–Goldilocks and the three bears. I think pink is a funny colour for bears, but Mama said it wouldn't work to try and colour them with crayons. When I use them to tell the story I pretend they are brown, like in the book.

Today Mama brought me a pad of writing paper, a pencil, and a stamped envelope with her address written on the front. This is the last day she can visit me in the hospital. She needs to go home to look after the rest of the kids. When I write a letter to her, she will answer it and send me another stamped envelope. She says I can give my letters to the conductor to mail when he comes to see me. She explains that it was the conductor who helped me pee on the train. She says the conductor knows that she is going home, and after she leaves he will try to visit me once a week.

§

I am watching the door with anticipation because I know the conductor is coming today. He always brings a treat to eat. The first time he brought a bag of oranges, my favourite fruit, and a box of nuts. The nuts were a mixture–peanuts, almonds, cashews, filberts, pecans, walnuts, and maca-damia nuts. I didn't know there were so many different nuts. The only ones I recognized were peanuts and walnuts. The conductor told me the names of the others so now I know which nut I am eating. For Easter, he gave me a green and yellow basket with a chocolate hen sitting on chocolate eggs. The eggs, wrapped in shiny red, blue, gold and silver foil, were hiding in a nest of skinny strips of green paper, pretending to be straw. Last week, the surprise was a bag of big, green grapes. They were the biggest grapes I have ever seen. When my teeth popped through the crunchy skin they were so-o-o delicious, sweet, and juicy. I ate so many I got a little sick to my stomach and kept the sisters busy the next day bringing me the bedpan.

He is here. I can hear him talking to one of the sisters. They think he is a kind man. I think he is the kindest man in the world. He is holding something round and flat in front of him as he comes through the doorway. Last week he said he was going to bring me a pie the next time he came–and he has! When I fold back the wrapping paper I see it is a cherry pie. I have never tasted a cherry pie. Mama makes apple and raisin and rhubarb and chocolate and lemon meringue pies, but she has never made a cherry pie.

The conductor asks the sister to cut a piece for each of us. Because I can't sit up he tucks a towel under my chin so I don't dribble any of the sweet juice on my gown. We eat our treat together and agree it is a perfect pie. We laugh because we both end up with lips stained cherry red. I do dribble a bit of juice on the towel, but I know the sister won't care. "We'll just throw it in the laundry," she'll say.

After we finish our pie, the conductor picks a story for me to read to him. He chooses *Cinderella*. Then I read him the last letter from Mama and give him my letter to mail. He gets up to leave, pats my shoulder, and says, "See you next week. And remember, only one piece of pie a day."

§

I am tired. I didn't feel like reading a book to the conductor today. When he asks me for the letter to mail to Mama, I don't have one. "I didn't feel like writing," I say. When the conductor gives my hand a little squeeze to say goodbye, he looks at my fingernails. I see him look at my other hand. "See you soon," he says and is gone. I lift my hands and stare at my nails. They have a lot of little white spots. I never noticed the spots before. I wonder if they were always there.

§

My mother receives a letter from the doctor. In part, it says:

> *We are having a great deal of difficulty getting Jean's blood built up as she is quite anaemic..................... In regards to this it might be very helpful if one of your friends or relatives, who are in the city here, would report to the hospital and have their blood matched with Jean's with a view to giving her a little bit of blood every day for about a week.....................Now this is not an emergency affair and I do not want you to get excited about it. It is something we do quite often in these cases. We are much more liberal with blood transfusions now than we used to be five or six years ago and we find it very helpful in building up people with infection who do not respond just as fast as we would like.*

My mother writes to the conductor and some cousins who live in Winnipeg. The conductor's blood is a match, so they do not need to test the cousins.

§

When the doctor came to see me today he said they are going to give me some blood in my arm to help me get better. Then he promised me he is going to put me in a cast and send me home. After the doctor left, one of the sisters came in with some blood in a bottle. There was a tube coming out of the bottle and on the end of the tube there was a needle. The sister stuck the needle into my arm, but it didn't hurt too much. She said I am going to get blood in my arm every day for a week. I don't care if it hurts every time they stick the needle in because I am going home soon. I am going to write a letter to Daddy and say, "Please come and get me as soon as possible."

§

I never saw my conductor after I received his blood because the doctor kept his word. I was put in a cast and allowed to go home.

I often wonder if the conductor came to see me after I was gone. I think he did. I know he would be glad I was able to go home, but I think he would be sorry that he didn't have a chance to say a last goodbye. I know I wish I could have told him I was going home and thanked him for all the treats he brought me. And if I had known that it was his blood that was helping me get better I would have said, "Thank you for your blood." But I didn't know.

I didn't fully appreciate this man's kindness and generosity until I was an adult. We had two relatives living in Winnipeg–a cousin of my dad's and her daughter. They each came to the hospital once. Meanwhile, the conductor, a stranger till he met us on the train, knowing how lonely I would be after my mother returned home, visited regularly.

For those many weeks that stretched into months, he was my Winnipeg family. How I wish that after I had returned home I had written letters to him as regularly as I did to my family when I was in the hospital. He deserved that. But I didn't do it. I was an eight-year-old child living in the present moment. I was so happy to be home with my mother and father, surrounded by my sisters and brothers and eating my mother's home-cooking, that the hospital stay and the conductor quickly receded into the past.

I think my conductor would have understood. He never mentioned a wife or children, so I believe in those hours we spent together, I was his family and I made him happy. I think he kept me close in his memory, as he is in mine.

I know what I feel when I remember him. Love.

Addendum to "My Conductor" Story.

When I began writing the story about the conductor I had no perception of the depth of my feelings for this man, but as I was describing his visits to the hospital so long ago, the tears began to fall. Then, as sorrow and guilt engulfed me at not having written to him after I returned home, I began to sob uncontrollably. The end of the story just wrote itself.

But more guilt and tears were to follow. My mother kept a daily diary from 1939 till shortly before her death in 1971. After I had been working on my memoir for some time, I turned to her diaries to check out some dates and ended up reading every volume. With a shock, I discovered how elusive and not to be trusted memory can be.

I found my conductor had a name–Mr. Sinclair. I learned that six months after I returned home Mr. Sinclair had come to the farm to see me. My mother wrote that she thanked him for donating his blood.

Incredibly, I have no memory of that visit. Did my mother tell me Mr. Sinclair had come to see me and did I fail to make the connection to my conductor? Or did the visit vanish from my memory because, after seeing I was looking healthier and happy, Mr. Sinclair spent the rest of his visit talking to my mother in the kitchen?

More humiliation was to come. A diary entry for December said that I had received a Christmas card from Mr. Sinclair. "Please, please, I hope Mum had me send him a card," I thought as I dissolved in tears.

There was an entry seven years later that raised more questions: *Eugene, Dorothy and Mr. Sinclair came to visit Harry and Sadie.* For the first time I realized my conductor had the same last name as Uncle Eugene and Auntie Dorothy. Did that mean there was a family connection and my conductor was not the total stranger I thought he was? Could he be Uncle Eugene's father, or perhaps an uncle?

I wrote to my Sinclair cousins asking about the relationship between a CPR conductor and their father. Nowhere in their extended family of carpenters and farmers could they recall a relative who had been a train conductor.

A subsequent search of census records supported this view, providing no link between my Sinclair uncle's family and anyone working for the railroad in any capacity. Therefore, it seems coincidental that my conductor and my uncle shared the same surname.

CPR personnel records are closed to the public, so the identity of my conductor remains a mystery.

Letters I Wrote to My Family

My dad and I were riding in the car following the hearse that was carrying my mother's body to the cemetery. "Your mother wanted you to have these," Dad said, handing me a worn looking envelope. Inside the envelope I found all the letters I had written to the family while I was in St Boniface Hospital. I did not know my mother had saved them. As I tucked this new-found treasure into my handbag, my hands trembled with emotion as I felt the "mother-love" that had preserved these missives for so many years.

Reading them was like time-shifting back to the eight-year-old kid I once was. I felt the loneliness and pain, but also the kindness and happy moments. Sometimes I choked-up with unshed tears and sometimes I laughed.

My spelling was frequently "original" as I had only been in Grade 2 from September to January, so to help you decipher what I was saying, the following is a glossary for some of the misspellings:

sprise–surprise	hude–heard
Braslite–rig and brch Bracelet–ring and brooch	fincy–finish
mrchmeloo–marshmallow	suse–such
scwey–chewy	uwez–usually
micjr–mixture	wot–want
buj–bunch	enething–anything
oreijs–oranges	doit no wote rog– don't know what's wrong
hpratinge–operating	cirfrm–chloroform
crde–card	operatude–operated
Aunt Sadiei–Aunt Sadie	wrs–worse
hacky–hanky	suck–stuck
posubl–possible	hrts–hurts
blud–blood	trae–tray
schll–school	orugus–oranges
lorneum–linoleum	frit–fruit
tow tabis–two tables	bnanus–banana
holed–hold	prsole–parcel
nurecs–nurses	popcrn–popcorn
gajuate–graduate	beucz–because

tonsis–tonsils	toot–took
whont–want	wates–weights
nerce–nurse	mite–might
Ucle Henner Uncle Henry	Aenety Dose Auntie Doris
wos–once	basckt–basket
Ester–Easter	docker–doctor
waithes–weights	fineest–finished
usly–usual	moth–month

Feb 16th

Dear Mamma,
Cousin Annie came to see me on saturday Feb 15th. She brought me a pair insyd was a beautife rig and book. And a glass came with the pair. When doctor Abel came he put a quarter in my hand, Cousin Annie brought me warchemelon candy they were scarce. ~~they were another x hae~~ on frieday Feb 14th. I hae 13 Valentine. I send love to daddy the kids and you.

Your
Jean

P.S. Thick you very much for the Valentine.

Feb 16th

Dear Mamma

Cousin Annie came to see me on Satrday Feb 15th She brought me
a sprise inside was a braslite rig and brch And a glass came with the
prise. When doctor Abut came he put a quarter in my hand Cousin
Annie brought me mrchmeloo candy they were very scwey They took
another x rae on Friday Feb 14th I hav 13 Valentine. I send love to
daddy the kids and you.

Your Jean
PS. Thick you very much for the Valentine.

Feb 19th

Dear Mamma

       I thot Dens wunt know you. I know they jiwud life ther prsenty. I gis bilfe thot I wuud be comeing home with you. My eczema is no worse then befor. You know those 2 girl that wven in this wud wen I come in they have ole gon out. Now ther aw 2 ethu girl in now. The conductor came to see me today. He brought me som nuts. It was a mic jr. He brought me a bij of oreijs to. You know I said I liked oreijs bten the apples. They stuck

          With love

            Jean

P.S. They tuc me to the hpratirge room. They put me under

Feb 19th

Dear Mamma

I thot Denis wunt know you. I know they wuud like there spris. I gis Billy thot I wuud be coming home with you. My eczema is no worse then before. You know those 3 girl that wer in this ward wen I come in they have ole gon out. Now ther are uther girl in now. The conductor came to see me today. He brought me some nuts. It was a micjr. He brought me a buj of oreijs to. You know I said I liked oreijs betr then apples. They stuck

With love
Jean

clafam. Then they stuck
a needl in my leg and
let out thy puss. god
pleas send two enavlopes
in with your nex letter.
on to put your letter in, and
one to put Ruby's letter in,
Did you git my frist letter
yet, and I have just wrot
finesh your next letter.
Did you git my frist
letter befor this one. I have
wrote Ruby a letter to
thats way I wont two
envelopes. and adres them
bothe as you did the authen
one.

X X x x x x x o o o o o o o o

P.S. They tuc me to the hpratinge room. They put me under clrfrm. Then they stuck a needl in my leg and let out the puss. And pleez send two envelopes in with your nexs letter. One to put your letter in and one to put Ruby's letter in. Did you git my frist letter yet and I have just about fineesh your necst letter. Did you git my frist letter before this one. I have wrote Ruby a letter to that's way I wont two envelopes. And adres them bothe as you did the author one.

X X X X X X X O O O O O O O O

Feb 20th 1941

Dear Mamma,
I was going to write to you on Tuesday but they operated on Monday and I didn't feel like writing then, but I feel better now. They operated on the 20th, I'm sry Mary's eczema is so bad becuz mine is no wors then befor. They suck a lot in my ty and it hurts wen the tube is. And not onless wen the tube is. It hurts wen they operated. I dont feel like writing eney mur now but will add mur after Dr's saturday. The ister said if I ate evrything on my tray for a hole week she tot I'd be abl to git up. I told her I'd try to eat evrything. The conductor brought me anuther bag of orrgus. I such a lot frit in the

Feb 28th 1941

Dear Mamma

I was going to write to you on Wednesday. But they Opratude on Monday and I didn't feel like writing then. But I feel better now. They Opratude on Feb the 25th. Im sorry Mary's eczema is so bad becuz mine is no wrs then before. They suck a tube in my leg and it hrts wer the tube is. And not onlee wer the tube is. It hurts wer they Opratude. I don't feel like writing eneey mur nuw. But will add mur after.

Mrc 2 Saturday The sister said if I ate everythig on my trae for a hole week she thot Id be abl to git up. I tolde her Id trie to eat everything. The conductor brought me anuther bag of orugus. I such a lot frit in the

fries. I have oranges bananas
and grapes. I have about
3 dozen oranges. Just after
I came down from the
Operateding room the nurse
came in with a big parsole
I didn't know whow ity
was from and I didn't
opun it but hazule and
anuther girl opend it.
I sae goby for now but
befor I sge goby I'l have
to thick very much for
the popcrn goby
                    love from
                        Jean

frij. I have orugus bnanus and grapes. I have about 3 dozun orugus. Just after I came down from the Opratude room the nurse came in with a big prsole. I didn't know whow it was from and I didn't opun it but hazule and anuther girl opind it. Il say goby for now but before I sae goby Il have to thick very much for the popcrn. Goby

Love from
Jean

Mar 4th 1944

Dear Mamma,

I was going to write to you on Monday but didn't. I got your letter on Monday 3rd. It's funny Denis didn't cut your hips. He would of cut your hips if you would of not took the knife away when you did he would of cut your hips. Lilias has gone out quite a while ago. Then a girl called Irene came in her bed. She went out last week.

With love,
Jean

Mar 4th 1941

Dear Mamma.

I was going to write to you on Monday 3rd but didn't. I got your letter on Monday 3rd. It's funny Denis didn't cut your hips. He would of cut your hips if you would of not took the knife away when you did he would of cut your hips. Lilias has gone out quite a while ago. Then a girl called Irene came in her bed. She went out last week.

With love
Jean

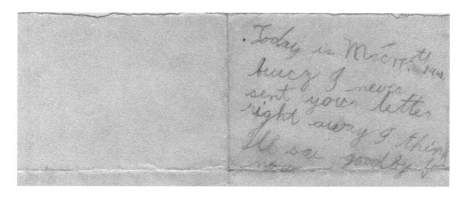

Today is March 17th 1941 beucz I never sent your letter right away I think I'll say goodbye for now

Mar 7th
1941

Dear Daddy.

I was going to write to you yesterday. But didn't. I have to write to Mary Lorna Billy and Rose today. How many little pigs have you. I guess there are just about 70 of them. I wish I knew when I was going home. But I don't know when I am going home. My leg is fine it only hurts a little when I move tell mamma to send six more stamps with her next letter.

With love
Jean

Dear Daddy

I was going to write to you yesterday, But didn't. I have to write to Mary Lorna Billy and Rose today.How many little pigs have you I gues there are just about 70 of them. I wish I know when I was going home. But I don't know when I am going home. My leg is fine it only hurts a little when I move. tell mamma to send six more stamps with her next letter.

With love
Jean

Mar 27th
1771

Dear Mamma,
They took the waters off Yesterday they mite put them back on agen. Old Hennes and Aanety Dose wire to see me on Wensday Aanety Dose and Hazel were to see me today Aanety Dose brought me a write pad a lead pencil some envlope and some stamps. I sill dont like the meells but I eat more then I dide befor. My doll is not brocken is it. Think you very much for the book. Is Denis over his cold.

With love
Jean

X X X X x o o o o o o

38

Mar 27th 1941

Dear Mamma

They toot the wates off Yesterday they mite put them back on again.
Ucle Henner and Aanety Dorse were to see me on Wednesday.
Aanety Dose and Haesl were to see me today. Aanety Dose brought
me a write pad a lead pencil some envelope and some stamps. I
sill donte like the meells but I eat more then I did befor. My doll is
not brocken is it. Think you very much for the book. Is Denis over
his cold.

> *With love*
> *Jean*

x x x x x o o o o o o

Arl. 3d 1941

Dear Mamma,

I can set up on the side of my bed now. It hurts a little to get out of bed but was I get out of bed its alrite. The condcter came to see me today. He brought me a baskt with Ester eggs and a hen seting on eggs in it. I got two dollers and 50 cents now. I got a letter from Aunt Edie Yesterday to. It munt not be so long before I can go home but my docter hasit told me yet. I hope Deny is well. I think I will close now so goodby.

With love,

Arl 3rd 1941

Dear Mamma

I can sit up on the side of my bed now. It hurts a little to get out of bed but wos I get out of bed its allrite, The conductor came to see me today. He brought me a basckt with Ester eggs and a hen siting on eggs in it. Ive got two dollars and 50 cents now. I got a letter from Aunt Edie Yesterday to. It mint not be so long before I can go home but my docker hasit told me yet. I hope Denis well. I thinck I will close now so goodby

With love
Jean

Apr. 5.th 1946

Dear Mamma,
                    I got your letter
Yesterday. Did you get a letter
from the docter lately did he tell
you when I could come home, I
asked hime twice but he just
said not yet Jean, since they
put the waithes back on I
haven't had any pain unless I
move. The condocter came to
see me Yesterday he brought
me a dozen oranges and some
nuts. He said next time he came
to see me he would bring me
a pie. One morning I had 11
bowls of corn Flakes. The
nurses said I was a good eater.
I think I'll close now so goodby.
              With love
                    Jean

Apr 5th 1941

Dear Mamma.

I got your letter Yesterday. Did you get a letter from the doctor lately did he tell you when I could come home. I asked him twice but he just said not yet Jean. Since they put the waithes back on I have't had any pain unless I move. The conductor came to see me Yesterday he brought me a dozen oranges and some nuts. He said the next time he came to see me he would bring me a pie. One morning I had 21 bowls of corn Flakes. The nurses said I was a good eater. I think I will close now so goodby.

With love
Jean

Apr. 4th 1941

Dear Mamma

I was going to write yesterday but by the time I finest folding papers for dressing it was to late. I sit up in a chair now. My leg was hurting now then until today. I hope I'll be home before nine moth. The girl in the bed has a radio she got it on Sunday. It was raining off and on yesterday. I don't know how day is. Thursday. I did'it freces your letter last night beause I had suse a pane in my leg. But it is biter today. Think you very much for the stamps. I thanck I will close now of godby

X X X X X X o o o o o o   With love
Jean

Apr 9th 1941

Dear Mamma

I was going to write Yesterday but by the time I fineest folding papers for dressing it was to late. I sit up in a chair now. My leg was hurting mor then usly today. I hope Ill will be home before nexe moth. The girl in the 1 bed has a radio she got it on Sunday. It was raning off and on Yesterday. I have' t hude how kay is.

Thursday 10 I did'it finees Your letter last night bcase I had suse a pane in my leg. But it is beter today. Think you very much for the stamps. I thinck I will close now so goodby

With love
Jean

XXXXXOOOOO

Apr. 17th, 1941,

Dear Mamma,
They put the water
back on Fideday 16th Because I had
so much pane in my leg, And wen
they put the water back on it
stopt the pane. And now I
havent as much pane in my leg,
the girl went home Yesterday
the one in the bed beside mine name
was Betty and the one in the
fast bed name was Noella. Bettys
Mother came at tow o'clock to
take her home and wen Noella
saw Betty getting redy to go home
she watd to go home to. There's
a boy in the boys room we have
so much fun with he can walk
and he every comes in our room
and wen we wot enthing we

Apr 13th 1941

Dear Mamma

They put the wates back on Frididay 10th Becose I had so much pane
in my leg. And wen they put the wates back on it stopt the pane. And
now I havit as much pane in my leg. Tow girls went home Yesterday.
The one in the bed beside me name was Betty and the one in the last
bed was Norlla. Betty Mother came at tow o'clock to take har home
and wen Norlla saw Betty getting redy to go home she watd to go
home to. Theres a boy in the boys room we have so much fun with
he can walk and he uwez comes in our room and wen we wot eneth-
ing we

get him to get it for us.
Theres to boys in the boys room,
something the same on there
legs one has a brocken leg I dot
no wots rog with the other
one. Its geting late now so I
thinck I will close. Think you
very much for the Ester bascht
and Ester cpde. Plese thinck
Aunt Nellie for the Ester bascht
and plese thinck Aunt dadeie
for the hacky. I thinck Ill
close now so goodby.
       With love
          Jean
     X x x x x x x x o o o o o o o

get him to get it for us. Theres to boys in the boys room something the same on there legs one has a brocken leg I doit no wote rog with the other one. Its geting late now so I thinck I will close. Think you very much for the Ester basckt and Ester crde. Plese think Aunt Nellie for the Ester bascht and plese think Aunt Sadeie for the hacky. I thinck Ill close now so goodby.

With love
Jean

x x x x x o o o o o o

May 7th th,

Dear Mamma,

Dorothy came to see me yesterday. I have just finished my supper. The doctor didn't come to see me to-day. There's only three beds in my room now. They took it out when they put a new wall on. Lorna and Muriel came to see me on Monday 5th. The boys have just finished having a fight. There's 8 boys in that room and they sure are noisy. I still have 2 dollars and 45 cents. I'm going to write a letter to Mr. and Mrs. Veal to-night to so I can send it with yours. So I think I'll close now so good-by

With love
Jean

May 7th 1941

Dear Mamma,

Dorothy came to see me Yesterday. I have just finished my supper.
The doctor didn't come to see me to-day. There's only three beds
in my room now. They took it out when they put a new wall in.
Lorna and Muriel came to see me on Monday 5th. The boys have just
finished having a fight. There's 8 boys in that room and they sure are
noisy. I still have 2 dollars and 45 cents. I'm going to write a letter to
Mr. and Mrs. Veal to-night to so I can send it with yours. So I think I'll
close now so good-by.

With love
Jean

May 9th 1941

Dear Mamma and Daddy,
                    I am just
writeing this litter to tell
you a sprise. The dockter came
to see me to-day. He askut
me if Daddy had been to
see me yet I said yes. He
spid it was to-bad becac
he was going to put me in
a cast and send me home
with Daddy so pleas
come and get me as soon
as posubl. Its soon supper
time so I will close now
good-bye for now.
                    Lots of love from
                                    Jean

May 9th 1941

Dear Mamma and Daddy

I am just writing this letter to tell you a sprise. The dockter came to see me to-day. He askut me if Daddy had been to see me yet. I said yes. He said it was to bad because he was going to put me in a cast and send me home with Daddy so pleas come and get me as soon as posubl. Its soon supper time so I will close now. goodbye for now.

Lots of love from
Jean

May 10th 1941

Dear Mamma,

I just got your letter a little while ago. They moved me into the last room Friday May 9th and then to-day they moved me into 32 becaus they are going to paint 34. They gave me some blud in my arm Yesterday, it didn't hurt much. I got a letter from Rose on Friday. And I got a letter from schll on Saterday. I think I'll close now so good-by.

With love

Jean

May 10th 1941

Dear Mamma

I just got your letter a little while ago. They moved me into the last
room Friday May 7th and then to-day they moved me into 32 becaes
they are going to paint 34. They gave me some blud in my arm
Yesterday it didn't hurt much. I got a letter from Rose on Friday. And I
got a letter from schll on Saturday. I think I will close now so good-by.

> With love
> Jean

May 14 19 21

Dear Mamma,
I got your letter
yesterday morning. They
moved me back into the
last room to-day. They
painted it different and
lonoreum on the floor. And
when they moved my things
I saw that I had so many
things that it took two
tables to holed all of them.
All the nurses but two
graduate on Saursday May 14.
A girl came in last night
and got her tonsils out this
morning. I think they are
going to give my blud in my
arm one more time but that's
all. I think I'll close now so
good-by
with love Jean

May 19 1941

Dear Mamma

I got your letter Yesterday morning. They moved me back into the last room to-day. They painted it different and lorneum on the floor. And when they moved my things I saw I had so many things that it too tow tabls to holed all of them. All the nurecs but tow gajuate on Tausday May 12th. A girl came in last night and got her tonsls out this morning. I think they are going to give me blud in my arm one more time but that's all. I think Ill close now so good-by.

> With love
> Jean

May 27th
1941

Dear Mamma

I am in a big room now they can put 8 beds in it but they have just 4 in now and there is only two girls in this room besides me. they moved me int anther bed last night. I about 1 games of Chiniese Checkers with anther girl and I won them all. A girl 1 yers old had a pil to take this morning she didn't whont to take it so she and the nuce had a fite I am going to write a letter to Row and send it with yours. Delore xo so good by

With love Jean X X X X X X O O O O O O

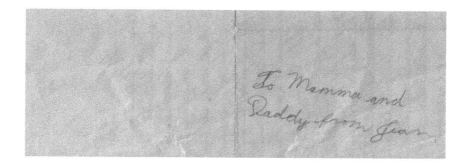

May 27th 1941

Dear Mamma

I am in a big room now they can put 8 beds in it but they have just 7 in now and there is onle two girls in this room besidess me. They moved me into anther bed last night. I playd about 27 games of Chiniese Checkers with anther girl and I won them all. A girl 7 yers old had a pil to take this morning she didn't whont to take it so she and the nerce had a fite. I am going to write a letter to Rose and send it with yours. I close now so good-by'

With love
Jean

xxxxxooooo

I Still Hate Adhesive Tape

For my first two months in hospital I was in traction on both legs, making me as immobile as if I were in a cast. Traction consisted of weights suspended from ropes that passed over pulleys at the foot of my bed. The other ends of the ropes were attached to footplates that were held in place by wide strips of adhesive tape going up and down, and then around and around, my legs. There had to be enough tape to withstand the pull of the weights. It was a lot of tape.

I was a happy kid the morning the doctor announced they were removing the traction and I would be allowed to move about in bed. I did not realize that removing the traction involved stripping off all that tape.

The nurses were apologetic and as careful as they could be, but there is no painless way to strip adhesive tape off skin soft and tender from weeks of being encased. Of all the "not-so-nice" hospital procedures I experienced this ranked as the worst, way above x-rays–even though they involved painful shifting from bed to stretcher to hard x-ray table–or the reeking chloroform masks, or the pricks of blood tests, or even the indignity of enemas.

The tape removal was agony, but the freedom from the weights was wonderful–at first. After about a week, as I was experiencing no pain, the doctor allowed me to try sitting in a wheelchair. I was sure that meant I would soon be able to go home. It was not to be. After only a few days the pain in my hip returned, I was confined to bed again, and when the pain persisted I was put back in traction.

I remember one difficult night before the traction was replaced. Unable to sleep I tried in vain to find a less painful position. At some point I twisted my body so that my cheek touched the cool metal of my bedside table. That mini-jolt of cold felt wonderful and helped to take my mind off the pain pulsing in my hip. That was when the sister making night rounds came by and wanted to know why I was lying with my head on the table. "My leg's hurting and it feels better when I lie like this," I said. Unfortunately, I didn't explain that it was the cold of the table that was helping.

"Oh, you poor dear," she said and bustled off, returning in a few minutes with a small square pillow that she gently placed under my head. It was too late to tell her that it was the sensation of the cold tabletop that I wanted. That would be rejecting her act of caring and kindness. So I spent the rest of that long aching night lying, softly cushioned, but in a very awkward position, wishing I could just move back to the pillow on my bed.

That's how it is with each of my hospital memories of loneliness or pain. There is always a flip-side–my hatred of the painful adhesive tape softened by a remembrance of caring and kindness.

Too Many Baking Powder Biscuits

With the first bite of one of my mother's baking powder biscuits, slightly crusty on the outside, light and flaky on the inside, dripping melted butter and sweet, tangy pincherry jelly, I knew I really was home.

It didn't matter that I was encased from waist to ankles in a combination cast and steel framework providing traction to my left leg. It didn't matter that I was flat on my back in a bed in the parlour while the rest of the family were gathered around the kitchen table. I could hear the rise and fall of familiar voices, the happy music of family laughter, the comforting clink of dishes. I was home.

I would spend a year confined to bed in that little room. The wonderful thing about being eight is the absence of concern about the future. I didn't wonder how long I would be bedridden, or if I would ever walk again. I simply accepted each day as it came. If any visitor was foolish enough to say, "Poor Jean," or words to that effect, my mother's firm response was, "She's doing just fine." And indeed, I was.

Although I spent a lot of time alone as the rest of the family lived their regular lives, I don't remember ever being bored. My mother ensured that I always had a book to read. When I had exhausted Liscard School's limited library, housed in one small cupboard at the back of the schoolroom, she begged and borrowed juvenile titles from relatives and friends until I was able to read her adult books.

My body couldn't leave my bed, but my mind could rove freely with young heroes and heroines. I travelled the streets of New York with *Ragged Dick* and all the other poor boys in Horatio Alger's books. The theme of every title in the series was as predictable and familiar as an old friend. He could be a bootblack or a newsboy, but through hard work, honesty, and courage each boy rose from scrabbling a life on the street to becoming a respected member of the comfortable middle class. I knew I could overcome all obstacles just as Alger's heroes could.

And there was Martha Finley's series about *Elsie Dinsmore*, a motherless young girl sent to live with grandparents while her father is overseas. This is an unhappy time for Elsie, unloved and bullied. Then her father, who blames her for her mother's death, returns and poor Elsie must contend with his many rules and harsh discipline. The stories would surely make any but the most deprived of child readers feel fortunate and appreciative of family. Father and daughter do eventually come together as the series takes Elsie from childhood to marriage and beyond. My young heart was thrilled when Elsie married the man who had loved her for so long. I could visualize the beautiful bride in her white gown with her flowing sheer veil held in place by a headdress of vivid orange blossoms. Imagine my disappointment when the first real-life bride I saw wore insipid white flowers in her hair. "Why isn't she wearing orange blossoms?" I whispered to my mother.

"She is," my mother whispered back. Seeing I was completely mystified, she added, "Orange trees have white flowers." My Elsie, however, will always make a bright splash at the altar with a crescent of orange-coloured blossoms in her hair.

There was no *Barbie* in my childhood, but flat cardboard dolls with clothes to cut out and attach to the figures with tabs were easy to dress and manipulate, even when you were lying flat in bed. Like *Barbie*, these dolls were young ladies, slim and alluring with flowing tresses and extensive wardrobes in the latest styles. However, they did not need a stand-up pink cupboard with pink hangers to store their finery. Dresses, jackets and coats, even hats and shoes, fit neatly in a flat brown envelope. And all you needed to create original additions to their wardrobes were paper, crayons, and scissors.

The Eaton's catalogue also gave me many hours of imaginative fun as I planned a complete wardrobe, furnishing a house or assembling a baby layette. I always began with a maximum amount I could spend which made the activity a mathematical challenge. Simply increasing or decreasing the funds at my disposal gave me repeated shopping sprees, while forcing me to prioritize. I never told anyone about the baby layette projects though.

The secret inner me was not sure if it was quite proper for someone my age to be planning for a baby.

My mother homeschooled me as I took Grades 3 and 4 through correspondence lessons from the provincial government. Despite how busy she must have been I never ever was made to feel that the extra work of tending to my physical needs or explaining my lessons was an imposition or a burden.

As a child I accepted everything my mother did for me without thought. That was what mothers did–looked after their kids. Now I am amazed at how my mother managed what must have been a most stressful time for her. I came home from the hospital on June 6th. On June 17th, just 11 days later, our sister, Leila, joined the family, baby number six. For the birth, and the 10 days of her "confinement," our mother moved to Uncle George and Auntie Lucille's place. Three days earlier Auntie Lucille had given birth to a daughter, so this enabled Auntie Sadie, the local midwife, to care for both mothers and babies.

I had been complaining of pain for several days, and the same day that my mother gave birth, my father took me to the hospital in Russell. After three pain-free days in the hospital I was home once more. I remained pain-free for almost a week before having another bad night. Then my mother came home with the baby. After two days of my crying all morning I was back in Russell Hospital for four days. Again, the hospital stay was pain-free, but followed by three sleepless nights at home. Sleepless nights for me would have been sleepless nights for my mother too, and she would have already been sleep deprived from night feedings for the baby. She must have been dragged-out weary, but I never heard a word of complaint, nor is there any in her written diary record of those days.

Finally, on July 10th, after consultation with the doctors in Winnipeg, Dr. Mackenzie and my father took me to the Russell Hospital once more, this time to have the cast and traction changed. As the cast was sawed open and removed, and the tape holding the traction in place was stripped off, the source of all my discomfort was revealed. It was a case of too many baking powder biscuits. I had gone from losing weight in the hospital to gaining weight as soon as I got home to my mother's cooking.

The pressure on my body, locked inside the plaster and tape, had caused the scar from the surgery on my hip to partially break open. In addition, both legs had many purple pressure sores, but worst of all was a big gash the tape had cut into my lower left leg.

Because of the injuries on my legs, the original intention of reinstalling a cast and traction was abandoned. After two-and-a-half weeks in the hospital I came home once more, to bed rest, but blissfully un-encased. An x-ray a month later showed that my hip, or what was left of it, was in the joint but far from well. I was instructed to stop moving around in bed so much. That is not easy to do without anything to keep you immobile, but dread of another cast was enough motivation for me to follow the doctor's orders.

My Magic Slough

Funny how little things stick in your memory–insignificant things, really, when you try to describe them, but you can see them, and feel them, as clearly as if it were yesterday.

A year after that fateful January morning when, unable to stand on my leg I slid down the stairs on my bum, I had progressed from bedrest to a wheelchair. By mid-April, when winter's snow and ice had melted, my mother said some fresh air would be good for me after being indoors all winter. It was a brilliantly sunny day, but because the spring air was still nippy, she muffled me head to toe in a quilt before moving my wheelchair into the screened porch. "Give a shout when you want to come in," she said. Because my hands were tucked snugly inside my cover I just sat, doing nothing, not even reading, which was unusual.

From my vantage point I had an unobstructed view of the large slough lying in low land to the east, maybe an eighth of a mile away. The water, moving in ripples as it was touched by a gentle breeze, was a brilliant eye-piercing blue. The sunbeams were playing a never-ending game of tag on the water, creating an incredible and ever-changing pattern of sparkling pinpoints of flashing light. The effect was hypnotic. I sat there mesmerized, just staring at the water, not noticing the passage of time till my mother came out to move me back into the house.

There were more sunny afternoons in the porch that month. Each time I was content to just sit, watching the play of dancing lights on the water. Each time I experienced the same almost "out-of-body" trance-like state. Such a simple thing–sunlight on water–but so beautiful, so wondrous when you took the time to really look, time I likely wouldn't have taken if I had been able to run about and play like other kids.

PART 1 OSTEOMYELITIS AND ME

I told no one how I felt about the slough, not even my mother. The experience was too special, too mystical, to share.

To my sisters and brothers I think it was just the big slough in the pig pasture, with the attraction any body of water has for kids. I don't remember them ever wading in that water as they did in a smaller slough in the farmyard. Perhaps its size was intimidating, or they were unsure of its depth. They would tramp in the squishy grass along the edge in their rubber boots, practice skipping stones on the water or just see who could throw a stone the farthest.

Even after I could join in their play, that slough kept its special magic for me. If I was having a bad day it was a place of refuge where I would go alone to sit on the big rock at its edge, and just stare at the water until peace of mind returned.

The big slough that I remember is no more. Partially drained by a ditch to provide pasture land for cattle, the area is now a sea of tall grass thriving in the moist soil. Like my childhood, my magic slough is gone forever. But I will never forget the wonder I felt as I watched that shimmering play of light on water–a memory that reminds me, as an adult, to take the time to truly see and appreciate the beauty in simple things.

Yes I Can

By mid-summer I was using crutches and my bed was moved upstairs to the big bedroom, where my sisters slept. The following January, now able to walk, I returned to Liscard School. It had taken two years, but I was a regular school kid again.

A year and a half later, I was back in Winnipeg–the Children's Hospital this time–for corrective surgery to my hip. Once again, I was in a cast from my waist to my ankle, but this time only my left leg was casted, leaving my right leg free. And in only five-and-a-half weeks, not months, I was home. Once more my mother was my teacher till the cast was removed and I could walk with crutches. Eager to rejoin my classmates, I convinced my family I could return to school while still on crutches. My case was helped by my school-age sisters and brother who willingly supported my plea, realizing it would mean getting a ride to and from school.

"You can't play. You can't run on crutches," the other kids shout when I join the starting line for Pom Pom Pull-Away.

"Yes, I can."

"No, you can't."

"Yes, I can. And you can't stop me."

It is my first day back at school. I have looked forward to this day with delicious, tingling anticipation. I will not be denied. I stay in the line.

Fuelled by hurt and determination, when the kid who is 'It' calls "Pom Pom Pull-Away," I "crutch" like I have never "crutched" before, making it to the other side without being tagged. When I am finally caught and join the others in the centre, I even manage to tag someone. No one ever again suggests I cannot play.

§

Today we are playing softball for the first time since I have returned to school. The two team leaders take turns calling out the names of the kids they want on their team. I am the last to be chosen, even after the little kids. The first two times at bat I strike out. The third time I stand further away from the base and lean forward a bit, balancing on my crutches. To everyone's surprise, including my own, I manage to smack the ball and make it to first base, running lickety-split on my crutches. After that I am no longer picked last, with my name now called before the youngest kids in Grades 1 and 2.

§

Dad is late coming to pick us up today. Standing around waiting is no fun, so we start a vigorous game of Pom Pom Pull-Away with the Brenner boys. They have been catching a ride with us every day and then walking the rest of the way to their home.

When Dad drives into the schoolyard with the horse-drawn wagon, one look at his face tells me he is not happy. I assume he is upset because we have had to wait for him.

"Instead of running around playing games why didn't you start walking home? You could have been halfway there by now." He is angry, and I realize it is my fault. Seeing me "crutch running" was not what he expected. I know he is right. I am capable of walking part way home, but I still feel hurt by the scolding. He should have been happy and pleased to see how well I managed on crutches.

After that Dad comes later and later each day. There are no more after-school games. We know we are expected to start walking home. The day that I get all the way home is the end of after-school pickups. The other kids aren't pleased, but I don't mind. I love the feeling of swinging along on my crutches, moving independently through space. And deep down inside I still feel injured pride, a determination to show my father I can do this. I even try to increase my speed, walking in the door a little earlier each day.

Pom Pom Pull-Away

Two goal lines are established about 30 feet apart. The person who is It stands in the middle of the space between the lines. The rest of the players stand behind the goal line on one side. When It calls "Pom Pom Pull-Away," all the players try to run across to the other goal line without being tagged by It. Any player tagged joins It in the centre and helps It tag other players. The game continues till everyone has been caught. The last person to be tagged becomes the next It.

Be Careful What You Pray For

When Rick Hansen traveled around the world in his wheelchair, my first thought was, "I wish Mum could have seen this."

This week I am watching the Paralympians scoot around the track in their long, sleek racing wheelchairs. I watch them turn and twist like mad-cap spinning tops as they compete for possession of the ball in games of basketball and rugby. I marvel at how attitudes and opportunities for the handicapped have evolved in 80 years.

As I watch the action on the television screen, I hear my mother's voice from the past. "I prayed if you were going to spend the rest of your life in a wheelchair, God would take you."

I have no idea how old I was when my mother told me this. I do know by then I was walking, having shed wheelchair, and finally, crutches. I do know I disagreed with my mother, thinking, "No, no, I'd rather have lived," but I never voiced that thought.

I did not feel hurt, rejected or unloved upon learning she had once been praying for me to die. I knew it wasn't because she didn't want to face a future of caring for me, because she had given me the best of loving care when I had been confined to bed, and later, a wheelchair. Also, I knew my mother's independent spirit. To her a lifetime of dependence on others would have seemed worse than death. And in 1940, when my prognosis was uncertain, it did not seem possible for someone in a wheelchair to live independently. Perhaps most important of all, I understood the depth of Mum's faith, even if I didn't share it. She truly believed I would be living in eternal happiness, flitting about in the heavens as one of God's angels.

Mum could never have imagined the technical advances in science, medicine, or space exploration we take for granted today, 80 years later.

Who knows what the next 80 years may offer? In fact, we cannot predict the future with any certainty, not even one day ahead.

If you believe in the power of prayer, be careful what you pray for. If you are asking for a specific outcome, can you be sure that what you are seeking is the best, or right, option? Should you, instead, be trusting your spiritual deity or leader to do what is best, and simply be asking for help in dealing with whatever happens?

If my mother were still here I think she would agree.

Osteomyelitis and Me

Antibiotics to fight infection did not exist in 1941 when I became ill with osteomyelitis, so I very nearly died. My mother's diary for January 24th records:

> *Saw Dr Abbot. No definite news. May recover, may not. Tell in 2 or 3 weeks.*

On February 10th as the doctor's diagnosis was more positive, my mother decided she could return home, leaving me in the hospital in Winnipeg. Her diary entry for that day:

> *J has pain in hip at night. Cheerful goodbye. Dr says abscess forming, will have pain. Must be drained in 7–10 days. Be in hospital a month.*

It turned out the doctor was too optimistic. I was still in the hospital on March 27th, when to my amazement, Auntie Doris and Uncle Henry walked through the ward door. They were in Winnipeg to take their daughter, Kay, to the Shriners Hospital for surgery. It was like an instant shot of adrenaline to see someone from home. They brought me a writing pad with lined pages, and wonder of wonders, a mechanical lead pencil. I had never seen such a marvellous pencil. You could turn the lead in and out. And the pencil didn't need to be sharpened–there were replacement leads you could insert. It was also beautiful–its smooth and shiny surface a pearly marbleized, soft shade of green. This gift roused me from weeks of lethargy. Up until March 7th I had been writing a letter to "Dear Mamma" or "Dear Daddy" every three or four days, and then for 20 days–not a word. After my aunt and uncle left,

I immediately picked up that magical pencil to write to "Dear Mamma." It was quite amazing how the pencil improved the quality of my script–each letter carefully formed and nicely rounded!

After Uncle Henry and Auntie Doris returned home and reported to my parents, my mother's diary says:

J fairly well but pale.

Only after I was safely home, my aunt and uncle confessed to my parents they had found me so pale, with almost white fingernails, that they did not expect me to leave the hospital alive.

Of course, I had no perception of any of this when I was in the hospital and I don't know exactly how, or when, I learned about it after I came home–probably in dribs and drabs over the years. Was it when my sisters told me they prayed for me every night because they thought I might die? Did I overhear snatches of adult conversation when visitors came to the house? Did my mother weave the information into family stories? I do know, since childhood, I have been keenly aware of how fortunate I am to be alive.

There is strength in that knowledge. Compared to what might have been, any hurdles in life are reduced to mere bumps in the road that you know you can navigate. It is a mindset that has helped me overcome, or adapt to, life's many challenges over the years. And there have been challenges.

While teaching full-time, I had been taking evening and summer courses at the University of Manitoba, working toward a Bachelor of Paedagogy. In 1969, I resigned from my teaching position to attend university full-time. Shortly after classes commenced, I began experiencing acute pain in my left hip. I managed to hobble painfully through the rest of the academic year, but then had to take a "gap year" for surgery to fuse my hip. The months in the hospital, first in a body cast and then working to regain mobility, were difficult not only for me, but for my husband who now had to look after all the household duties while caring for our children, ages 16, 13, and 10. There was no Home Care at that time so we had to manage on our own, but manage we did. Though I was still using crutches when I came home, I was able to make meals and wash dishes. Gradually I progressed from crutches to cane to independent walking, which became my favourite recreational activity.

Beginning in my late 70s, arthritis in my knees and back increasingly limited my mobility. My daily walks continued but I needed a cane, then two canes, and finally a walker to keep me upright. At age 85, after two years of excruciating pain in my right knee, I had knee-replacement surgery. The surgery was a success and once again I could go for pain-free daily walks with my walker. Now, three years later, my left knee is starting to complain, so there will likely be a second knee-replacement surgery in my future–if I should live long enough. My "Yes, I can" attitude, adopted in childhood, has helped me deal with every physical challenge.

I do think the years of immobility and "aloneness" while recovering from osteomyelitis contributed to my becoming somewhat of a loner. Unlike my sisters, I have never had a best friend/confidante, nor have I felt the need for one. In fact, I realize in my writing, I am sharing more of my thoughts and feelings than I have ever shared with anyone outside of close family members, maybe more than I have ever shared with anyone.

While I relished the intellectual stimulation of educational conferences when I became a teacher, and later a teacher-librarian and library consultant, I dreaded those inevitable evening "meet and mingles." In truth, social situations with a large group of strangers are my version of torture. I am in awe of those who can "work a room." My "cup of tea" is a small group getting together for a particular purpose, for example, the meetings of the writing group to which I belong. The sharing of stories and constructive feedback in these sessions leaves me refreshed, stimulated, and motivated to keep on writing.

Through all the alone time I had in those childhood months stuck in bed and wheelchair as the rest of the family lived their regular lives, the characters in books became my best friends. Now, I cannot imagine a world without books.

In fact there is only once in my life, since I learned to read, that I have not had a book or some other reading material readily available. It was 1966 and my family (husband and three kids) and I were on a two-week fishing trip with my mother and father. The plan was to stop at several lakes, ending at Jan Lake in northern Saskatchewan. The clothes in my suitcase shared space with a cache of books, more than enough for any "free" time for reading, I assumed. However, as Dad's boat would only hold five and I didn't fish anyway, I volunteered to stay ashore with my five-year-old daughter Lynn. And as we stopped at only one lake that had a beach accessible to the water, I ended up with a lot of time for reading. By the second day at Jan Lake, I had read every book I had brought with me.

So, after the rest piled into the boat for their morning fishing trip, Lynn and I trudged along the rocky shoreline to the store. "Sorry," they said. "We don't sell paperbacks or magazines." On to the gas station and the same story, except to my desperate plea they added, "No newspapers either." As for the spanking new lodge–"We expect people to bring their own reading material." I was dumbfounded. Did the people who lived and worked here never read? I did survive the next four days till we were back home–but with severe withdrawal symptoms. I made sure that never happened to me again.

Now I live surrounded by books. There are books in my study, the living room, and the bedrooms, with the overflow filling a wall of shelves in the basement. The topics reflect my interests over the years. In addition to literary fiction–the majority of my library–there are titles on Canadian history, Indigenous issues, biography, politics, architecture, energy-efficient house design, landscaping, gardening, financial planning, self-improvement, healthy living and cooking, dealing with death, and lately, memoir and the craft of writing.

In addition to an early love of reading, planning and prioritizing became the warp and weft of the fibre of my being. The Eaton's catalogue is no more, but those long-ago, make-believe shopping and budgeting activities I devised with the catalogue while bedridden may have started it all. The imaginary problems have been replaced with real-life challenges–planning budgets, trips, wardrobes, exercise routines, menus, housekeeping schedules, landscaping, vegetable gardens, and flower beds. Unbelievably, I spent 14 years planning the house of our dreams, happily drawing and redrawing floor plans as the family's needs changed with the passing years! Files and lists are my indispensable tools. Daily to-do lists organize my days, even in retirement. My grocery lists are organized to match the aisles of the store where I shop. Attached to my freezer are a map and a checklist which enable me to find what I want in a flash and tell me immediately how many meals I have of any item.

I realized not everyone shares my passion for planning after the day I proudly showed my sister-in-law, Doris, my recently completed diagrams for a five-year rotation plan for our new raised-bed garden. I was completely deflated by her reaction. "I've won lots of prizes for my gardens and I didn't need a plan," she said. I had seen her gardens–brilliant patchworks of bursting bloom. I had pictures of some of them.

My "planned" garden

Doris' "unplanned" garden

Upon reflection, I realized Doris worked instinctively, her pleasure was in the planting while, for me, the hours of planning were far more fun than the mucking in the dirt required to implement my plan.

Osteomyelitis may have had both positive and negative influences on my life, but there is one priceless gift it gave me—time with my mother. During the years I was homeschooled, I longed for the day when I could rejoin my classmates. Now I realize how fortunate I was to have those hours with my mother as we worked on my lessons. She was a great teacher—knowledgeable, patient, supportive, and motivating.

In a wheelchair or on crutches, I could help with some of the household tasks, so when I could walk once more, I fell naturally into the role of "mother's helper" while the other kids did the outdoor chores. Because of all those hours we spent working together, just the two of us, discussing lessons, preparing meals, working in the garden, or picking berries, I had a special, close relationship with my mother. I might never have had that without osteomyelitis.

While osteomyelitis has had a great impact on my life, I realize that the total of the person I am today was shaped by many other factors as well–the genes I was born with, my parents as role models, my extended family, growing up on a farm, a childhood spanning the Great Depression and the Second World War, and the myriad of experiences of a long life.

I almost died when I was eight years old. I am now 88 and realize the number of years I have left are relatively few. As I contemplate the end of my life, I share this sentiment expressed by the German poet Ludwig Jacobowski in 1899:

"Don't cry because it's over.
Smile because it happened."

PART 2
In The Beginning

Love, Death, And A Dream

This is the only photo I have of my mother and father in their courting days, of just the two of them, when they are not part of a group of family and friends. Based on the leafless shrubs in the background, I imagine it is a warm spring afternoon, they have decided to go for a walk in the countryside, and coming upon the wooden bridge, have stopped to pose for a picture.

The bridge is a puzzle. I don't know where it is or why it is there. There is no discernable cut in the ground to indicate a creek or a ravine running under the bridge. I wish I had asked my mother or father about it. Now it is too late. There is not even one family member of their generation left to ask.

It is a Sunday, I am sure, as my father's farmer overalls and heavy boots have been exchanged for neatly pressed trousers, a cardigan and dress oxfords. As my father helped my slim, trim mother perch on the railing, she made sure her narrow skirt demurely covered her knees. She is smiling down at my father, tall and handsome with his dark, curly hair. He is smiling up at her as he stands beside her on the boardwalk. Lost in each other's eyes, they are paying no attention to the person taking their picture.

My mother was engaged to marry someone else when she met my father. She was a schoolteacher and had accepted a position in the school district where my father and his older brother helped their father tend the farm. She boarded at a neighbour's, but it was a small community and they soon met and eventually fell in love, my mother breaking her prior engagement. A romance, and a mystery story too, as my mother would never divulge the name, or the slightest crumb of information about the man she had been about to marry.

While my mother and father were falling in love, tuberculosis, known as TB, was stalking her family. The infection, traced to a hired girl who had been living with the family, claimed a younger brother, Cecil, age 16, in 1928. Both my mother and her sister, Velma, were diagnosed with latent or inactive TB. This indicated they had been in contact with the germs, but as their immune systems were keeping the bacteria from growing, they were not contagious. People could live a normal lifespan with inactive TB, but there was always the possibility that it could become active.

At that time there was no cure for TB other than plenty of rest and  fresh air, and Velma's shift work as a nurse made it difficult to get either. My mother decided to move to another school in the area that had a cottage, so Velma could stay with her.

Realizing they would need some mode of transportation to live independently, my mother became the proud owner of a Model T Ford.

A cantankerous machine, it sometimes needed repeated hand cranking to get it to start. That didn't faze its mechanically inclined owner. She learned to fix flat tires, a common occurrence back then, and soon became familiar with the vehicle's inner workings, boasting just a little about identifying and fixing a broken wire on an occasion when the car refused to start, and they had arranged to pick up friends.

This was a happy time as the sisters continued to have no symptoms to indicate their latent TB infections were becoming active. On the other hand, their love lives were obviously active, as both my mother and Velma became engaged, my mother to my father and Velma to my father's older brother, George. Their betrothals were sealed with identical diamond rings and a double wedding was planned.

But sorrow was waiting in the wings. First, the sisters learned their mother had active TB. Then Velma's immune system lost the battle with the TB bacteria and she died in February 1931. Grief-stricken, George gave my mother Velma's diamond ring to pass on to her first-born daughter.

My parents' wedding, December 29th, 1931, was not a gala event. Tuberculosis and the economic depression cast a double pall over the ceremony, which took place in the living room of my mother's parents' home in Swan River. As no pictures were taken to record the event, my mental images are based on my mother's stories. Neither my mother nor my father had new clothes for the occasion, so they wore their Sunday best. As it was winter there were no garden flowers to make a bouquet for the bride. Only her mother, father and a teenage brother witnessed the couple take their vows. The newlyweds spent their wedding night in one of the upstairs bedrooms, with my mother having to get up several times during the night to tend to her ill mother.

What conflicting emotions my mother must have had the next morning knowing, as she said goodbye, that she might not see her ailing mother again, and at the same time looking forward with hopeful anticipation to married life with her husband.

As the train carrying the newlyweds chugged into the station at Churchbridge, they saw that George was there to meet them. The last stage of their journey to their new home was by horse and cutter over the snow-crusted fields to the Benthall farm, which they had contracted to rent.

Our mother always ended the story of their wedding with, "When we got married we had a horse, a plow, $5.00 in our pocket, and a dream of someday owning our own farm."

And as we children listened we knew that, even if it seemed impossible, you could achieve your dreams if you worked hard enough. Our parents had done it.

One, Two, Three–and Counting

November 8, 1932–the date I decided to leave the warmth and safety of my mother's womb. I have heard the story of that day retold so many times I almost feel like an observer of the event, not the contraction-inducing instigator.

The repeated ringing of the phone woke Uncle Harry from a sound sleep. Two long rings followed by one short ring meant the party-line call was for them. His sleepy, "Hello," was answered by my father's frantic voice. "Get Sadie here quick. Doctor's on another call."

"Fast as I can. Snow's mighty deep."

"Yeah, I know. Just get here."

By the time the team of sturdy Clydesdales were hitched to the open sleigh, Auntie Sadie was ready at the door, muffled in winter woollens, midwife bag in hand. The winter of 1932 had arrived early and with a vengeance. Roads and fields were indistinguishable, one white sea of undulating drifts. As Uncle Harry headed across the fields, taking the shortest route to my parents-to-be, he flicked his horses' rumps with the ends of the reins, urging them forward as they lunged and plunged through snowdrifts up to their bellies. To everyone's relief, Auntie Sadie arrived in time to catch me as I made my entrance into the world. The doctor did not.

With Auntie Sadie's arrival, my father would have retreated to the kitchen to await news of the birth–was it a son or a daughter? Back then husbands were expected to stay out of the way, and indeed, they wanted no part in what they considered messy women's work. In fact, I imagine my father went out to help Uncle Harry put his team in the barn and then, because it was morning, he likely would have milked the cows before returning to the house.

That house, my new home, an uninsulated frame building heated by wood stoves, was a cold and drafty shelter from winter winds that whistled under eaves and rattled windows. My mother said when she put me down to sleep she bundled me up in layers of blankets and even put a knitted bonnet on my head. Maybe that is why I hate anything woolly on my head today!

In 13 months I was joined by a sister, Mary, and when I was exactly two-and-a-half years old, Lorna was added to the family. We were all born on the eighth of the month—November 8, December 8, and May 8. We always thought that was quite special.

Me, Dad holding Lorna, Mary, Mum

There must have been some sibling rivalry between Mary and me. Our mother said that when she couldn't stand our fighting anymore, she would tie both of us to the foot of their bed, just far enough apart that we couldn't touch one another, and there we stayed till we promised to get along. A 1930's version, or at least my mother's version, of time-out!

Mary, Lorna, Me

I was too young to really remember living at the Benthall house. All I have are the stories I have been told. My memories start when we were living at the Jenson place, which we moved to before Billy was born.

Mum holding Bill, Mary, Me, Dad holding Lorna

Auntie Sadie, Penises, and a Plate

The other day a broken dish brought back one of my earliest memories.

I am four-and-a-half years old. My younger sisters, Mary and Lorna, and I are standing on chairs pulled up to the table, so we can watch as Auntie Sadie bathes our newborn brother, Billy, in an oval basin on the kitchen table. We are eyeing with wonder and curiosity this tiny, wriggling, red and wrinkled addition to our family. As Auntie Sadie soaps and then rinses one part of Billy's body after another, our curiosity leads to our first lesson in "family life education" as Auntie Sadie explains exactly what makes our baby brother different from a baby sister. It is the first time we hear words for what everyone seemed to delicately refer to as that area "down there". Penis! Vagina! What a revelation!

When we were older and wondered why Auntie Sadie and Uncle Harry had no children, our mother told us the story of their three babies. All were "blue babies" born with a blood condition for which there was neither a diagnosis nor a cure in the 1920's. The first child survived until nine months of age while the others died at two months. After the third baby died Auntie Sadie said she could not bear to lose another baby and would have no more. I don't know how old I was when I connected this to the fact that, unlike all the other married couples I knew, Auntie Sadie and Uncle Harry had separate bedrooms.

But Auntie Sadie did not succumb to her grief. Instead she became a midwife and devoted her life to helping other women have their babies. She assisted at the births of most of her nieces and nephews and many neighbourhood children, totalling over 50 in all.

Until the late 1940's, rural women had their babies at home. Country doctors came to the house when called but frequently, due to weather conditions or distance to travel, did not arrive as quickly as the baby did.

A midwife had to be prepared to handle a birth on her own. It was also her job to care for the newborn and the mother, who was kept in bed for 10 days after giving birth. In addition, if the family had no "hired girl," the midwife had to care for the other children in the family as well as cook the meals and do the laundry. It was truly a labour of love because the pay was only a dollar a day, and that was if the family could afford to pay. For Auntie Sadie it was doubly a labour of love, for these children she helped birth became her children too.

I have a picture of Auntie Sadie stand-ing in front of her house, holding our brother, Billy. He looks to be about three or four months old and Auntie Sadie is holding him towards the camera in her outstretched arms. It's as if she is saying, "Look at this bonny baby boy I helped bring into the world."

During the summer holidays each of their nieces, one at a time, would be invited to spend a few wonderful days at Auntie Sadie and Uncle Harry's. You had Auntie Sadie's undivided attention as she let you help as she cleaned the house, cooked the meals, and worked in the garden. As we worked she would explain "how" or "why" or pass along an interesting nugget of information. One of the morning tasks, emptying the chamber pots under the beds, became a health lesson–pee that was too yellow meant you needed to drink more water.

She also changed the way I thought about housework. At home I thought my mother had the right idea–furniture should be straight-sided so dust would fall off–but at Auntie Sadie's I happily dusted every crevice of the plant stand's "spool" legs. No cake ever tasted better than one I helped make–happily beating the eggs till they were thick and yellow and tirelessly stirring the batter till it was well mixed. In the garden my favourite job was picking peas. We would go out in the early morning, while the plants were still wet with dew and the plump pea pods cool and crisp. Carefully,

I followed Auntie Sadie's example and held the vine stem with one hand while I pulled off a pod. Otherwise, she explained, you could break off a piece of the plant or even pull it right out of the ground.

Breakfasts in their home were a child's wildest dream come true. Every morning, instead of porridge, we had Uncle Harry's favourite breakfast–macaroni and cheese! This was not one bit like the box of macaroni and cheese, with its packet of bright orange powdered cheese, you can buy today. This was homemade macaroni and cheese with a rich and creamy sauce made with real shredded cheddar, topped with buttered bread crumbs, and baked in the oven till bubbly hot with a golden crispy crust. I have never had a better breakfast–ever.

If the day was hot Auntie Sadie would sometimes make a picnic lunch which we would eat down by the creek. Then I would wade in the refreshingly cool water under her watchful eye. When we returned to the house there might be a special treat, like homemade ice cream, which I could help make by turning the handle on the ice cream maker. This creamy, icy magic was possible because, during the winter, Uncle Harry would have filled their ice house with huge chunks of ice from the creek and covered them with a thick layer of sawdust so it would stay frozen all summer.

Looking back, I now marvel at how Auntie Sadie's loss and sorrow didn't turn her into a bitter and withdrawn woman. Instead she reached out and turned the tragedy of her life into a triumph of love. As children we knew Auntie Sadie loved us and we freely returned her love.

When she died in 1972, Auntie Sadie left instructions that each of her nieces be given a piece of her china collection. My Auntie Sadie's plate, with its sprays of misty roses bordered by soft green and gold leaf that had developed the patina of age over the years, reminded me of all those wonderful holidays I had spent with my aunt. I loved that beautiful plate and it gave me great pleasure every time I used it to serve cookies and cakes to family and friends. And because I shared the story of my aunt and how she had triumphed over the tragedy in her life, "Auntie Sadie's plate" became a special family treasure to my children and grandchildren.

Shortly after our son Lloyd and his future wife Karen started dating, we had a family supper, and when it was time for coffee and dessert our beloved Auntie Sadie's plate, heaped with fudge brownies, was brought to the table. As the brownies disappeared and the plate's pastel and gold leaf decorations were revealed, Karen dissolved in laughter. "All the penises," she gasped, pointing at the plate.

We reacted in shock and disbelief. How could she make fun of our treasured plate? There was a chorus of, "What do you mean?"

"The gold leaf," she said. "Gonads and penises."

We looked at the plate with new eyes and there was a ripple of surprised laughter. Now we saw it too. Around the edge of the plate–between every two rounded scallops–there was a sausage-like shape with a needle-point end.

"Only a Fine Arts grad would see that," we laughed. We shared Auntie Sadie's life story and the history of that special plate with Karen–and forever after that the plate became "Auntie Sadie's penis plate." It was irreverent, but I don't think Auntie Sadie would have minded. Now the plate reflected both family love and laughter.

Years passed and when my 80th birthday was approaching I realized it was time to start planning for the passing of the torch to the next generation. The children were invited to identify any items they would like left to them. Karen requested Auntie Sadie's plate. It seemed only fitting as she had added a provocative new dimension to our relationship with the plate.

Sadly, Karen will not be getting Auntie Sadie's plate, nor will the plate ever be a part of another family gathering. To my horror, when taking it out of the cupboard a few weeks ago, the plate slipped from my hand and fell to the floor. I felt sick as I saw the shattered pieces at my feet. My eyes filled with tears as I swept up the last tangible link to my beloved aunt.

I miss that plate, but my memories of Auntie Sadie are as beautiful as ever. I can't bequeath her plate to future generations, but I can leave her story.

"Here's to you, Auntie Sadie. May your story live on!"

A Moment in Time

I remember the day this picture was taken. It was a Monday because my mother is doing the laundry. It was summer because my mother is doing the laundry outside.

The wash tub and the rinse tub are sitting on a couple of old chairs that are missing their backs. Attached to the wash tub is a wooden contraption with a plunger which my mother is moving up and down by hand. Attached to the rinse tub there is a wringer with rollers and a handle. The handle must be turned by hand to squeeze the water out of the clothes as they are fed into the rollers.

I can tell my mother is cross at my father. "Eddie, I don't want my picture taken," she says.

She is tired. She has carried the pails of water for the laundry from the well and heated the water in the copper boiler on the wood-burning range. The hot stove has probably turned the kitchen into a stifling oven, so she has decided to lug the chairs and the tubs outside and carry the pails of hot water from the boiler to the wash tub.

Behind my mother you can see a grey, unpainted, two-story structure, with a lean-to that looks like it was added on as an afterthought. The screen door has a definite sag. It is the rented farmhouse that is our home. The landscape is barren except for one stunted, straggly tree at the corner of the house. The parched ground in front of the house is a combination of pebbly soil, sparse grass and low-growing plantain and dandelion weeds. You can just make out the corner of a little wooden wagon, which says there are children in this family. In fact, there are four of us, age six and under, which means there is a lot of laundry.

My mother would have been moving that plunger up and down for hours. Outside the range of the camera, the whites and the light-coloured clothes would be pegged to the clothesline, sagging motionless on this hot and windless day. It is a good thing there is no wind. A wind would sweep up the soil from the rain-starved fields and fill the air with a murky cloud of gritty dust.

I imagine the reason my father is taking the picture is because he thinks my mother is smart to take the laundry outside. He wants to record the event even though my mother does not want her picture taken. She is not only tired–she is hot, perspiring, and untidy. Her flimsy home-sewn housedress is clinging damply to her plump body. Strands of hair have escaped from her bun and are straggling limply about her face.

I have another picture of my mother. This picture was taken 10 years before, in the 1920s. She does not look anything like the person who is at the laundry tub. In this picture she is standing proudly in front of her beloved Model T Ford. She is a rural school teacher and in the background you can see the cozy cottage where she lives. Her hair is bobbed in the latest style, and she is wearing a slim flapper-style dress with a tiered skirt and a white collar. I'm sad that I never had the chance to know this fashionable, slim, and pretty woman. The depression of the 1930s–and perhaps four babies in five years–seemed to erase her.

When I look back at that bleak 1930s picture, I wish I could speak to that woman at the laundry tub. I would tell her, "Times will get better," because they did. I wish I could tell her, "You will not rent forever. You will buy your own farm and you will make it a place of beauty with groves of leafy trees, a lush lawn, a bountiful vegetable garden and a prize-winning rose garden."

I know my mother usually had faith in the future. One of her maxims we heard many times over the years was, "All things work out for the best in the end."

But, in that moment by the laundry tub, captured forever by my father's camera, I don't think my weary, bedraggled mother had much hope in her heart.

No More Storytelling

It was early morning, December 27th, 1939. My two sisters, brother, and I were awakened by the sound of agonized groaning. Before we could react to the terrifying sound, the hired girl's head appeared in the faint light that was creeping up the stairs from a kerosene lamp below. Without a word she unlatched and lowered the heavy trap door at the top of the stairs, leaving us in inky darkness.

Huddled under heavy patchwork quilts in that uninsulated attic room, we lay there stunned into silence for a moment before letting out our mystified and worried whispers.

"What's wrong?"

"What's happening?"

"Why'd she shut the door?"

In intervals between the cries of pain we heard unfamiliar voices. More questions: "Who's here? What're they doing?"

Eventually, as the dim winter dawn entered through our one small, square, frost-crusted window, those terrifying sounds of agony ended. As we lay there hardly daring to breathe, wondering if the suffering we had heard was over, the hired girl pushed up the trap door, latched it open, and announced, "You have a new baby brother."

That was it. We had never been told that a baby would be joining our family. The hired girl could have explained what was happening before closing the attic door, but she said nothing. Apparently there was no concern that, without an explanation, we might be frightened by the sounds emanating from below. Did we suspect, or instinctively realize what was happening, though we never dared whisper our suspicions? I don't know. I do know that we were terrified by those sounds of pain that resulted in the arrival of our brother Denis.

It was a time when big families–six to 12 children, or more, were the norm, so news of an aunt or neighbour woman having a baby was commonplace. When we were told the infant had been left in the cabbage patch or a stork had brought it, the explanation depending on the season, we knew that was adult "storytelling." After all, we lived on a farm. We knew cows had calves, mares had foals, and sows miraculously produced litters of piglets, though we were never allowed to watch the births.

However, from bits and pieces of overheard conversations, children pick up more information than adults realize. Although we never had the birthing process explained to us, we had repeatedly heard the story of my arrival on an unusually snowy November–how Uncle Harry's horses had plunged through snow up to their bellies to get Auntie Sadie to our house before the doctor arrived–and barely in time for my birth. One of the make-believe games I remember my two sisters and I playing was "having a baby." The patient, discreetly covered by a blanket, would have her doll lying atop her stomach. The doctor's job was to reach under the blanket, extract the doll, and hand it to the midwife. Rubber balls stuffed inside our dresses created breasts for the mother and midwife. As we had only three balls we were faced with a problem. We dealt with the dilemma by giving the mother two breasts as she had to feed the baby, while our midwife made do with one breast in the middle of her chest. Such is the ingenious imagination of children! Our "new mother" gave no evidence of discomfort, so I am sure we were playing this game before Denis' birth. I know that I did not associate pain with having a baby till that frightening morning in December.

That was in the 1930s. Sex, and anything related to sex, including pregnancy and the birthing process, was a taboo subject for polite discussion among adults, let alone children. When going out in public, a women who was pregnant would hide her "condition" as long as possible by wearing a loose coat past the time to need a coat, or when summer heat precluded that stratagem, carry a coat or jacket folded over her arm in front of her bulging belly. If we noticed our mother's gradually increasing girth, we just assumed she was getting fat.

Pregnancies among unwed girls or women were viewed as shameful and "covered up" as much as possible. There might be a quick "shotgun" wedding–the term originating with the concept of the girl's father using a gun to force the reluctant groom to the altar. A pregnant teenager might be sent to "visit" an out-of-province relative for the required months, returning without the baby who had been "put up" for adoption. Another ruse was to keep the pregnant girl in seclusion for the duration of the pregnancy, with her mother claiming to have given birth to the baby, who could then remain a part of the family. Though they were illegal, backdoor abortions were also an "out" for women who could afford them.

Then, in 1960, the approval of the birth control pill as a contraceptive led to a sexual revolution and women's liberation. Engaging in sexual activities no longer meant an unplanned pregnancy, freeing women to join the workforce in increasing numbers. In 1960, approximately 30 percent of women aged 20 to 30 were part of the workforce in Canada. By 1970 the number had doubled to 60 percent. In 1971, the federal government amended the Canada Labour Code to include 15 weeks of maternity leave benefits paid through the Unemployment Insurance system. Women gained more control over their own bodies in 1988 when abortion became legal in Canada and was funded through the Canada Health Act.

Today, in 2020, parental leave has been extended to 12 months, or 18 months with the same amount of unemployment benefits spread out over the longer period. The change in name to parental leave is noteworthy as now either partner may choose to take the leave to care for their child. In many industries, labour unions have negotiated longer parental leave times for their members by topping up the EI benefit amount as well as guaranteeing that women can return to the same job they had before their maternity leave.

Families of two or three have now become the norm. Also, as women can delay starting a family until they are established in their careers, the average age of first-time mothers has increased. Currently, 70 percent of women with children under five years of age work outside the home, creating an increasing need for affordable, quality childcare options. This has become a political issue, with some provinces subsidizing costs to keep them affordable, while others do not.

There has also been a huge societal change in attitude to sexual activity before marriage. Now most young couples live together for months, even years, before getting married, or may choose to live "common law." As the stigma attached to unwed pregnancy has evaporated, couples may even have a child or two before getting married. In addition, most "single" mothers now choose to keep their babies, resulting in fewer children being available for adoption.

This, in turn, has led to medical advances in helping couples who are having difficulty conceiving. In intrauterine insemination (IUI), sperm is inserted into a women's womb. The in-vitro fertilization (IVF) process involves eggs being fertilized with sperm in a laboratory. The fertilized embryo is then placed in the women's womb. Eggs, sperm, and fertilized embryos can now be frozen for future use, leading to the creation of donor banks for eggs and sperm, as well as the emergence of gestational carriers or surrogates. The first IVF baby was born in 1978. Now there are millions of "test tube" babies.

Society's changing sexual mores have led to a gradual change in attitude toward the LGBT community. Same sex relationships became lawful in Canada in 1969. In 1982, LGBT people were guaranteed basic human rights under the Canadian Charter of Rights and Freedoms. In 2005, same sex marriages were legally permitted. Now same sex couples, both lesbian and gay, have the same rights as heterosexual couples to adopt or raise children. Today Canada is rated the most gay-friendly country in the world.

How has the sexual revolution affected children? Sexual education classes are now part of the school curriculum, focusing on safety, mutual respect, and the right to say, "No"–with information appropriate to the age of the child.

As parents are having fewer children, I think each one is individually more cherished. There is more attention paid to the importance of early childhood experiences and learning, beginning with a child's first year.

Just as mothers no longer hide their "baby bumps," children in the family are no longer shielded from the realities of pregnancy. They are informed in advance of the impending arrival of a brother or sister and encouraged to feel the baby moving in their mother's tummy. Depending on their age, they might be shown ultra-sound pictures of the baby as it develops. While most babies are now born in a hospital, if a mother chooses to have a home birth with a midwife, other children in the family will understand what is happening. And as prenatal classes now train couples in techniques to control pain, the sounds of childbirth may not be as agonizing as those my siblings and I heard so long ago.

Now there is no more "storytelling" when babies arrive. There are no more questions unanswered. And no more fear.

Grandpa and Grandma's Log House

Unlike the house where we lived until I was seven–an unpainted grey clapboard building squatting on bare, hardscrabble prairie–our grandparents' home was a place of beauty.

Both Grandpa and Grandma were immigrants from England, and here on the prairies they had created an English country garden.

Their cozy whitewashed log house was nestled on two sides by a hill and surrounded by mature trees. Hop vines, covering the front of the house from ground level to the eaves, formed a leafy background for the flower beds with their bright blooms. The lawn was a soft green carpet inviting bare feet and childhood play while curving gravel pathways led to the front door or to a bench under the trees. The maples with their low, forked, and wide-spreading branches invited kid-climbing. And enclosing the yard was a neat wire fence, almost hidden by more twining vines, and a wide metal gate.

In winter the log house was heated by wood stoves and by the sun streaming in through the south-facing windows. Both the hill and a large poplar grove protected the house from buffeting winter winds. In summer, the rooms were dim and cool, protected from the sun's hot rays by the earthen berm on the north and east sides and the vines and deciduous trees that filtered the light from the south and west.

This was an energy-efficient house built in 1893!

Behind the kitchen, extending further into the hillside, was the cold room. Its walls were earth and its floor carefully laid, flat, split rocks. Here our grandmother stored the crocks of whole milk, waiting for the cream to rise to the top so it could be skimmed off. Around the perimeter there were shelves holding the little tubs of butter she made from that cream, as well as all the vegetables, fruits and preserves that needed cool storage.

The hill that hugged the house extended into a plateau for some distance to the north. Here, in addition to the usual large vegetable garden, our grandparents had created another prairie rarity—a thriving orchard with apple and crabapple trees and raspberry, gooseberry, and blackberry bushes.

I loved our weekly Sunday visits to Grandpa and Grandma's farm. I knew our cousins would be there too. While the men sat under the trees and talked about the weather and crops and prices and politics, the women admired the flower beds and toured the orchard and garden, and then went inside to make the meal. We children would loll about on the grass, or try to do summersaults and headstands, or see who could climb the highest in our favourite maple tree. If they begged, we would pull the smaller kids about in the wagon.

We might play one of our favourite games—hide-and-seek, blind-man's-bluff, or tag. I remember one day our feisty, one-legged grandfather—he had lost his leg due to a tragic childhood accident—couldn't resist and got up with his crutches and joined us in a game of tag. "No fair!" we said when he reached out with his crutch and tagged us.

"What do you mean—no fair?" he said. "You've got two legs, I've got one." We couldn't argue with that logic, so with lots of screaming and giggling we used evasive tactics to avoid his reach and tried to tag him from behind.

I thought that log house would be a wonderful place to live, and not just because of the beautiful flowers or the soft grass, climbing trees or orchard fruit. The upstairs bedroom windows opened at ground level to the hill behind, and it seemed magical to me when my dad, or uncles or aunts, described how, on warm summer evenings, those windows provided an easy escape when they wanted to play outside in the twilight. Nothing, I thought, could be more perfect.

My grandparent's log house is now gone. Only the stone foundation remains. A photograph, taken in the 1930s, has become a family icon. It has been reproduced on the cover of a family reunion cookbook and on plates and mugs that are family keepsakes. That picture taken so long ago is black and white, but when I look at it, I see it in color just as I remember it.

My Putland Grandparents

These are my favourite pictures of Grandma and Grandpa Putland.

In this picture the camera has captured them at a relaxed moment, not staring fixedly at the camera or unsmiling–as in most pictures taken back then. You can see Grandpa's crutches on the grass at his feet. I am standing beside Grandpa, Mary is beside Grandma, Lorna is in front of Grandpa, and Grandma is holding our cousin, Barbara, on her lap. Uncle Henry must be the photographer as in the next picture we have been joined by our father, mother, Auntie Doris, Auntie Sadie, and Uncle Harry. This is how I remember my grandparents–always surrounded by family.

In fact, if I had to choose one word to describe Grandpa and Grandma Putland, it would be "family." They had 10 children, nine of whom lived to old age. Their farm was truly a family farm as the three eldest, who were girls, and the three boys (numbers six, eight and 10) left school before completing the elementary grades to help their one-legged father with the farm work. My father said he only went to Grade 5, and he thought his three oldest sisters stopped at Grade 3.

As well as helping with all the outside chores, the three girls had to perform many of the demanding physical tasks usually reserved for boys. Auntie Violet, in the forward to the *Baimbridge/Putland Centennial History Book*, describes how her eldest sister, Nellie, helped fetch winter wood by loading the trees onto the horse-drawn sleigh after her father had chopped them down. The three younger girls, who were able to continue their schooling, two becoming teachers, realized their education was achieved on the backs of their older sisters. That sense of being part of a family enterprise, working together for the common good, was a powerful bond uniting parents and children.

Whenever they weren't needed for outdoor farm work, the girls assisted their mother with household tasks, including helping to care for the younger ones. This could, upon occasion, call for meting out a little discipline.

Our father liked to tell the story of what happened when he tested the sharpness of a new jackknife on his pant leg, slicing through the cloth and cutting a deep gash in his leg that left a permanent scar. An older sister, more upset by the cut in his pants than the blood trickling down his leg, decided such wanton carelessness deserved a good spanking.

Despite the odd spanking, or the 18-year-age span between the oldest and the youngest, the sisters and brothers were a close-knit group. It was a family that played together as well as worked together–skating and tobogganing parties in the winter and pickup games of softball and horseshoes in the summer. In fact, I had difficulty finding a picture of only my mother and father in their courting days. At the beach, on a picnic, or posing for silly pictures in the home yard, they were always part of a family group.

After the children were married and raising families of their own, "Ma" and "Pa" were still the nucleus of the family with regular Sunday gatherings at the old log house that I remember so fondly. After Grandpa and Grandma and the log house were gone, the familial ties that bound their children lived on, with much "inter-visiting" among the families. The three boys, who all became farmers, lived within a few miles of one another and often worked together, even jointly owning their first tractor.

As my dad was the third youngest in that family of 10, my grandma and grandpa were already in their late sixties/mid-seventies in my earliest memories of them. By then their youngest son, Henry, had taken over the farm and Uncle Henry and Auntie Doris lived in the log house with Grandma and Grandpa. My grandparents now spent their time tending their front yard and large vegetable garden and orchard.

When, with little-kid curiosity, I first asked my mother, "Why's Grandpa only got one leg?" she gave me the short version. "His leg got badly burned in an accident." In my little-kid imagination I saw Grandpa's leg flaming into ash like a stick in our stove.

When I was older, and had been joined by sisters and a brother, we were given the complete story of the accident, probably as a caution so we would never do what Grandpa did.

The accident happened when Grandpa was 12 years old. He and his older sister, Rose, were home alone as their mother, father and brothers were all at work. Rose wanted the fire lit, probably to cook the family meal.

Grandpa had watched his older brothers using kerosene to start the fire in the stove, so he tried to do the same. He must not have known there were live coals in the stove or did not realize the danger.

Suddenly the can of kerosene he was holding burst into flame, badly burning his leg. Rose quickly grabbed the flaming can and ran towards the river.

Unfortunately, Rose never made it to the water. She was severely burned and suffered for several hours before dying.

Grandpa's burned leg never healed properly, causing him problems all his life. But despite his injured leg, Grandpa came west as a homesteader, cleared and plowed his land, built a sod shanty and, before his marriage to Grandma, a log house and barn.

After Grandpa and Grandma had been married several years he injured his burned leg again when a log fell on it. When the sore on his leg would not heal, and the leg became so painful he could no longer do his farm work, Grandpa decided the only solution was to have it amputated at the hip.

The burden of guilt for his sister's death was not so easily removed, however. "That," our mother said, "he bore for the rest of his life."

Grandpa liked to reminisce about his days as a homesteader and Uncle Henry wisely recorded many of his stories. After Grandpa died Uncle Henry would often share these stories as the family lingered over a Sunday dinner table. That is probably how I first heard the story of Grandpa's botched amputation surgery. Grandpa's doctor was from Saltcoats, but the surgery had to be performed in the nearest hospital, which was in Yorkton. The doctor was drunk when he arrived at the hospital to do the surgery, so it was postponed for two weeks. The second time the doctor was sober, but he proved to be inept. First, he neglected to tie off the main artery, resulting in a great loss of blood, and then, he missed the hip socket, breaking the point of his knife off in the bone. Fortunately, the hospital surgeon intervened and completed the surgery. However, by that time Grandpa had lost so much blood he very nearly died.

Sometime in the 1970s, I added Heather Robertson's book, *Salt of the Earth–the Story of the Homesteaders in Western Canada,* to my collection of Canadiana. The "contents" list indicated the book included the pioneers' trek west, homesteading experiences, and the development of communities and towns, ending with the First World War. As I was perusing this collection of photographs and first-person stories I was seeing history as it was lived, described by the homesteaders through excerpts from their diaries, letters, and reminiscences.

As I began the section called "Community" I did not know a surprise was waiting for me. On page 152, under the heading "Doctor," there was a description by Dr Patrick of a surgery performed on a woman by a doctor from Saltcoats (Dr. S). The word "Saltcoats" caught my attention. Could that be the doctor who had done Grandpa's surgery? When, in Dr. Patrick's opinion, Dr. S "showed a lack of knowledge of the progress made in surgical technique," I felt sure this must be Grandpa's doctor.

When Dr. Patrick went on to describe a second surgery, which was on a 33-year-old man who had a severe burn that had never completely healed, I knew this had to be the story of Grandpa's amputation, written by the surgeon who had intervened to save Grandpa's life. And to think, if I had not chosen this book from the hundreds in the bookstore, I might never have discovered this first-person record of a piece of our family history!

Checking dates, I realize there is a discrepancy in Grandpa's age between Uncle Henry's records and Dr. Patrick's reminiscences. Uncle Henry writes that Grandpa had his amputation surgery in the winter of 1905. Grandpa would have been 44 years old, not 33 as indicated by Dr. Patrick, but except for this discrepancy, the details of the surgery are identical in both of their accounts.

In 1905, when Grandpa had his amputation surgery, my grandparents had a family of six, the five oldest being girls, and my grandmother was pregnant with number seven. As she nursed Grandpa during his recovery from the surgery, I can imagine how Grandma must have worried about what the future held for her large family. How could her husband, now with only one leg, do the hard, physical work that farming required? The three oldest girls were only 11, nine and seven years old. Could they manage all the farm work with one hired man? If not, how could they afford more help?

She need not have worried. Grandpa proved a one-legged man, with determination and ingenuity, could indeed farm and support his large family. (See Uncle Henry's stories of his father's life in the Appendix section.)

I was almost seven years old when Grandpa Putland died in 1939 at the age of 79, so I have only a few years of memories with him. On our Sunday visits to Grandma and Grandpa's he would usually be seated on the bench in the far corner of the yard, in the shade of the overhanging trees. His crutches would be lying on the ground at his feet. Sons and sons-in-law would be gathered around him—sitting on benches or squatting on the grass—as they discussed farming issues spiced with a sprinkling of politics and local gossip. Sometimes there would be posing for family pictures. Sometimes he paid attention to our games, shouting an encouragement or a warning to us, and occasionally joining in the fun.

When our mother explained that Daddy was sad because Grandpa had died, I don't remember feeling sad myself, but rather, uncomfortable with the changed mood in the house as well as mildly curious. If Grandpa was now an angel in heaven, how come Daddy was sad?

We younger grandchildren did not attend Grandpa's funeral, spending the afternoon with Auntie Lucille who was nursing a one-and-a-half-month-old baby. I imagine it was a simple affair, held in the log house that was filled with so many memories for Grandma and her family, with Grandpa's body, perhaps in a homemade coffin, transported by truck to the Churchbridge cemetery for burial.

In the years after Grandpa's death our mother would, from time to time, bring Grandma to our house for a day-long visit. Quiet and unassuming, Grandma was happiest if Mum had some task for her to do. I remember only this one snippet of a story she shared after Mum urged her to tell us about life in England. I am sure there must have been more, but this is the only picture that has stuck with me.

At the end of the day, you would see the factory girls walking home from work. They'd be four or five abreast, singing loud and bawdy songs.

This was clearly something Grandma found shocking, not something she could imagine doing, but a little bemused shake of the head was as far as she went in expressing her disapproval of the behaviour. Now I wonder, as she stared out the window, did she envy those girls their carefree camaraderie just a wee bit?

Uncle Henry and Auntie Doris continued to live in the log house with Grandma till March 1945 when they moved into a frame house they had purchased and had transported onto the property. Grandma chose to remain in the log house, but she was in failing health. Our mother's diary reports that by January 1947 she was spending all day in bed, but she must have still wished to be independent, as a granary on Auntie Nellie and Uncle Herman's farm was adapted to make a small two-room house for her.

I will never forget the visit my mother and I made to see her on a July afternoon that summer. Grandma, covered in a quilt, was lying in bed in the tiny bedroom. Auntie Violet was there when we arrived and there was barely room for the three of us to stand around the bed. It was a hot day and the temperature in that bedroom was stifling. I have never seen anyone perspire as much as white-haired, plump little Auntie Violet perspired that day. I watched, fascinated, as droplets the size of big raindrops formed on her cheeks and ran down in rivulets before dripping off her face.

As we left, Auntie Violet said, "She's not staying in that hot-box another day." I could not understand how anyone would have ever thought that ugly, uninsulated little shack was a fitting home for Grandma.

Frail and failing, Grandma spent the final four months of her life once more surrounded by family, living with her daughters in turn–the last month at Auntie Sadie's. I knew that Grandma must be seriously ill when Auntie Sadie was coaxing her to swallow a spoonful of brandy as she pressed it to her lips. I knew that Auntie Sadie, just like our mother, thought all alcoholic drinks were evil, so she must be desperate to be using brandy as medicine for her mother. That was the last time I saw Grandma. She died November 25th, age 78.

Grandma's funeral was my first. All I was conscious of was Grandma lying dead in the open coffin at the front of the room. When the time came for the family to walk up to the front to say goodbye to Grandma, my gut tightened in fear. I had never seen a dead person. I did not want to see Grandma dead. As I stopped in front of the coffin I kept my eyes lowered, unable to look, and quickly walked by. I was back in my seat as I watched my younger cousin, Barbara, approach the coffin. She stopped and stood for what seemed minutes, looking down at Grandma. And I felt ashamed that Barbara, who had lived till she was eight in the log house with Grandma, seemed to love Grandma more than I did–loved her enough to want to say a last goodbye to her.

That night when I went up to bed, the first thing I saw as I stepped into my room was the stack of cards lying on my desk. I was hand-painting Christmas cards for the family that year and there on top of the pile was my card for Grandma, a card I could now never give her, inscribed,

Merry Christmas to Grandma
With all my love,
                    Jean

My Fraser Grandparents

Grandma Fraser, my maternal grandmother, died before I was born, so she exists only as a creation of my imagination based on information gleaned from my mother's stories and this one mother/daughter photo.

I choose to think the snapshot is not kind to her, that what looks like a stern frown and squinting eyes is just an instinctive reaction to facing the sun. She is not smiling, but when I cover the top half of her face with my hand I think I see the possibility of a smile at the corners of her mouth. I do know when I look in the mirror I see those same strong lines running from my nose to my mouth.

Realizing she was dying of tuberculosis, my grandmother's last words to my just-married mother as she was leaving for her new home were, "I hope I live to see my first grandchild." My mother and father did their best–I was born 11 months after they were married–but my grandmother died on September 5th, 1932, age 56, two months and three days before I made my entry into the world.

Grandpa Fraser, though infected with latent or inactive tuberculosis, fulfilled Grandma's dying wish, and more. He lived to see, not just nine grandchildren, but a great-grandchild, our son, Darryl.

I don't know when Mum told me Grandpa and Grandma were first cousins. It was one of those things I felt like I always knew. It was unusual for first cousins to marry back then, and it wasn't allowed anymore, she said. In response to my "Why?" she explained there was a greater risk of their children inheriting a bad family trait, like certain diseases.

Since I grew up surrounded by cousins on the Putland side of the family, I assumed that Grandpa and Grandma, being cousins, had known each other since childhood.

However, genealogical research my sister Leila did a few years ago proved that assumption wrong.

The story of my Fraser grandparents begins with the two Montgomery sisters–Mary and Margaret.

Mary Montgomery married Alexander Fraser and they settled in Cumminsville, Ontario, where Alexander taught school for 37 years. Their fifth child, William, born in 1869, was my grandfather.

Margaret Montgomery married William Burton, who had grown up on a farm in Ontario, but around 1900 he moved his young family to Manitoba where he became a farmer himself. Their third child, Janet, born in 1876, would become my grandmother.

In 1895, Alexander Fraser, now a retired teacher, sold the house in Cumminsville and the family made the move to a farm in the Lansdowne area of Manitoba. I suspect it was at the urging of his wife, Mary, who wished to be closer to two of their daughters who had recently married prairie farmers after a visit with their Aunt Margaret. At last, 20 years after leaving home to start their own families, the Montgomery sisters, Mary Fraser and Margaret Burton, were now living in the same district.

Within three years of the Fraser and Burton families becoming neighbours, my grandparents, the cousins William Fraser and Janet Burton, had fallen in love and married.

For the first 10 years after their marriage, William and Janet stayed close to their families, continuing to live in the Lansdowne area. In the 1901 census report, William earned $300 working as a grain buyer for six months and $200 from other unspecified jobs.

According to my mother, Grandpa Fraser was a "jack-of-all-trades," working as a telegraph operator as a young man in Ontario, and after he came west, as a railway station master, a carpenter, and a farmer.

I don't know how much success Grandpa had as a farmer. Although Grandma had grown up on a farm, Grandpa was a "town boy," having lived in Cumminsville till he was 25. As he moved his family from a farm in Lansdowne to one in the Dauphin area, then back to Lansdowne, and finally to Swan River, it would seem to indicate he was continually searching for a better opportunity.

I do know money was always in short supply. My mother said that Grandma complained that if someone asked Grandpa for the shirt on his back he would give it away, even if it was the last shirt he owned.

Through the generations the Montgomery, Fraser and Burton families shared a Methodist/Pentecostal faith, emphasizing personal witness, spreading the gospel and missionary work. And when Grandpa and Grandma moved to the Swan River area, joining relatives–Grandpa's sister, Jessie, and Grandma's brother, Walter–they found an established Pentecostal faith group.

The Jessie and William Fullerton and Walter and Pauline Burton families both had farms, and my grandparents also settled on a farm once more. However, by 1930 Grandpa was no longer farming, having moved his family into Swan River where he worked as a carpenter. They would not move again.

In September 1940, Grandpa Fraser, now 70 years old, was working on a building when he fell from a ladder, severely injuring his back. Our mother stayed by his side in the hospital till he regained consciousness, but returning home to her family, she did not know if her father would ever walk again.

In a diary entry in January 1941, she reported that Grandpa was improving, now able to sit up.

The following excerpts of a letter Grandpa wrote in May 1941 reveals a great deal about Grandpa as a person as he describes his struggle to survive, his increasing mobility, and hope for the future.

> *But up till the time of my accident I was still well and able to do just as much as any of the men I had working with me and able to get there first in the morning, for all of which I was and am truly thankful, although I am now according to the Doctor's verdict, a cripple for the balance of my life. I find cause for thankfulness in the fact that I was under compensation when I got hurt. That compensation is all I have to live on but its lots better than having to live on relief, and the old age pension would not be enough to keep me going as I have to have someone with me all the time. You see I cannot use my fingers to button or unbutton my clothes. But although the Doctors give me no hope whatever of being able to ever do any work at all, I am not losing hope that the good Lord will see fit to*

give me enough use of my hands that I can dress and undress myself. He can do what the Doctors call impossible for they only gave me a few days at the most to live when I went into the hospital and four times after that when I took that many set-backs, they pronounced my recovery impossible. But – Here I am, still alive, and much better than I once was.

Summarizing the next section of Grandpa's letter:

In his delirium Grandpa felt he was crossing the "River of Death" but when he started to climb out on the "Other Side" his hands were gently pushed off and he was carried down the river and thrown out on this side again.

Since then I have had a hope that I would get well enough to look after myself without any help and am still clinging to that hope. I will be glad of your prayers to that end. I can walk around outside to a very limited extent and can feed myself for which I am very thankful.

Grandpa achieved his wish and, though his fingers remained permanently bent at the knuckles, resembling giant claws, he was eventually able to live independently in his own home.

We made our first family visit to Swan River to see Grandpa in July of 1942. I was nine and had graduated from wheelchair to crutches that spring. My mother's diary notes that one-year-old Leila and I stayed with her at Miss Latimer's while the rest of the family were at Hogg's. Our hosts were not relatives, so I assume they were friends of my mother and grandfather.

I have only two memories of that visit. It was our first family visit to the cemetery where Grandma Fraser, Uncle Cecil, and Auntie Velma were buried. This was a ritual that would be repeated on every visit to Swan River. We took no flowers, just stood by the three graves in silent contemplation till our mother would share a memory or two and then we would know it was okay to talk.

Miss Latimer has faded from my memory, I regret to say, but her piano made a lasting impression. I can still see the wood grain in the pale beige of its natural oak cabinet. It was the first piano I had seen, and years later when my parents bought a piano I assumed it would look exactly like Miss Latimer's beautiful instrument. When our new piano's wrapping was removed I stared in disbelief. Its finish was a flat dark brown, the ugliest thing you could imagine, compared to the natural oak beauty that I had pictured in my mind. Today I still prefer light-coloured wood, as you would see if you stepped into my house.

On subsequent visits to Swan River we stayed with Uncle Walter and Aunt Pauline, who had now retired and moved from their farm to a house in town. Their strict religious rituals gave me a sense of what my mother's upbringing might have been like. Heads were bowed for a grace that thanked God for what seemed like everything possible before eventually getting around to the food we were about to eat. After breakfast Uncle Walter would read from the Bible. Next, a little box of cards with quotes from the Bible was passed around the table with each person selecting a card, and then reading it aloud. I sat there hoping I would draw a card with something short and simple as you were expected to memorize the passage and live according to that tenet for the day.

After our first visit to Swan River in July 1942, Grandpa came to our place for two weeks in August. Then he was back to celebrate Christmas with us in December, staying till March of '43.

Watching Grandpa spend a good portion of every morning reading his Bible, I realized he was a religious man. I became even more convinced when I heard him tell my mother he took a God's kidney pill every day. It was many years later, when I saw an ad for Dodd's Kidney Pills, that I realized my grandfather was not quite as close to God as I had imagined.

In those first three months that Grandpa lived with us, he helped Mum build a closet and bank of drawers in what she complained was "wasted space" in our roomy upstairs landing. Grandpa couldn't hold a saw or hammer with those bent fingers, but he could give advice and instructions, use a tape measure, and hold boards in place.

This pattern of visits was repeated with Grandpa returning in December '43 and staying till March. He helped Mum wallpaper a bedroom and worked with Dad building kitchen cupboards and Mum's dream–a dumb waiter. What looked like a trap door in the kitchen floor was a lift with shelves to carry food between basement and kitchen, saving many trips up and down the stairs.

Whenever Grandpa visited it seemed there were always things needing fixing–chairs, doors, windows–or a planned renovation needing his guidance. One of the last big projects made with the help of those misshapen hands was the built-in bed, closet, dresser, and drop-down desk in the small bedroom I shared with five-year-old Leila. I loved that bedroom. I could lie in bed, and looking out the low old-fashioned casement window, find my starry night-time friends, Orion and his dog Sirius, points of brilliance in the dark southern sky. That nifty little desk meant I could study and write in the privacy of my bedroom. And with no furniture to sweep under, the bedroom was transformed from the most inconvenient to the easiest in the house to clean.

After Grandpa, age 82, was hospitalized with the flu, his health declined. His visits became fewer and Mum made more short visits to Swan River. He did spend Christmases in '51 and '52 with us, but in September '53 his latent tuberculosis became active and he was admitted to the sanatorium in Ninette. The following is an excerpt from a letter written while he was in Ninette to a niece, Irene Young.

The biggest drawback I find here is that there is no Christian atmosphere at all. I was talking to one attendant today who has been here for a day or so, and it was quite an uplift to talk to one who had the more important things at heart. There is a man over in the next building to us who belongs to the brethren. He comes over occasionally and that helps.

The others here are all very nice to get along with and are very kind but they have very little desire to talk about personal Salvation, quite a few of the better class are Church members but that seems to be all they think necessary for Salvation. I have settled down to the conclusion that about the only witness that a person can bear here is the witness of as clean a Christian life as you can live.

In October '54, Dad and Mum made the parlour into a downstairs bedroom for Grandpa and brought him home from Ninette to live with them for about a year. After celebrating Christmas with the family, he wrote the following in a letter to Irene, and husband Will:

> *All the folks here, including myself, are quite well and the Lord is good to everyone. We have great reason to be thankful in this wonderful Canada of ours. And so few people seem to show any sign of gratitude. Jean, Vera's oldest girl, has a baby boy, about three weeks old. She calls him Darryl John. I don't know if I told you that Harold's girl had a baby last fall, also a boy, but he only lived about three weeks and smothered in his crib. So I am now a great-grandfather for the second time.*

A few days later, Mum and Dad took Grandpa to Yorkton for a medical check-up. On their way home, they stopped in at our place for a short visit so that Grandpa could see his 21-day-old great-grandson, Darryl.

In April '55, we made our first Sunday visit to Mum and Dad's since Darryl's birth. Grandpa had been ill with a bad cold and was still weak, spending most of the day resting on his bed. This would be the last time I saw Grandpa.

In May, he moved back to Swan River but sometime in '56 he was readmitted to Ninette. Mum and Dad brought him home for a visit on August 19 and returned him to Ninette on September 2. It would be Grandpa's last visit and their last "goodbye."

December 7th, Mum got a message that Grandpa was in the Swan River hospital, having suffered a stroke. She rushed to his side, but he never regained consciousness, dying at 6:30 a.m. on December 9th. He was 87.

Reading Mum's diary, I think how lonely she must have felt in the four days till the funeral. She had no siblings by her side to share her grief–she sent a telegram to Uncle Harold in the U.S. and phoned a radio station to send a message to Uncle Bob, now in Beaver Lodge, northern Alberta. Cousins Irene and Will Young would not be able to come from Minnedosa, MB.

She was alone to make funeral arrangements, look over papers in the house, meet with a lawyer, pay the hospital bill, and clean Grandpa's house.

Dad arrived the morning of the funeral. After the funeral at 2:00 p.m. the mourners gathered at Aunt Pauline's for lunch. By the time Mum and Dad got home that night at 9:30, Mum must have been exhausted both emotionally and physically.

One thing I know–Mum could not have done more to make Grandpa feel loved and useful in the years after his accident. As for Grandpa, Mum said he was easy to live with, never criticizing or interfering in the raising of the kids.

What is my favourite memory? The Grandpa I knew was kind, but not demonstrative, quiet and serious, almost dour. So I was stunned the day he made a joke–and even more shocking, he was making a joke about the Bible.

"Jean reads too much. That's in the Bible," he said.

"Grandpa," I said, hardly believing what I had just heard come out of Grandpa's mouth. "That's not in the Bible."

"Yes, it is," Grandpa said. "That's in the Bible." And he showed me his open Bible with his finger firmly placed under the word "that's."

Exploring Our Fraser Ancestral Roots

In 2012 John and I, with my brother Bill and sister-in-law Vel, spent about a week in Burlington, Ontario, visiting our sister Leila. She became our tour guide as we explored locales related to our Fraser, Montgomery, and Burton ancestors, who had settled in the area as early as 1836.

A leafy drive between stands of majestic maples led to the Kilbride pioneer cemetery, located in what is now the city of Burlington.

Past and present–an awareness of the impermanence but continuity of life–came together as we walked the ground once trod by our ancestors as they buried and mourned their dead. Leila led the way to a group of six markers, one Fraser and five Montgomery stones. Some were standing straight and true, but others were tilting or lying on the ground.

The information on the monuments showed the ravages of erosion over the years, with some almost illegible.

JOHN ALLAN
son of
WM.& MARGARET
MONTGOMERY
died 6 Oct. 1872
aged 1 yr.6 ds

ALEXANDER J.
son of
ALEX'R & MARY FRASER
died May 8, 1869
aged 5 years 1 mo &
17days

These two stones are a sad reminder of the rate of infant and child mortality in those by-gone days.

Leaving the Kilbride cemetery and the memorials to our Fraser and Montgomery ancestors, we drove to the Carlisle cemetery where the Burton side of our family had been buried. The Carlisle cemetery is large and still in use today, so there is a mix of very old and new stones. Here, again, was evidence of baby deaths and women dying young, quite probably in childbirth.

A day or two after our cemetery excursion, we took another trip back into the past with a visit to the schoolhouse where Alexander Fraser, our great-grandfather, had taught for 37 years. Along the way we pulled over onto the side of the road to have a look at the home where Alexander and Mary had raised their family of eight.

My grandfather William is second from the left in the back row.

This 10-acre treed property was the home where our grandfather, William, with his seven brothers and sisters, spent his childhood and early adulthood. Alexander provided a very settled and stable life for his family that was not echoed in the adult life of some of his children, including William, who tried farming in several districts before finally moving to town and working as a carpenter.

After that quick look at the Fraser family home, we moved on to our main objective–the schoolhouse. Four years after our great-grandfather began his long tenure in Cedar Springs School District #10, the original log building was replaced by a stone structure, which is now a Burlington building designated "of heritage interest."

The current owners of the schoolhouse-turned-residence are a young couple with three children, and when contacted by Leila, `they very graciously agreed to a tour of their home.

In fact, they seemed delighted at the opportunity to point out carefully preserved features of the building, such as the original floorboards in the kitchen and the section of slate board, the precursor to a blackboard, they found discarded in the yard, now framed and hanging on the wall. Harking back to a simpler time, their kitchenware was stored on open shelves and in an antique oak hutch.

As I stood there on those wide floorboards where our great-grandfather had walked the aisles between his students' desks over a hundred years ago and gazed at the slate board where he would have written his daily lessons, the present collapsed into the past. And, floating in the ether was a sense of the transitory nature of life, the short time span of a generation, or even two–my present and my future soon to be the past. A hundred years from now who will stand where my feet have been?

Over the years the conversion of the schoolhouse to a residence has resulted in several changes to the building. The schoolhouse door, which faced the road, has been replaced by a side door. Now, only the sign with the school's name marks the location of the original doorway. Two large dormers added to the rear of the building have converted a former storage area into a liveable second half-story. While planning more renovations, this couple are committed to maintaining the historical integrity of the building.

I also learned the family's three children are being homeschooled by their mother. So, 61 years after it closed, the old schoolhouse is a schoolhouse once more. I can imagine Alexander, the schoolmaster, approving in his Scottish brogue, "Aye, Aye!"

Auntie May

"Auntie May's coming to visit," our mother announced. This was more of a warning than an announcement. It meant my sisters and I needed to make sure our books were stowed upstairs so that we could hide out in our bedrooms and read when our work was done. Auntie May, a veritable workhorse, was a firm believer in the adage, "the devil finds mischief for idle hands to do." Reading, in her view, was "idling"–so if she saw you with your head in a book, she always found something "useful" for you to do.

Auntie May was our Dad's sister. Born in 1895, the second child in that family of 10 born to Grandma and Grandpa Putland, a strong work ethic would have been bred in her bones. There was her "never-give-up" father, who after a leg amputation, devised ways to continue farming in that non-mechanized age when all implements were horse-drawn, for example, building a little harrow-cart he could ride when using a harrow, an implement with no seat.

Then there was her efficient mother, who tended to the needs of a large household which, in addition to her husband and children, included her blind mother, the teacher who boarded with them, and a hired man. It was also a time when everything was homemade, from bread and butter to sausages and ham, to clothes and bedding.

The three oldest in the family, all girls–Nellie, May, and Sadie–worked hard from a young age, helping their one-legged father with outside farming jobs and their mother with household tasks and caring for younger ones. Dad recalled spankings he got from Auntie Nellie and Auntie Sadie, "but never from May," he said. "She had a soft heart."

May's older sister, Nellie, married at 19, and a younger sister, Sadie, at 23. Two years later, at age 26, when younger sisters and brothers were old enough to help at home, May left to work as a housekeeper for John

Galbraith, a widower, with three children, ages seven, six, and five, and a newborn baby. A year later she and John Galbraith were married, giving her an instant family of four children. Over the years three more children were added to the family.

With her tireless energy Auntie May had no trouble tending to the physical needs of her large family. However, there are times when a stepmother needs to tread lightly and that was not Auntie May's style, so conflicts were inevitable with young people struggling to find their own identity.

When Uncle John retired from his job as an elevator agent, the couple moved to Qualicum Beach in B.C. with the three youngest children. But every year the prairies and family drew Auntie May back for a summer visit.

The years did not change Auntie May. She remained a one-woman hive of worker bees. Shortly after my marriage to John, a Sunday visit to my folks coincided with Auntie May's stay. Sometime during the afternoon John had several coins drop down his pant leg to the floor. He had just met my aunt, so he was not prepared for what happened next. "A hole in your pocket," Auntie May said. "I'll fix it right now."

"It's okay. I'll put them in my other pocket," said John.

"Git your pants off so's I can mend that pocket."

John froze, not knowing what to do.

"I'll do it tomorrow," I assured my aunt.

Auntie May ignored me. "Git in there, git those pants off and give 'em to me," said Auntie May, pointing to the bathroom off the kitchen. John was 5' 8" back then, or at least insisted he was. Auntie May was 5' 2" if she stretched. If there really is something called force of personality, Auntie May could harness it. The upshot was John ended up in the bathroom, taking his pants off and opening the door a crack to meekly pass them to Auntie May. He stayed there till his pants reappeared with Auntie May's satisfied comment, "There–mended."

After Dad retired to Qualicum Beach, we always popped in to see Auntie May on our yearly visits. She was 89 the last time we saw her, still living in her house with an unmarried son. Cheerful as always, she had slowed down a bit, but she still bustled about as she made us "tea and crumpets." That is how I want to remember her, but unfortunately, I have one last image of her.

Before our next visit, her failing health required a move to a nursing home. Sadly, she had to be restrained in a wheelchair. The reason–the staff could not keep her out of the kitchen.

What a sad way for my feisty aunt to spend her last days. A needle, thread, and some pockets to mend could have kept Auntie May so busy she would not have had time to head for the kitchen.

The Two Uncle Bobs

"Bob Fraser?" the woman said. "Everyone in town knows Bob Fraser. He's one of the old-timers. But I'm sorry, he isn't here. He's in Dawson City."

It was 1999. My brother Bill, his wife Vel, and John and I were leaving Whitehorse, in the Yukon, on our way home from our trek to Alaska. We decided to make a side-trip to Atlin to try and find an uncle we hadn't seen or heard from since 1957. Since Atlin was in the northwest corner of BC, the only road access to the town was from Whitehorse or Skagway, Alaska. While Bill knew Uncle Bob had lived in Atlin for years, we had no address or phone number and decided to start our search at the town museum.

"Never heard him talk about his family," the woman at the reception desk said, when we explained who we were. "Bob was a town character–he drank too much and, with his bushy white beard and floppy felt hat, was a favourite photo subject for visiting tourists. He spent his life moving from cabin to cabin searching for gold."

The photo of Uncle Bob is from The Prospector, June 6th, 2003 issue.

As we were leaving, she added one last piece of information. "Your uncle was a good carpenter," she said. "If you visit the Pine Creek Campground while you're here, your uncle made those picnic tables and barrel fire-pits."

That evening as we sat around one of Uncle Bob's fire-pits, talking and eating smores and jam-jams, I thought, "So that's the end of it. We're never going to meet our elusive uncle."

I admit my disappointment was tempered by relief. Since Uncle Bob never talked about his family, he might not have wanted to see us. It could have been an uncomfortable, even upsetting, meeting.

Uncle Bob was my mother's youngest brother–an age gap of 17 years separating the two. His childhood had been repeatedly saddened by death–first, his 16-year-old brother Cecil, then his sister Velma, and finally his mother, leaving him, in his early teens, with a widowed father. In the 1920s and 30s deaths happened more frequently than today and would have been accepted as God's will in that evangelical home, but still troubling, I imagine, for a young child.

Bob did come to live with my parents for a while when he was 15. However, relations between my father and the teenager were difficult, and Bob returned to live with his father until he joined the army, eventually being sent overseas in World War II.

My mother's diary records that Bob, home from the war, visited us for five days in October 1945. I would have been 12 at the time. I don't remember Uncle Bob paying any attention to us kids. Nor do I remember him talking about his war experiences, though I do recall my mother saying his girlfriend had died in the bombing of London.

Uncle Bob then vanished from our lives for the next six years, reappearing with Grandpa Fraser to celebrate Christmases with us in 1951 and 52. In 1953, with Grandpa now in the Ninette TB Sanitorium, Uncle Bob came alone for Christmas, leaving shortly after to visit Grandpa.

Three years later Grandpa had a stroke, dying on December 9, 1956. Unable to contact Uncle Bob by telephone or telegraph, Mum sent an announcement to the radio station. Uncle Bob did not make it to the funeral, or our Christmas or New Year's celebrations, but on January 6th he arrived in Churchbridge. After a two-day visit he left for Edmonton with his truck, to disappear from our lives forever.

My memory of the Uncle Bob who visited in 1951 and 52, when I was 19 and 20 years old, is of a quiet and serious man. That's it! Hoping for at least a glimmer of insight into Uncle Bob's personality, I called my brother, Bill. After all, Uncle Bob had slept in the big bedroom with the boys, and in that informal situation he might have been more relaxed and talkative. Zilch! Bill recalled nothing more than I did about our uncle.

Bill had been around home longer than me, so he did have a few nuggets of general information. He was the one who knew that Uncle Bob lived in Atlin, that our folks couldn't understand why he had moved to that northern wilderness, that our mother had a mailing address (probably a post office box number) and she had written to her brother when she was diagnosed with cancer. Bill didn't know if Mum ever received an answer to her letter.

And then, unexpectedly, we "met" our estranged uncle, but not till 2016, years after his death.

In 2012 our youngest sister, Leila, had compiled a history of our mother's family from the 1800s onward. However, she was unable to find any statistical information about Uncle Bob as he was not listed in the 1916 census, the most up-to-date census released to the public at that time. Finally, in 2016, with access to the 1921 census where Bob was listed as two years old, she was able to estimate his birth year. "Panning" for information about Robert Fraser, born in 1919, she hit "pay dirt" when she was directed to a cemetery record in Atlin for William Robert Alexander Fraser, also known as Bob, who died in May 2003.

The next link in the chain of events was contacting Carolyn Moore, editor of the official Atlin town website. When Carolyn posted Leila's request for information about our uncle on the Atlin Facebook site, we received the mother lode–pictures and comments from several people who had known him.

Local author Terry Milos generously shared photos and a chapter on Uncle Bob that would appear in her soon-to-be published book, *North of Familiar*. Rick Nesgaard and his father, John, one of Bob's close friends, contributed their memories, as did 17 others on Facebook. Elizabeth Clarke, Vera Kirkwood and Bea Bonnell had also published pieces in memory of Bob in the June 6, 2003 issue of *The Prospector*, the town's local newspaper.

We met the uncle that no one in the family had ever seen–a hard drinker, cigarette smoker, poker player, and occasional hearty cusser, who revelled in telling WW II stories.

This was not the uncle I remember. When he visited us in 1945 and the 1950s he did not drink, smoke, play cards or swear–or at least, not when he was in the company of his father or his sister, neither of whom would have accepted such conduct.

Reading Terry Milos' book, you get a sense of my uncle's time in the North as an era of working in the camps, punctuated by parties with drinking and storytelling. There was also an easygoing ethos of generosity and sharing. If you needed a place to stay and someone had an empty cabin, it was yours for as long as you needed it. After a drinking party, if you needed to crash for the night before going back into the "Bush," there would be a bed for you.

It was a way of life that seems to have been a perfect fit for Uncle Bob. Despite his drinking, the Atlin folks described him as "always the perfect gentleman," "a gem of a man," "the sweetest man ever," and "our beautiful Bob." He was known for his generosity, willingness to help anyone in need, sense of humour, loyalty, and enduring friendships.

Joe Ackerman was one of Bob's good friends. For several years Bob lived in a cabin on Joe's property near Surprise Lake. Terry Milos said the two "were similar in character" and "like an old married couple squabbling about things." Not all Bob's friends were his vintage. Terry Milos and her husband met Bob in 1974 when she was 23 and Bob was 55, yet they became good friends over the years. She said Bob was "always friendly, smiling, glad to see you, loved kids and telling stories." John Nesgaard, who was 22 years younger, said that Bob was like an older brother "willing to share his thoughts if I needed advice." Others said Bob had a "strong opinion about what was right and was not afraid to say so" and he could "wax philosophical at times" saying, "You can never stop learning. I'm old, but I'm disappointed if I don't learn something new every day." Still others, young adults now, remembered Bob fondly from their childhood days.

We learned that in the 1950s Bob worked in the mining industry in the Grande Prairie region, likely as either a miner or a camp cook, moving to Atlin sometime in the early 60s.

Uncle Bob became well known in northern BC and the Yukon as a camp cook but liked nothing more than prospecting for gold on the several streams where he had claims. In those years, he seems to have lived in several cabins in and around town, and later, the cabin at Surprise Lake. Terry Milos said to get away from all the drinking in town, Bob lived for a few years with one of her friends and children at their trap-line cabin, helping with the work in exchange for a place to stay.

Eventually Bob moved into the low-cost housing in Atlin, next door to John Nesgaard, and whenever John was back in town from the mining camps they would get together for dinners and partying.

As age and arthritis took their toll, Bob realized he needed to move into senior's housing. Not wanting to go to any BC retirement home in the south, he established Yukon residency by living at the Salvation Army hostel in Whitehorse for a year and then moving to the McDonald Lodge in Dawson City. Whenever he could, he would "hop a bus" to Atlin to visit his friends when they were back from the camps, "staying as long as he wanted or until they had to go back to work."

When Bob could no longer travel to Atlin, Rick Nesgaard said his father, John, made the trip to Dawson City at least once a week–a two-and-a-half-hour drive one way–to see his old friend.

It was John who ensured Bob's last wishes were honoured and he was brought back to Atlin for burial. Another friend, Bob Kirkwood, worked with the federal Veteran Affairs Department to pay for burial costs and a headstone. It seems Uncle Bob had total confidence that his friends would respect his last wishes, as shortly before his death he had a notice printed in the local paper, saying, "A BIG THANK YOU TO THE PEOPLE OF ATLIN FOR BRINGING ME BACK HOME."

And now, years later, John Nesgaard writes that "after eight years of trying I have poppies growing at his gravesite along with fireweed and strawberry plants. We keep it maintained and I visit quite regularly."

I'm afraid Uncle Bob's father, sister, and relatives in the faith community where he grew up would have disowned the "Atlin Bob." Would even we, his nieces and nephews, have been able to see beyond the heavy drinking to the generous, kind and gentle core of the man? Generous, kind and gentle, and oh yes, a good carpenter too–ironically, all words that could have been used to describe Grandpa, Bob's father.

I'm happy that in Atlin Uncle Bob found, for the first time, a community where he felt at home. The people of Atlin not only embraced him, they became his family.

PART 3
Growing Up On The Farm

The Hunter, The Hunted, and the Haunted

I am five. I am standing at the window in the rented Jensen farmhouse. I am mesmerized by the large lacy snowflakes floating lazily down to the white drifts in our yard. A small movement catches my eye and I watch as a coyote steps warily out of the distant bush, then begins to lope across the open field. "Hurry," I think. "Daddy might see you."

It is too late. A blur of bay horse, my father riding bareback, rifle held at the ready, flashes past the window. The coyote, suddenly aware of impending doom, veers sharply, changing direction. I watch as horse and hunter streak across the snowy field in hot pursuit of the frightened, fleeing animal. My father, motivated by the need for money in these depression years, is a skilled hunter. The coyote does not have a chance.

When my father returns with the dead coyote slung behind him over the horse's back, I know what will happen next. The coyote's skin will be carefully cut off its body and scraped to remove all the flesh. Then the skin will be fastened, fur side down, around a shaped board. This happens to all the animals he hunts and traps for their fur–coyotes, foxes, muskrats, weasels, and rabbits. I know this because these boards with their dead, inside-out animals are brought into the warm house and ranged around the walls of our parent's bedroom to dry.

In winter, my sisters and I do not have to use the freezing-cold outhouse and can use the chamber pot in our parents' bedroom at night. I fear going into that room filled with all those animal skins, but as I desperately need to "go," there is no alternative. I feel throat-tightening fright as I leave the bedroom door ajar, allowing the yellow rays of the kerosene lamp in the living room to reduce the darkness to a murky gloom, while casting huge, flickering, eerie shadows on the wall. Fright becomes heart-thumping terror as I squat there in the almost-dark surrounded by those ghostly, once-alive animals.

§

I am older, ten, I think. It is summer holidays and I am spending a few days at Auntie Sadie's and Uncle Harry's. Uncle Harry is not happy with all the gopher holes in his pasture as his cattle and horses can injure their legs if they step in a hole.

"Two cents for every gopher tail you bring me," he promises. "Take a pail of water and Shadow. Pour water down the gopher hole. Gopher'll pop his head out. Shadow'll grab it. Gopher won't know what hit it. Cut off the tail, you got two cents."

I end up spending part of each day in the pasture. I lug pail after pail of water with Shadow by my side, an eager black and white mutt of inde-terminate heritage. I do my part–I pour water down each hole till a sleek, drenched and frenzied head appears. A quick snap of Shadow's jaws breaks the gopher's neck. I cut off the tail with Uncle Harry's jackknife and add it to my collection in the covered jar. We repeat this gory operation over and over. The dog and I are partners in this killing field, though I try to absolve my guilt by thinking, "Shadow is doing the killing, not me."

§

I'm a teenager. I am sitting in the back-corner booth at Baskin's café with my two sisters. It's quiet now that the after-school crowd has left to go home to their supper–no more giggling as we tease each other with friendly insults and quick come-backs. Mary checks her watch. "6:00," she informs us. "Should be here soon."

"Colossal waste of our time," I complain grumpily. I have homework and a half-read book in my bag and I'm itching to take them out, but when Dad gets here, he won't want to wait for me to gather my stuff together.

"Dad'll be happy. Must be having a good hunt," says Lorna, trying to make peace.

"Coyotes won't be happy," I counter. "Don't see what fun he gets out of running the poor animals into the ground."

A few moments later we hear a distant roar that quickly increases in intensity as Dad glides up to the café in his snowplane. We shrug into our heavy hooded jackets, pull on wool toques and mitts, grab our bags and rush out into the frigid air. Dad opens the door in the side of the snowplane and we cautiously crawl inside over the coyote carcasses piled on the floor of this miniature "house" on skis. We settle on the bench at the back, our feet resting on dead animal bodies. As the motor-driven propeller at our rear efficiently skims us along over snowy fields and drifted-in roads, the noise reaches ear-splitting levels. The sound is so intense it prohibits thought, let alone attempts to talk.

Our father no longer hunts from necessity to augment our meagre income. He is now hunting for the thrill of the chase and the kill. I have a picture of Dad and three hunting buddies, cradling their rifles, as they kneel beside the snowplane. Completely covering the shed wall behind them are their trophies—a row of 20 coyote skins, hanging as if from a clothesline. These skins will be de-fleshed and stretched over drying boards, just like the animals in my parents' bedroom that caused me so much fear when I was younger. They will not end up in our house to dry, however. We now have electric power, thanks to our wind turbine and the bank of batteries in the basement, so the skins will be stored in a heated outbuilding.

§

Looking back, I realize that I was, and still am, ambivalent about the killing of animals. While I wanted the coyote to escape and feared the animal skins in my parents' bedroom, I shared the family's pride in my father's hunting prowess and the speed of his two bay "hunters," acknowledged as the fastest horses in the neighbourhood.

I also do not like remembering all the gophers I killed that fateful summer. I wonder, if the dog had not nabbed them, would I have been capable of clubbing them over the head? Was I doing it for Uncle Harry's approval, as much as for two cents a tail?

As a teenager I thought it was unsporting of Dad to run coyotes to the ground with the snowplane, but I never voiced my reservations to him.

To this day, I have never shot an animal. I do not even fish. I do not like the thought of a deer or a moose being felled by a bullet, a muskrat or a beaver being clamped in the jaws of a trap, or a pickerel gasping for breath with a hook in its mouth. However, during the first 10 years of our marriage we lived on a farm and raised cattle and pigs destined for the slaughterhouse. I could never bring myself to chop the head off a chicken, but when my husband had done the deed, I plucked, cleaned, cooked, and participated in consuming the bird.

I do not approve of the inhumane way many animals are confined on today's large corporate farms. However, I still eat meat. With vengeance in my heart, I trap mice that dare to invade my house or camper. As for flies and mosquitoes, I swat them without a qualm.

It makes me wonder, am I the hunter, the hunted or the haunted?

Christmas Without Cash or Credit Cards

It was Christmas Eve. I was five and my sisters, Mary and Lorna, were four and two-and-a-half years old. We had spent the day making decorations for the Christmas tree–stringing macaroni Mum had dyed red, green and yellow with food coloring, cutting gold and silver stars out of foil saved from chocolate bar wrappers and making paper chains from strips cut from brown grocery bags and coloured with wax crayons. After supper we helped decorate the tree with our creations, reaching as high as we could, while Dad helped with the top branches. I was one year older than Mary, but to my surprise, she could reach as high as I could.

Before going to bed each of us carefully positioned one of Dad's big socks under the tree, mine to the left, Mary's in the middle and Lorna's on the right. There was no sock for our brother, Billy, as he was just a baby. We didn't leave cookies and milk for Santa Claus, as I later discovered many other kids did. We always knew the story of Santa Claus was make-believe, just like a fairy tale, and it was our parents who gave us the gifts we would find in the morning. Snuggled into bed after our bedtime stories–the story of Jesus' birth followed by *"T'was the Night Before Christmas"*–we were tingling with anticipation, thinking about the surprises that would be waiting in our stockings. We did not need an imaginary, fat bearded man in red coming down a non-existent fireplace chimney to make us excited.

Waking Christmas morning, we didn't take time to dress but rushed downstairs in our flannel pyjamas. Hugging our Christmas stockings in our arms, we knelt in the circle of warmth radiating from the wood-burning space heater. We each discovered not one, but two Christmas oranges at the top of our socks! Next to emerge were little brown paper bags with hard Christmas candies, striped in red, green, and white. We didn't take the time to pop a single candy into our mouths. We wanted the surprise we knew would be waiting at the bottom of each of our socks. There were three simultaneous squeals of amazed delight, "It matches my pyjamas!" as we extracted our familiar little dolls, now wearing new flannel nightgowns and wrapped in flannel blankets. While I don't remember the patterns or colours of my sisters' pyjamas, I can clearly see the sliver-thin stripes in brown, white and red my doll and I were wearing. Also vivid in my memory is the maternal glow I felt, cradling my blanket-wrapped doll in my arms. With its nightgown and blanket it was just like a real baby!

In the afternoon, our family and all the uncles, aunts, and cousins who lived close enough to come by horse and van or sleigh, gathered at Auntie Nellie's and Uncle Herman's for a family Christmas celebration. They had a rambling two-story house with a living room that seemed huge, compared to ours. A long table had been set up for the traditional Christmas dinner of turkey, goose, mashed potatoes, gravy, stuffing, creamed corn, buttered peas, cranberry sauce, cucumber pickles, plum pudding with sauce and mince tarts. There were so many people that two sittings were needed to feed everyone. Those that were waiting did a bit of before-dinner snacking at the side table with its bowls of Japanese oranges (what everyone called mandarins), nuts in shells and homemade fudge and caramels. After dinner, while the women, including Auntie Nellie's three older daughters, cleared the table and did the dishes, the men disassembled the long table to form three tables so they could play crokinole. We younger ones wisely disappeared upstairs where we could play a noisy game of hide-and-seek, undisturbed.

At the call, "Time for presents," we emerged from our hiding places and raced down the stairs to gather around the Christmas tree decorated with twisted crepe-paper streamers and homemade paper ornaments. There had been two stipulations the families agreed upon–gifts were to be homemade or could cost no more than 25 cents. The children's gifts were handed out first. I gasped with pleasure and disbelief as I tore away the paper on my parcel to reveal a tea set! Arranged on a tray were tin lids for plates, sardine cans for serving dishes, small cans with handles soldered in place for tea cups and larger cans for jugs, all painted a delicate shade of mauve. Mary was sitting on the floor beside me. "I've got one too!" she exclaimed. It was a replica of mine, painted sky-blue. I have no recollection of the gifts any of the other children received. I do know there was much hilarity as the adults opened the gifts they had chosen from the wicker clothes basket–packages of tacks, nails, paper clips, toothpicks, matches or gum, chocolate bars, pencils and notebooks. Scarves, hats, and mitts, knitted from recycled yarn, were modelled for all to admire.

Mary and I later learned that Auntie Nellie had made our treasured tea sets. We used them for many years–for tea parties with real food indoors in the winter and for mud-pie confections in our summer playhouses.

Along with that special Christmas I also remember the year Mum helped us learn the pleasure of giving. We were still living on the rented Jensen farm, so I would have been six. She had purchased a quantity of eraser-tipped pencils and scribblers with a variety of pictures on the covers. In the evening, two days before Christmas, she invited each of us, one at a time, into our parents' bedroom. I was curious and intrigued by the mystery when I stepped through the door into the room, dimly lit by the mellow glow of a small kerosene lamp. Whispering to give the aura of secrecy, she displayed the scribblers and pencils, explaining that I should carefully look at the pictures on the covers of the scribblers and pick two for each of the other kids. I carefully debated what each of my siblings would prefer before choosing. Once I had my turn, I realized the other kids would be going through the same process, but I was still excited by the secrecy and suspense. No one knew which pictures I had chosen for them. I didn't know which ones they were giving me. Mum had the wonderful gift of making the simplest event momentous.

Fast forward eighteen years. My husband and I were renting his parents' half-section farm. After a disastrous crop, due to too much rain combined with an early frost, we were facing Christmas celebrations with my family with no money to buy gifts. I spent days, probably weeks, pondering the problem before I had an eureka moment.

I liked to cook and had many recipes collected from magazines and newspapers. With a supply of recipe file cards and many hours of hand-printing I made gifts for all the women in the family. Then, a few batches of creamy homemade chocolate fudge, studded with nuts, solved the problem of what to give my dad, brothers, and youngest sister.

Despite my worries about not having money for gifts, it ended up being one of our more memorable Christmases, in part I think because of the personal time invested in it. Many times over the years, my mother or one of my sisters would say, "Remember the year you made all those recipe cards?" and then tell a story about a recipe that was still a family favourite, or had been shared with someone, or even had ended up a culinary disaster! I no longer have any of those hand-printed recipe cards but there are a few dishes that have survived my periodic recipe-file purges over the years and are now family classics.

Potato Salad

4 c chopped potatoes (approximately 6 potatoes)
1 c finely chopped celery
1/3 to ½ c finely chopped onion
4 hard-cooked eggs, sliced
For firm potatoes for salad: Boil red potatoes in their skins just till tender. Then peel and cube.

Dressing:
½ c mayonnaise
3 T sugar
2 T vinegar
1 t salt
¼ t pepper
2 to 3 t prepared mustard
Optional: Can add ¼ to ½ c sweet green pickle relish

Mashed Potato Loaf

2 to 2¼ lb. potatoes
Optional: 3 garlic cloves, peeled and sliced
½ c sour cream
¼ c skim milk
1 T butter, melted
½ c old cheddar cheese
1 bunch green onions, sliced or 1 T minced fresh parsley

1 t dried thyme leaves

½ t dried rosemary, crushed

½ t salt

¼ t pepper

Sprinkle of paprika

Cook potatoes (with garlic, if using) till tender

Drain and mash potatoes.

Add rest of ingredients, except paprika, mashing till well mixed.

Put in oiled loaf pan or casserole. Sprinkle with paprika.

Bake uncovered, 350° F, 45 minutes.

Serves 6 to 8.

Note: Also great as a topping for Shepherd's Pie

Potato Gratin

2 lb. potatoes - Russet or Yukon Gold, unpeeled, thinly sliced

1 large onion, thinly sliced

1 garlic clove, minced

½ c grated Swiss or cheddar cheese

3 T flour

¼ t salt

¼ t pepper

1 1/3 c beef or chicken broth

3 T parmesan cheese

Preheat oven 375°

Oil large shallow baking dish (minimum 13" x 9")

In large bowl toss potatoes with all ingredients except broth and parmesan cheese.

Place potato mixture in baking dish. Pour broth over.

Bake, covered, 35 minutes.

Uncover and bake another 10 to 15 minutes. Sprinkle parmesan cheese on top and bake 15 minutes longer or till potatoes cooked.

Serves 6 to 8.

Braised Chicken

For each 3 or 4 lbs. of chicken pieces use: ½ c flour, combined with 1 t salt, ½ t pepper and 1 t paprika.

Brown floured chicken in oil, med-high heat.

Put in shallow roaster, cover, and bake in oven at 325° or 350° F for 45 min. to 1 hour.

Add 1 or 2 T of water, as needed to prevent sticking.

Barbecued Chicken Casserole

3 to 3½ lbs. chicken breasts or legs

Mix ½ c flour, 1 t salt, ½ t pepper and 1 t paprika.

Coat both sides of chicken pieces in flour mixture.

Brown in oil, med-high heat.

Place chicken in casserole.

Remove all but 2 t oil from skillet.

Add I med. onion, chopped or sliced. Saute till golden brown.

Add the following to the onion:

½ c finely chopped green pepper

½ c chopped celery

1 c ketchup

2 T Worcestershire sauce

1 T brown sugar

1/8 t pepper

1 c water

Pour mixture over chicken.

Bake, 350° F for 45 min. to 1½ hours, depending on whether using breasts or legs and size of chicken pieces.

Spanish Pork Chops with Rice

4 pork chops
½ c plus 2T rice
1 c sliced or chopped onion
½ c chopped green pepper
½ t salt
¼ t pepper
¾ t paprika
1 t sugar
1 – 28 oz. can diced tomatoes
Brown chops on both sides in 1 T oil, med-high heat
Arrange chops around sides of 2 qt. casserole.
Add rice in centre. Note: Use rice with regular cooking time of no more
than 15 minutes, or partially precook and drain thoroughly before adding
to casserole. Otherwise, chops will be overcooked by time rice is done.
Add remaining ingredients to pan in which chops were browned and stir.
Pour over pork chops and rice.
Cover and bake at 400° F for 45 minutes

Brownie Pudding

Mix dry ingredients together:
1 c flour
2 t baking powder
½ t salt
¾ c sugar
3 T cocoa
Combine:
½ c milk
1 t vanilla
2 T melted butter
Add wet ingredients to dry ingredients and mix till smooth.
Pour batter into greased 8" x 8" cake pan.

Mix:
¾ c brown sugar
¼ c cocoa
1 ¾ c hot water
and pour over batter.
Bake 350° F 40 to 45 minutes.
Serve hot with cream, ice cream or whipped cream.
8 servings

Fun for Free

Each year the spring run-off formed a temporary slough in the low spot where our long driveway dipped down before rising again to meet the municipal road. Until it drained away, my sisters, brothers and I tugged on our high rubber boots and headed for that slough every day after school.

The game was to see who could wade the farthest into the murky, icy-cold water without getting a boot-full. The uneven muddy bottom made the game a challenge. You might be wading confidently along and step in a low spot or a hole and get an unexpected boot-full. If you were lucky you would wade till the water almost reached the bottom of the red line that circled the top of your black rubber boots. Invariably, you would be tempted to try another little step and "Whoops!" you'd have a boot-full.

The game sounds simple and silly, but it makes me smile every time I remember the fun we had—the tingle of anticipation, the shrieks of surprise when that icy water spilled over the tops of our boots.

In summer, my two sisters and I spent hours in our "playhouses" in the bush just north of the house. We each had our own designated spot and visited each other by invitation only. Lorna and I used twine tied from tree to tree to define our territory. Mary staked her claim with curtain walls made from pieces of worn cotton sheets tie-dyed in delicate pastel colours.

We transformed wooden apple boxes into cupboards, tables, and chairs. An assortment of tin lids and cans served as dishes for delicacies, including stone soup and mud pies decorated with berries. When the vegetables in our individual garden plots matured, we were able to offer our invited guests: carrots, peas, and green beans, while wild Saskatoon trees in the bush provided berries for dessert.

With a little imagination, sticks about three feet long, with a string tied to one end for a halter, became horses. We gave our steeds names and would gallop around the yard, urging them on–"Come on Blaze!" "Come on Diamond!" "Come on Queenie!" When we needed a rest, we would tether our horses to the veranda rails and feed them piles of sand as a stand-in for oats. Sometimes our mother would say, "I just swept the floor!" but she never forbade this activity as she encouraged our creative play.

When I had children of my own, I was thrilled to discover hobby horses with stuffed fabric heads in a toy store. I anticipated all the hours of fun my kids would have with these more realistic horses. To my disappointment my children did not share my excitement and seldom played with their horses. I found this hard to understand when I remembered all the fun we had with plain old sticks. Years later, my sister Mary described a similar experience with her grandchildren. After some thought, we realized horses were an essential part of our life on the farm and we children were, in fact, playing out the adult roles we saw daily. For our children and grandchildren, living in a world dominated by machines, the hobby horses had no meaning.

Every Saturday in summer, after chores and supper, our family would pile into the car, two-deep in the back seat, and go to town. It was the highlight of the week for all the farm families in the neighbourhood. The women shopped for groceries while the men gathered in the café, pool hall, or on the street corners, discussing the weather and crops. Young children stayed close to their mothers in the grocery store, while older siblings ran about on the sidewalk and teenagers promenaded down the main street, sometimes holding hands. Our mother loved ice cream, and reading her diary many years later, I discovered that in those nickel-and-dime days of the depression, an ice cream cone on Saturday night was sufficiently significant to be recorded. "I had an ice cream cone with Sadie tonight."

The arrival of the train Saturday night was also a big event. Seeing the postmaster, a veteran of World War I with one wooden leg, stomping along as he pushed his wheelbarrow to the station, was the signal the train would be arriving shortly. Young and old would congregate on the station platform. At the first faint sound of the steam whistle there was a chorus of, "Here she comes!" As the train chugged into the station the conductor would be standing on the step of one of the cars, swinging his lantern to signal to the engineer when to stop.

I now wonder what the passengers thought as they looked out at that gathering on the platform. Did they assume we were there to meet an arriving loved one or local celebrity, or did they scoff at the thought that watching the train come in was Saturday night entertainment for these country bumpkins?

After the mailbag had been unloaded and trundled away, the adults would gather in the post office as they waited for the postmaster to raise the little half-door that separated him from the crowd, signalling that the mail was sorted into their individual boxes. Mail in hand, it was time to gather the family and head home with the week's groceries.

In winter no roads were kept open, so all travel was by horse. Our father, like the other men in the district, would make the long trek into town for groceries by himself. Our family weekend excursion became visiting nearby family and neighbours, travelling by van or sleigh.

A van was like a little trailer, or a fishing shack, on skis. There was a small stove at the front, a door at the back, and benches along both sides, with firewood stacked underneath. A window let the driver keep an eye on the horses, controlled by the reins that were passed through two holes at the front. Travelling by van felt closed-in, stuffy and uncomfortable with the heat from the stove and the winter-dressed bodies pressed close together on the short, hard benches. And all you could see through that small front window was the horses' rumps.

Travelling by open sleigh was a completely different experience. In preparation for a trip, our father would pile deer hides on the bottom of the sleigh while our mother warmed bricks in the oven and heated thick blankets and quilts hung over chairs by the wood-burning stove.

When we were all settled on the prickly hides, wrapped in warm blankets with hot bricks at our feet, Dad, standing at the front of the sleigh, would slap the reins and we would be off across the snowy field. I loved the bite of the cold, crisp air on my face while the rest of me was toasty warm; the beauty of millions of stars brilliantly flashing in the dark night sky arching overhead; the rhythm of eight hooves moving in unison; the sound of sleigh runners slicing through snow; the jingle of steel traces; and even the pungent smell of manure when the horses relieved themselves. I loved it all.

There were no overflowing toy boxes, elaborate jungle gyms or trips to Disney World in my childhood. In those lean depression years, both children and adults made their own fun for free. Would I trade the memory of wading in the slough, riding my stick horses or going on a winter sleigh ride, for a memory of standing in line at Disney World? Never!

Harvesting in the 1930s and 1940s

Looking down from an airplane window, I can appreciate the beauty of a swathed field with its ribbons of golden grain. When viewed at ground level as I drive by on the highway, however, that field looks flat and uninteresting compared to the harvest-time fields of my childhood with their uniform rows of upright stooks.

While farmers in the 1930s and 1940s did not have the swathers and combines that make harvesting today fast and easy, they did have machines called binders, which were pulled by horses or tractors. These machines cut the grain and bound it with twine into bundles called sheaves. Then the physical labour of stooking began. Each stook was made from eight sheaves, picked up two at a time, and formed into a tepee shape so it would shed the rain. This involved bending over thousands of times in a day.

Dad usually hired a man to help with the stooking. I remember the first year he decided we four older kids could handle the job. That first day was torture. Our backs ached from the repetitive bending, the sheaves did not always stand properly when plunked into place, the thistles pricked our arms, the twine rubbed our fingers raw, and the sun's rays were blazingly hot as they beat down on our toiling bodies. Our misery was so great the possibility of dying of sunstroke seemed very real! So, as we continued working, each of us took a turn telling the others which of our belongings they could have–that is, if they should be lucky enough to survive. Quitters we were not! Giving up or complaining to our dad was never an option. We had a job to do and we did it.

It was always an exciting day when the threshing crew came rattling into our yard with their horse-drawn racks. The threshing machine would already have been set up in the field. The men would be facing days of hard physical labour but there was a feeling of camaraderie as they worked side-by-side, pitching the sheaves onto their racks and then pitching each sheaf off the racks into the thresher that separated the grain from the straw. After the harvest season it was no wonder our dad could impress us when he flexed his arms and presented his bulging muscles for our inspection!

While the men needed physical strength, farm women needed stamina for the long hours required to prepare the meals for eight to 12 ravenous men. As soon as my two sisters and I were old enough to help, we were kept home from school to assist my mother.

We gathered the vegetables from the garden and peeled, shelled, or shucked them as required. We fetched water from the well and washed the mountains of dishes after every meal and baking session. We carried armfuls of wood from the woodpile as the kitchen range was in use all day. Our favourite task was churning the butter, as you could read while moving the dasher up and down in the cream. However, we were never allowed to do any of the cooking. Our mother could not risk burned potatoes, a fallen cake, or a tough pie crust. She knew the crew would be moving on to another farm and the men would talk!

The meals our mother cooked were monumental by today's standards. She would be up before dawn to prepare the breakfast of porridge, bacon, sausages, eggs, fried potatoes, and toast. By noon she would have mixed that day's batch of bread and have a dinner, including meat, potatoes, two vegetables and freshly baked pies, on the table. At the end of the day supper was another meal as hearty as the noon one, but with a hot pudding instead of pie.

I remember an incident that made me wonder if the men realized the number of tiring hours the women spent cooking and baking at harvest time. The noon-hour meals were always convivial with friendly teasing and joking among the men. This was a day the teasing turned into horseplay, and one of the fellows picked up a lemon meringue pie and mashed it into my uncle's face. I heard my mother's gasp of dismay and a sharp intake of breath. I saw her bite her bottom lip and blink back the tears as she watched her perfect pie slide in lemon-yellow and meringue-white drips down my uncle's face, and all her time and care used to make it were for naught.

Our favourite time of day was mid-afternoon when we would help our mother take a lunch of hearty sandwiches, cake, and cookies to the men in the field. There would also be a big covered pail of steaming hot coffee, already mixed with sugar and cream. The men would gather around the food as if drawn by a magnet.

As we lunched with the crew it was the only time we were permitted to drink coffee. I never liked the taste of that sweet, creamy brew but, nevertheless, I always drank it because it signified that we had joined the adults, if only for a few days.

The Singer Salesman

In rural communities in the 30s and 40s, travelling salesmen regularly came calling with their wares. We frequently saw the Fuller Brush man, as well as the Watkins and Raleigh men, with their salves and ointments and non-prescription drugs. But one special day, a Singer sewing machine salesman stopped at our house. Invited in, he proceeded to demonstrate the wonders of his modern treadle sewing machine.

"Would you believe," he said, "it has a reverse lever, so you can go backwards and forwards at the flick of a finger! Just think of the time you'll save not having to turn your work around to finish off a seam. And you can darn a hole in a jiffy." His practiced fingers were smoothly demonstrating each task as he gave his enthusiastic sales pitch.

But there was more—he told my mother not only could she use this wondrous reverse feature to speed up her everyday sewing and mending, she could use it to express her creativity. By now, our little-kid curiosity had drawn us three girls around the machine. We were mesmerized by this man's nimble fingers as he rethreaded the machine several times with different colored thread and created multicolored designs on brightly coloured squares of cloth he drew out of his bag. When he had completed designs on three different coloured squares, he handed one to each of us—yellow to Lorna, blue to Mary, and red to me. What a treasure! And because they were different colours, there would be no argument about which was ours.

He was a good salesman. By the time he left we had a new Singer sewing machine. That treadle machine was used to make and mend our clothes for many, many years. Our mother often commented on the convenience of that reverse lever, but I don't recall her ever using it to make decorative zig-zag designs. Rickrack tape was inexpensive, came in many different colors, and could be quickly sewn on collars or cuffs as a creative trim.

After the power grid reached their farm, our parents proudly purchased an electric sewing machine, disguised to look like an end table in its walnut-coloured cabinet. However, that new store-bought machine did not come with the magic memories that were part of that old treadle machine.

An Unexpected Ingredient

As kids, one of our favourite days was pig-butchering day. We never considered what the pig thought of it.

We would get to snack on crackles—pig rind baked in the oven till deliciously crisp. And for supper there would be full-length spareribs, which would have been sprinkled with salt and pepper and baked in the oven till the meat was dark brown. Unlike today's barbecued ribs, there was no sauce to detract from the marvellous flavour of the crunchy meat as you chewed it off the bone.

One of our favourite breakfasts was "oven toast," homemade bread smeared with the solidified fat leftover from cooking bacon, sprinkled with salt and pepper and baked in the oven until golden brown. Somehow, we managed to survive all that fat and salt without clogged arteries and high blood pressure by the time we were teenagers!

After supper on butchering day the kitchen would become a sausage-making factory. Earlier in the day our mother would have carefully cleaned the pig's intestines to use for the sausage casings. A machine with a hand-turned crank was used to make the sausages. One gizmo was attached to grind the meat, which our mother would then mix with spices, and another attachment was used to squirt the seasoned ground meat into the casing. We older kids could help by turning the crank on the machine. Grinding the meat was hard work, but we all vied to do the squirting. First, it was easier to turn the crank now that the meat was ground, and secondly, it was fun to watch as the meat squirted into the casing and our mother or father twisted it at regular intervals to form perfectly uniform sausages.

There was one day when our sausage factory's quality control did not meet its usual high standards. As the last sausage was formed, our mother's scream of disbelief and horror tore the air. "My rag!" she cried, holding up her bare pointer finger. Earlier, when cutting up the meat she had been a bit overzealous and sliced her finger. In those pre-band-aid days she had tied a little piece of cloth around her finger to staunch the bleeding–and now it was gone.

A frantic search of the floor and every other flat surface in the kitchen turned up nothing. A visual inspection of the sausages also revealed nothing. There was only one conclusion: The rag was hidden in one of the sausages.

"I can't feed those sausages to company," our mother wailed. "And what if someone stops by unexpectedly when we're having sausages."

Luckily, no one did stop by as our family ate its way through a lot of sausages—until the day, to our father's chagrin and our mother's immense relief, the rag turned up in one of Dad's sausages. At last, our mother could serve the tasty links to guests without having heart palpitations.

Doing It Right–We Thought

The first week of July 1945–Auntie Lucille, Auntie Doris, and our mother were all admitted to the Russell Hospital. Each was there to deliver her seventh baby–the first hospital birth for all three.

Our mother who was 43—the oldest of the three—went to the hospital on June 30th to await the impending birth. She was joined the next day by Auntie Lucille, who gave birth to a son, Keith, in the Langenburg doctor's car as they were on their way to the Russell Hospital. On July 5th Auntie Doris delivered a daughter, Janice, and on the same day a brother, Leslie, was added to our family.

I was 12 that summer. Mary was 11. For the two weeks our mother was in the hospital the two of us were responsible for looking after a household of seven, including our younger siblings: Lorna–10, Billy–8, Denis–5, and Leila–4.

Mary and I were determined to do things right. Mostly we followed our mother's routine—laundry on Monday, baking on Friday, cleaning on Saturday. I don't remember doing the ironing on Tuesday, but I hated ironing so maybe Mary, who was more meticulous, looked after it. It was summer holidays, so we could have broken with tradition and said, "Sorry kids, you're wearing un-ironed clothes till Mum gets home," but I doubt we would have been so daring. The Wednesday task of mending I am sure we left in the basket awaiting Mum's return. As Mary continued to help with the outside chores as usual, meals were my responsibility.

There was one day when my hygienic standards weren't quite as high as my desire for punctuality. It was almost noon when I heard the tractor, and looking out the kitchen window, saw Dad coming down the road with the grader. Dad did not like to waste time waiting for dinner and the vegetables still needed to be cooked. I grabbed the dish of freshly shelled peas, and in my haste, spilled the lot on the floor. Aghast, I watched as miniature green marbles rolled in every direction. What was to be done? Between the floor and the cooking pot came a broom and a dustpan and a quick rinse in a colander. No one noticed I ate no peas.

Mary and I did set high standards for ourselves, even if we didn't always manage to meet them. We were acutely embarrassed on a Monday afternoon when Auntie Lucille, with blanket-bundled baby Keith, stopped by unexpectedly to find us still working on the laundry. After all, our mother always finished this Monday task by noon. As we apologized profusely for being so slow, our aunt assured us we were doing just great.

Remember, this was long before automatic washers. Thanks to our wind turbine and the bank of batteries in the basement, we did have an electric machine with an agitator that swished the clothes in the tub of soapy water. It also had an attached wringer that swivelled. Each item of clothing was fed through the wringer by hand, falling into a tub of clear water as it emerged from between the twin rollers of the wringer. The clothes were then swished and punched by hand to rinse out the soap. The wringing and rinsing were repeated with a second tub of clear water. After the second rinse the clothes were sent through the wringer again and into a laundry basket. The final step was lugging the basket outside and pegging the clothes on the clothesline. This process was repeated for every load of laundry–and we learned seven people make a heap of laundry in a week.

Remembering that long-ago Monday, I now realize that our aunt's visit was probably at the request of our mother, who was wondering how we were coping in her absence

Four-year-old Leila was more of a challenge for Mary and me than the laundry. We would lay her down on the couch in the sunporch for her afternoon nap and she would be up before we were out of the room. After half-a-dozen repeats of this performance, one of us would hold her down while she kicked and screamed until she wore herself out and went to sleep. This ritual continued daily for the two weeks till Mum came home from the hospital with our baby brother. When Mum asked us how we had managed in her absence we said, "Good, no problem–except Leila. She wouldn't take her afternoon nap unless we held her down. And then she kicked and screamed."

"Oh," Mum said. "She hasn't had an afternoon nap for over a year."

All seven of us

Back row–Me, Lorna, Mary
Middle row–Denis, Leila, Billy
Front–Leslie

Going and Coming

Joining a tour of the Winnipeg Art Gallery's exhibition, <u>American Chronicles: The Art of Norman Rockwell</u>, felt like stepping into a time capsule, taking me back to my childhood.

Rockwell's *Saturday Evening Post* cover, *Going and Coming, 1947*, instantly evoked memories of our Lake Day. The nine of us, two adults and seven kids, piling into that square 1940s car, would be heading for Round Lake to the south, or Madge Lake to the north. In those pre-seatbelt days, we were sitting two-deep, but no one complained. We were going to the lake! The air in the car crackled with excitement.

Days before the annual event we would be aquiver with anticipation tinged by dread. What if the day was cold and rainy? What if the car wouldn't start? The weather had always cooperated in the past, but there was a year when the car had stalled and refused to start. With disappointed, wailing kids in the background, Dad had convinced a neighbour to lend us his vehicle.

It wasn't a special day for only our family. Dad's brothers, George and Henry, and their families would be there too. There would be 21 cousins in all, ensuring a splashing good time.

Wearing bathing suits under our clothes, we kids would strip on the beach and dash headlong into the lake, that first smack of cold water taking our breath away. The adults would cautiously inch into the water, we young folks teasing, and sometimes, daring to splash.

I don't remember any of us kids being able to really swim. There were wildly flailing attempts at dogpaddling and Uncle Henry taught some of us to float. Mostly, we invented our own water games, involving a ball and lots of good-natured dunking and splashing. Our original version of water polo would continue until the call, "Lunch is ready."

And such a lunch it was! Our busy mothers would have loaded picnic tables with potato salad, coleslaw, devilled eggs, cold baked beans, sliced ham, canned chicken with its jellied goodness, crusty home-baked buns, all the pie we could eat, and to top it off, the tangy homemade beverage, Saskatoon vinegar. There was only one drawback. We were not allowed back in the water till an hour after we had finished lunch. The parents said it was to avoid deadly stomach cramps that could cause us to drown.

Finally released to "go jump in the lake," the free-for-all water antics would resume. Getting out of the water and lying on the beach was unthinkable. We spent all the other days of the year on dry land. In the water we stayed until ordered out for supper. We must have looked like shrivelled prunes by then.

Now, as I study Rockwell's split-canvas painting, I smile at the humour in the contrasting facial expressions and body language.

The *Going* pictures a family, their car topped by a canoe, on their way to the lake. The father and mother are sitting tall, father's hat planted four-square on his head, new cigar firmly held between his lips, mother's hair tidy, scarf neatly tied. Father has a self-satisfied expression. "Good. Everything's loaded and we're on our way," I can imagine him saying. The children and the family dog, playfully leaning out the windows, are bursting with energy and anticipation. Only Grandma, sitting stoic and composed in the back seat, staring straight ahead, seems untouched by the excitement.

The *Coming* panel shows a different family. The father is hunched over the steering wheel, his hat pushed back on his head, a short stub of cigar hanging from his mouth. The mother and the little one on her knee are leaning against the window, sound asleep. One boy stares soberly ahead, while his sister sits with chin resting in her hands. Their brother sleeps in the back seat. Even the image of the dog, tongue hanging out, says, 'weary and hot.' Only Grandma seems unchanged.

Suddenly, I realize that my Lake Day memories are about the fun of the 'going' and the 'there.' Images of the 'coming' home are kept tucked away in an inner closet of my mind. They do not fit my fun-day focus.

On the drive home everyone is tired and a bit cranky. The car seems smaller as we squeeze together in the back seat. The younger ones seem heavier when they lean against us as they sleep. Sunburned backs, pressed against the seat, sting. And someone is sure to get car-sick, especially Mary, who once violently ejected her lunch and supper while standing directly behind Dad. Thereafter she had to sit, a basin at the ready in her lap.

It is long past dark when we drive into the yard—home at last. But the day is not over. The cows are standing outside the barn door, waiting to be relieved of their full udders. Sleeping young ones must be roused and hustled into bed. Leftover food must be unloaded from the car and put away. And when that is done, there is still the milk to be run through the hand-turned separator.

However, by next July, as Lake Day approaches, we kids will have forgotten all about the 'coming' and will once more be agog with delicious anticipation of the fun of the 'going' and the 'there.'

Rockwell said he showed life as he would like it to be. Just as an artist selects what he or she wants to put in a picture, I realize our minds are equally selective in what they store on the canvas of our memories.

Saskatoon Vinegar

This recipe uses a ratio of 2 to 1 so is easily adapted to the quantity of berries you have. For 8c of berries you need 4c of water and 4c of sugar with 2c of water.

Working with two or three cups of berries at a time, use a fine metal sieve and a potato masher to squeeze as much juice as you can out of the berries. Repeat till all berries have been juiced. Combine the juice and 4c of water and bring to a simmer, Cook for 10 to 15 minutes. Cool to room temperature.

Combine the sugar with the 2c of water and bring to a boil, stirring constantly, to dissolve the sugar. Cool to room temperature.

When cool, mix the berry juice and the sugar syrup together and store in the refrigerator for up to three days or put in sealers and process in a hot water bath for 20 to 30 minutes as you would any fruit.

To make the refreshing drink we called Saskatoon Vinegar, you add some of the Saskatoon berry syrup, to desired taste, to a pitcher of cold water.

Red, Blue, and White Ribbons

There were two 4-H clubs operating in Churchbridge in the 1940s—a grain club and a calf club. Their purpose was to interest young people in farming, develop related skills, and contribute to positive personal emotional growth.

Our dad enrolled us four older kids in both the grain and the calf clubs. Our membership in the grain club did not last very long. The four of us were unanimous in our dislike of roguing (pulling the weeds in our plots) and after two years staged a family revolt, refusing to join for another year. The only positive memory I have of the grain club is winning the competition to design a community bulletin board, which did get built and was used for many years.

The calf club was completely different. I loved it. You were responsible for looking after your own calf—a living breathing creature with feelings and a distinct personality. Feeding and grooming your calf was a daily ritual. In spring, in addition to brushing, that grooming would involve squeezing out any warbles (parasitic flies) that had formed a swollen cyst under your calf's hide. The warbles were the pupa stage that began with a heel fly laying eggs in the hair of the animal's lower leg. The larvae migrated through the body till they reached the animal's back. There they formed a hard covering around themselves. When the pupa was fully mature, the warble would fall to the ground and open to release the adult fly. We did not wait for the warbles to mature, however. We would squeeze them out before they were ready to emerge on their own. That may sound gross, but it was great fun, my favourite grooming chore. It was just like squeezing a giant pimple–great training for when you were a teenager and had pimples you pinched, even though you knew you shouldn't!

The year would culminate with a calf show where your animal would be judged on its qualities as a good beef animal—broad, straight back, well-fleshed in the loin area, and good depth of body. At the same time, you would be judged on your showmanship—how well your calf responded when being led or standing for inspection. The show would begin with everyone leading their calf around in a ring while the judges evaluated how they walked. Then you would line up in an orderly row so the judges could take a closer look at each animal. It was important that your animal stand with all four feet placed squarely under the body, so training your calf to lead, turn, and stand properly was an important part of your daily care routine. You had an aid–a stick with a pointed end–which was used to lightly poke between a cloven hoof to persuade your animal to move a leg to a desired position. You could take that stick with you in the show ring.

Red, blue, and white ribbons were awarded for first, second, and third place beef animals, and for showmanship. Our family won many ribbons over the years, but the ones I prized the most were the ones I won for showmanship.

There was one year when I had a particularly strong-minded calf. As I was attempting to get him to join the line after walking in a circle, he decided he didn't want to move in response to my tug on his halter. Our local Agricultural Extension Representative was leaning on the rail fence beside my dad as they watched the show. When my calf was refusing to move, Dad heard the Ag Rep say, "Push him," under his breath. In the next second that is exactly what I did, giving up pulling and instead changing direction and pushing my calf's head to get him to turn. I ended up winning the showmanship red ribbon that year despite my balky partner, or maybe with his help, by showing I could manage a difficult animal.

After our local calf club show there would be a larger regional "Fat Stock Show" in our neighbouring town, Langenburg. Again, our calves were judged for their quality as meat producing animals while we were judged on our showmanship skills. The show would culminate with an auction sale of the animals.

That was the hard part. Once your calf was sold, you led it to one of the holding pens where you removed its halter, knowing you were leaving it to be shipped away for slaughter. This was an animal you had given a name, cared for all year, and formed a bond with, and now you were abandoning it. You knew there would be a new calf again next year, but this parting still hurt.

Time passed, and we four kids aged out of the calf club, while the younger ones in the family took over and continued to win many ribbons.

I realized how closely those ribbons had become interwoven into our family life on the day John and I got our wedding picture proofs from the photographer. Our pictures had been taken in front of the living room drapes. Studying the prints, I burst into laughter as I spied, pinned to the floral-patterned drapes, a calf club ribbon! This was in 1953, before the advent of coloured film, so the picture was in black and white, but I am sure it was a red ribbon, as it had gone unnoticed among the drape's red roses. Although it was doubtless a ribbon won by one of the younger kids, it still seems an appropriate part of our wedding picture, a "stand-in" for the many red ribbons I won over the years.

Reading, Writing and 'Rithmetic

My younger sister, Mary, and I ended up in Grade 1 together. This is how it happened. The legal age to start school was five, if you would be turning six before January 1st of the next year. As my mother thought this was too young, that another year of maturity increased your readiness to learn, she did not enroll me at Liscard School, our local one-room Grade 1 to 8 school, till I was six, to be seven in November.

I was eager to start school. It meant one thing to me—I was going to learn to read stories, just like my mother did. Each day I came home from school excited to share what I had learned—the names and sounds of letters and putting them together to make words.

This was too much for Mary to bear. She wanted to share in the fun. She begged and begged to go to school too. And then she begged and begged some more. As she was five years old, with a birthday in December, she was the legal age to start school. Finally, my mother caved, and Mary joined my class a few weeks into the school year.

Years later she admitted she hated it, but after all the begging she had done, she didn't dare tell our mother she wanted to stop. Learning never did come as easily to Mary as it did to me, and I have often wondered if my mother's theory was right, and another year would have made a difference in her confidence and attitude to school. Also, we would not have been in the same class, and in a sense in competition, which might have improved our sisterly bond.

There were advantages and disadvantages to being a beginner in a one-room, eight-grade classroom. One of the advantages was you got to eavesdrop on what was happening in the older grades, sort of learning by osmosis. However, the older students could also listen to your lessons, and if you made an embarrassing mistake you could count on being unmercifully teased at recess. In fact, recess could be a difficult time for beginners until you developed an "I don't care" attitude. One of the boys' favourite ways to tease the girls, who had to wear dresses in those days, was to push us higher than we wanted to go on the swings and then sing out, "I can see your underpants." Usually, it was the kids in the middle grades who did the teasing, while the Grade 8 students, who were "too mature" for such behaviour, would come to our rescue.

Every day in Grade 1, after the noon-hour break, we were given a card with a picture of a person from another country, dressed in an elaborate traditional outfit. These blue-gray cards, with the figure outlined in dark blue, came in boxes of Shredded Wheat cereal, separating the layers of cereal biscuits. On the back of the card were specific instructions for colouring the picture. Other than developing hand-eye coordination, the cards were basically "busy work" to keep us occupied while the teacher worked with other grades, because we never talked about the countries where these people lived. Too bad we didn't—it was a learning opportunity missed. My reaction to the activity was amazement. How could the teacher and his wife eat that much Shredded Wheat? Did they have cereal for every meal? I was older and wiser to the ways of the world before I realized the savvy company had supplied schools with packs of cards as an advertising gimmick.

I enjoyed the mile-and-a-half walk to and from school–unless the neighbour's bull was in their pasture which bordered the fence. I had an irrational fear of bulls—in my mind they were wild and angry beasts that would charge you, head down, nostrils flaring, hooves tearing up the turf. After all, I knew that bulls had rings in their noses because the only way you could control them was by jerking on this sensitive part of their body with either a rope looped through the ring or a stick with a hook on the end.

At the sight of the bull, I would trudge through the ditch on the other side of the road and climb through the barbed wire fence, dragging my lunch pail behind me, into another neighbour's field. Even with two ditches filled with high grass, weeds and wildflowers and two barbed wire fences separating us, I still walked warily keeping my eye on the bull, ready to detect the slightest sign of aggression. Only when I was well past that pasture, I would climb back over the barbed wire fence, through the ditch and up onto the road once more. When Mary started school, she joined me in this maneuver at first, and then deciding the bull was paying no attention to us, she stayed on the road, scorning my timidity.

In January of my Grade 2 year, the osteomyelitis virus attacked my left hip and it would be two years, in hospital and recovering at home, homeschooled by my mother, before I rejoined my classmates. Then, when I was 12 years old, it was back to the hospital for surgery to straighten the hip. During both hospital stays I got letters, written as an English assignment I am sure, from my classmates. And each time, while I was recovering at home the teacher would bring the school kids for a visit. I ended up looking forward to the letters and visits as they helped me feel connected to the school.

My first attempts at independent writing were the letters I sent to my family during that first hospital stay. I had no idea my mother had saved them till my father gave them to me after her death. Reading them so many years later was a very emotional experience. They are now a precious treasure, a window to the child I was.

Mary and I stayed an "extra" year at Liscard School, taking Grade 9 by provincial correspondence courses under the direction of the teacher–and with help from our mother. Our sister, Lorna, who had skipped a grade, was now in Grade 8, just one grade behind us. The next year all three of us attended the high school in Churchbridge. At that time, you had to take either French or Latin for entrance to Normal School. I had opted for Latin in Grade 9 as our mother was a Latin scholar. Later, when I found out that French, not Latin, was taught at the Churchbridge high school, I had to take Latin by correspondence again in Grade 10.

I successfully petitioned my parents to let me attend the collegiate in Yorkton, our nearest city, for Grade 11, where Latin was taught. I also wanted educational opportunities beyond what were available in our small-town high school.

At the Yorkton Collegiate the excellence of the teachers and the challenges of the programs were all I had hoped for. I focused on studying, determined to get recommended in every subject so I wouldn't have to write final exams in June.

My fondest memories are of Miss Gould, our English teacher, who shared her love of literature while motivating us to become better writers. On a bookshelf in my study sits a binder with all the creative writing I did in high school. I was proud to have two pieces of my writing published in our Grade 12 yearbook—one a satirical send-up of our teachers, which I still think is funny, and the other a sappy, sentimental story that shows fiction is not my forte. Miss Gould's parting words to me were, "Keep on writing." I did in a way, though not how I think she hoped–long letters to family and friends, detailed journals recording family holidays, countless essays for English, history and sociology university classes, and during my working years, curriculum outlines, program guides, workshop presentations and reports on meetings and conferences.

However, in that Grade 11 year, Latin—which I had wanted to master—turned out to be a pesky thorn under my fingernail that I couldn't remove. Try as I would, I could not get my average mark to the 85 percent needed for exemption. Having to write the final exam for that one subject kept me in the city for the last two weeks in June. I did nothing but study, subsisting on cereal or sandwiches and sleeping only as much as my body demanded for those two weeks. That was when I discovered a drug-free trick to help me stay awake when I was nodding off. Rubbing an ice-cube behind your ears gives you an instant jolt of energy. Reapply as needed and it will keep you going for another hour or two.

In the end, all the studying was worth it, as my final mark of 84 percent surprised both me and the school principal. However, upon discovering a second language was no longer a requirement for entry to Normal School, I got rid of the prickly nuisance by dropping Latin in Grade 12.

On the social side, my move to the city school was akin to a frog jumping from a pond directly into the ocean. I felt like a nerdy country bumpkin—a misfit among the city kids. The first two months of Grade 11 were the loneliest time of my life.

My mother had arranged for me to stay at a boarding house. There were three other boarders—women I imagine were in their late twenties, early thirties—old enough that I considered them spinsters, as no men came calling. (The concept of career women, single by choice, was many years in the future.) As I had made no friends among my classmates, no one came calling on me either. I spent all my after-school time in my room studying, emerging only for meals. After two months my landlady took me aside and said, "This is not the right place for you. You need to be with other young people." I phoned my mother immediately and told her the landlady wanted me to move, neglecting to say why.

My mother arrived, consternation (and disbelief I choose to think) in her voice as she asked the landlady, "What has my daughter done?" Recognizing the wisdom in the landlady's assessment of the situation, my mother found a light-housekeeping place–facilities to cook your meals and responsibility for cleaning your living space—which I would share with three other young people, one of whom was in my class at school. The second floor of the house had two bedrooms opening onto the landing at the top of the stairs. This space had been outfitted as a simple kitchen with a small table and chairs, cupboards, a counter and a hotplate. As the hotplate had only two burners, timing the cooking of our meals required cooperation and negotiation among the four of us. We also shared space in a refrigerator in the basement, where we did our laundry and ironing.

Our landlady was an accomplished baker. Once a week we came home to the tantalizing aroma of freshly baked rolls–crusty rolls, cloverleaf rolls, crescent rolls, breadsticks and twists–golden-brown tops shiny with glaze. Cool enough to be stacked, they would be heaped in a huge tin kneading pan in the basement. My classmate was the landlady's niece and we would often be given a roll as we came in from school. When her niece left for "personal reasons," (code in those days for being pregnant), the landlady's weekly gift of rolls left too. But that "come eat me" invitation wafting up from the basement on baking day was irresistible. Each one of the three of us still living upstairs secretly snitched a roll thinking, "One won't be missed in such a big container." Maybe one wouldn't have been, but three were. We were accused of stealing, which we couldn't deny. Thereafter, baking day was olfactory torture and we tried to avoid going down to the basement.

Before she left, my classmate and I became "school friends" and hung out after school going for coffee or a coke. However, a blind date with her and two male friends revealed a gulf of so-called sophistication or experience that prevented us ever becoming close personal friends. While she and her partner "made-out" in the front seat, I spent a miserable interminable evening defending myself from persistent unwanted advances. That was the first and the last blind date I ever went on. I was also shocked by my classmate's treachery when I discovered the man she was with was her best friend's boyfriend. I wasn't surprised when she left school in January because she was pregnant.

That first year in Yorkton, the CPR train was my lifeline. Every weekend I would climb aboard for the 50-mile ride to Churchbridge, where I could count on either my mother or my father meeting me for the drive home. One unforgettable stormy Friday in February, I came home from school to a message from the landlady, "Call home, Jean." Dread was clutching my stomach as I made the call.

"Hello." It was my mother's voice.

"Hi Mum. What's up?"

"Storm's blocked the roads. No way we can get to town."

"What about the snowplane?"

"In the repair shop–again."

I kept the tears in check long enough to say goodbye to my mother. Once upstairs, I erupted in a gut-wrenching, homesick bawl in front of my roommates.

Happily, the next year–my Grade 12 year–was very different as my sisters Mary and Lorna joined me in the city, Lorna in Grade 11 and Mary taking a secretarial course. Now I had someone to share shopping, cooking and mealtimes with, and hang out with on weekends.

Our mother had found another light-housekeeping place. Here we cooked on the landlady's kitchen range and had space in her refrigerator. With three of us living in the city, we were on a "shoestring" budget, but on the plus side we brought the tastes of home with us. To help keep our grocery bills down we hauled jars of canned vegetables, meat, fruit, rice pudding and milk from home. Yes, to save money, our mother even canned our cows' milk.

Our living quarters were two small bedrooms opening onto a dining/ studying/sitting area. In those pre-computer, pre-smart phone with camera days, when working on an essay you took notes from references by hand, and if you wanted to change the order of paragraphs you had written it was a cut and tape procedure. In the process of writing essays for English and history classes, I would invariably end up with the floor littered with pages of discarded writing. Mary was not happy with my messy habit and it did cause some friction between the two of us. When her secretarial course ended a month before we graduated and she was hired as a stenographer in a lawyer's office, she immediately used her first paycheck to move into a bed/sitting room of her own—with nary a scrap of paper on the floor.

Sometime in the winter of that Grade 12 year, I realized my boyfriend was getting much too serious and I broke up with him. We had both belonged to 4-H calf clubs and met at a regional rally, but except for our shared experience of growing up on a farm, we really didn't have that much in common. Parting at the door, it took some time to convince him this was really the end for us. I don't remember the month, but I know it was cold because my landlady scolded me for keeping him standing out in the cold instead of inviting him in.

Breaking up was the morally right thing to do, as I sensed he felt we were moving toward a "permanent relationship," and it would not have been fair to keep his hopes up. However, it left me without an escort for the graduation dance in June. Nevertheless, I went ahead and ordered a gown, confident someone would ask me to be their partner. No one did.

So, as the date for the dance drew near, I screwed up my courage and asked a boy from our hometown. He turned me down. Oh, the ignominy of not having a partner for the graduation dance.

But it's funny how things work out, because a few days later, when I was shopping for groceries with my sisters, we came out of the store to pouring rain and our brown paper grocery bags were soon soaking wet. Suddenly, the bottom of my bag gave way and a bottle of ketchup crashed to the pavement, breaking into sharp shards of glass, one of which cut a huge gash in my foot. We stood there, stunned at first, not knowing what to do as my blood pooled with the rain on the sidewalk. Luckily, this happened right by the school and a teacher, heading to her car, saw my predicament and drove me to the emergency room for stitches, and then drove me home. Walking with crutches, and a bandaged foot, I realized I now had an "out" for my grad dance predicament. I was even able to cancel my order for a gown.

Saved by a bottle of ketchup!

Normal School

I attended Normal School in Moose Jaw, Saskatchewan, in 1951/52, the last year it was called "Normal School." The name was derived from the definition for "normal" as conforming with, or adhering to, a norm or standard. So Normal School was a school whose methods of instruction were a model for imitation—an institution for the training of teachers.

I suspect they got tired of having to explain the rationale for the name. By the time my sister Lorna came tripping along behind me in 1953/54 it had been renamed the "Teachers' College."

Like My Grade 11 year in Yorkton, at Normal School I was on my own again—no sisters to keep me company—but as all my classmates were also swimming in unfamiliar water, it was easier to form friendships. I shared a light-housekeeping space with three other students, and we shopped and "hung out" together after school and on weekends.

A group of us became rabid fans of the Moose Jaw hockey team, never missing a home game. It was the beginning of a lifetime of cheering on sports teams as my husband, kids, grandkids, and great-grandkids played baseball, football, hockey, ringette, rugby and curling games.

And unlike my Grade 12 predicament, at the end of the Normal School year I had a date for the graduation dance–no ketchup bottle savior was needed!

My roommate came from a small town on a spur railway line from Moose Jaw. One weekend she invited me to go home with her on the train. The dated, shabby passenger car we boarded was a far cry from the main-line railway cars that went through my hometown of Churchbridge—it was so old it still had a stove at the front for winter heat. My friend knew two of our fellow passengers and the young men joined us on the seat facing ours. The other three decided they wanted to pass the time playing a game of whist. The game required four players, and despite my protestations that I had never played cards, they insisted that I had to play. I'm sure they did a good job of explaining the game to a neophyte, but I had never even seen a deck of cards before—they were not allowed in our family home at the time as our mother was adhering to her strict evangelical upbringing—and the instructions went way over my head. After the game my partner remarked, "We should have won that game," the implication being my playing had caused us to lose, which of course it had.

That was only the beginning. I discovered I was visiting a fun-loving, card-playing family. We even went to a community whist drive one evening. This was an "equal opportunity" event, where after every hand, you moved to another table and played with a different partner. There were prizes for the three highest scores and a booby prize for the lowest one. I pitied my poor partners if they thought they were heading for first prize before they ended up teamed with me. I was not surprised when they announced the winner of the booby prize. I was presented with a package of chocolate exlax tablets (for constipation relief), to much laughter. For one horror-stricken moment I thought I was expected to swallow some.

During that year at Normal School, homesickness did hit me from time to time. I never knew what might trigger it, some events more memorable than others. There was one day I will never forget. I had eaten my favourite lunch–canned tomato soup and a grilled cheese sandwich–and it was time to head back to class. Stepping out of the house, I paused to soak up the promise of winter's end in this warm mid-April day. The snow was melting, puddles were everywhere, the air had that softly caressing, moist, spring feel. Just at that moment a farm truck drove by, a rather dirty truck. In the back was a lone cow, a rather dirty cow, obviously stressed by the trip, because as the truck went by the pungent smell of fresh manure wafted in my direction. A mighty wave of homesickness engulfed me. My eyes filled with tears and at that moment I wanted nothing more than to be home on the farm as the smell transported me away from the cityscape before me.

What I saw was the farmyard where the melting snow was revealing the mounds of horse and cow manure dropped over winter, the warm sun thawing it, releasing that familiar barnyard odour. A younger me, home from school, had changed my clothes, pulled on my rubber boots and was heading to the barn to groom my 4H calf. I was stepping carefully to avoid those smelly humps emerging from the snow. I was happy that the melting snow was signalling the end of winter, and I was paying no attention to the rich aroma emanating from those warming clumps of winter droppings. It was just there, the familiar barnyard smell. Little did I know how sweet that smell of spring would seem to me one day.

Fortunately, I found the classroom work both challenging and interesting. Our instructors used a variety of teaching strategies, modelling what they hoped we would adopt in our classrooms. We were involved in numerous small group activities, including a major project they called an "enterprise." We could choose a topic from a list of suggestions or submit a topic of our choice to our supervisor for approval. This activity culminated in a presentation to the whole class, with a specific number of minutes allotted for each group presentation. We were warned that a group would be cut off when their time elapsed, even if they weren't finished. In other words, plan your group presentation carefully. Our group did, establishing the sub-topic each person in the group would present, the number of minutes they could use and a hand signal that would give the speaker a one-minute warning to wrap it up. All went well till our second last presenter ignored our warning hand signals and kept on speaking till the group's time limit was up. It left the last speaker (me) unable to present our group's conclusions and summary. After spending weeks of hard work on the project it was an extremely frustrating experience. Lesson learned--I should have taken control of the situation, thanked my group member, cutting him off, and then made my presentation.

Two three-week practice teaching sessions were the highlight of the year. We were sent out in pairs to work with one of a group of specially selected master teachers. Some of these teachers taught in Moose Jaw, but many were working in small towns scattered around southern Saskatchewan. Board and room were provided for all out-of-town student placements. Instructors from Normal School visited each school periodically to observe our performance and confer with the classroom teacher. I was sent to two small towns, Pence and then Milestone. In each instance my teachers were helpful mentors, explaining their lesson objectives and giving constructive feedback on lessons I taught.

Many years later, working in Winnipeg schools, I was surprised to find that student teachers were sent to a school, not a specific classroom, for their practice teaching. They spent time observing in every classroom, with the possibility they could be observing some less skilled teachers. In addition, they received feedback on their performance from many teachers. The focus here was on breadth of experience versus the consistency I experienced as a student teacher. There are advantages and disadvantages to both approaches, but I think I still prefer the "master teacher" concept.

There were 222 of us enrolled in Normal School that year, divided into six classes. Although we represented many nationalities, we were a "white" group. At some point during the year, I asked an instructor if an Indigenous person would be accepted if they applied. There was a long pause before he said, "I don't know." In fact, I didn't say, "Indigenous." In 1953, we were still referring to Canada's first people as "Indians." Times have changed, though slowly. Today we do have many Indigenous teachers and are actively working to recruit more.

Drama was one of the extra-curricular activities encouraged at Normal School. Each year, the school would stage a major theatrical production, directed by two teachers—in 1953 it was Thornton Wilder's *Our Town*. In addition, each of the six classes would present a short, student-directed one-act play of their choice. Our class selected *So Wonderful in White*, a play about the trials and tribulations of student nurses. As a male nurse was unheard of in the 50s, it had an all-female cast, with the boys in our group having roles in directing, set design, lighting and props. Our production was reviewed by the *Moose Jaw Times Herald*, which noted that it involved "a large variety of near hysteria and copious quantities of weeping, with the matron, played by Jean Putland (me!), outstanding for the dignity of the portrayal." The girl in the lead role was commended for a "workmanlike job", the director for "handling the grouping with efficiency" and the décor and lighting as "convincing." I must have known it would be the only rave "acting review" I would ever receive as I saved the press clipping, the newsprint now darkened with age, the edges a bit tattered and worn, showing the passage of time, just like me.

"SO WONDERFUL IN WHITE" AT NORMAL SCHOOL

PART 4
A New Family

I Had a Dream

When I was a preteen, I dreamed of teaching in a school by a lake, of being able to repeat, every hot summer day, the wonderous splashing cold-water fun of our family's once-a-year trip to the lake.

In my early teens, I imagined a second possible career path. I would still be a teacher, but now I would go into the far north to teach, marry an Indian chief (nothing less than a chief would do!) and bring my husband home to my father's disapproval, and the shock of all the family. However, actions speak louder than dreams. When I graduated from Normal School, I sent an application to a small country school less than 50 miles from home—with nary a lake nor an Indian chief in sight. In truth I was a homebody who had missed my family when I went to high school in Yorkton and Normal School in Moose Jaw. And I was a country girl—the farm, not the city, was my happy place.

My application was accepted, and I began my year of teaching at Shamrock School. I boarded with Dave and Doris Tulloch and family. I was given a warm welcome and it turned out to be a happy place to live. Dave and Doris were a compatible couple who enjoyed each other's company. Although I never saw outward signs of affectation, such as hugs or kisses, I could sense their mutual love for one another. While Doris was the more serious one, Dave had a wonderful dry sense of humour that added spark to the relationship. Their baby, Grant, was two years old, but still not talking, much to their concern. They need not have worried as he was a chatterbox by the time I left in June. The two older boys, Lorne, 12 years old, and Bruce, eight, were as well behaved as boys could be and respected their parents. I never saw discipline exercised, beyond an occasional scolding from their mother.

That's why I was so surprised when Bruce, now 75, was visiting me recently, and he recalled a "licking" with a big strap he and Lorne got from their dad after they had done something to make him very angry. Bruce couldn't remember what they had done, but he could still recall the sting of the strap. They didn't want that to happen again, so after their punishment, the two boys got the strap and buried it. So maybe that is why I never saw any physical punishment!

Doris was a great "country cook." The meat, potato, and vegetable meals were delicious, as were the lunches she packed for me each school day. The tantalizing aroma of fresh-baked bread, buns, pastry, or desserts was often a comforting welcome home from school. I ate well all year.

The house was an original log house with a second story added. There were two bedrooms upstairs, one with finished walls and linoleum on the floor, the other with bare uncovered studs and a plain board floor. I later learned my arrival had turfed Lorne and Bruce from the finished bedroom to the unfinished one. I wouldn't have blamed them if they had felt some resentment.

It was not luxurious accommodation, however. There was no electricity and the walls were not insulated. In the winter the water in my wash basin froze overnight. Every morning Doris would bring me a pail of water, steaming hot from the kitchen stove. I did my lesson planning and preparation at a table in my room by the dim light of a kerosene lamp. In winter, I worked with a sweater and my heavy terrycloth housecoat on over my day clothes and was still cold. I admit I wasn't quite prepared for this. With a wind turbine that powered batteries in our basement, we had electric power at home from the time I was 12 and running water soon after. I had become used to insulated walls, a warm house and hot water at the turn of a tap. I was more citified than I realized.

At school, conditions were just as rudimentary as the rural electrical power grid was still a few years in the future. To make duplicate copies of seatwork for my students I used a hectograph, a gelatin pad in a metal tray. A master copy was made on paper, using a special pencil or pen. This copy was then placed face down on the pad to transfer the image to the gelatin. Copies were made by smoothing blank paper over the image on the pad and then puling the paper off. When you had the number of copies you needed, the gelatin pad could be wiped clean using rubbing alcohol to remove the ink, leaving the pad ready to use again. It was a messy slow process, but at the time, the only non-mechanical way you could make three or more copies.

The Tullochs lived one-and-three-quarter miles from the school. In summer, I walked the distance carrying books and papers in a bag, switching the bag from one arm to the other as each tired of the load. Packsacks were far in the future, as were running shoes or sneakers. My low-heeled leather shoes sometimes gave me heel blisters. If this happened, I would remove the offending shoes, add them to my bag, and walk barefoot along the grassy edge of the gravel road, hoping no one would drive by and see me. When I got close to the house, ignoring the pain, I would put my shoes back on. It would have been unseemly for the teacher to be seen walking barefoot.

In the winter the boys and I rode to school on a horse-drawn toboggan, Lorne doing the driving. We didn't use the road, shortening the distance by cutting diagonally across the snow-covered fields. The toboggan made a crunching, sliding or squeaking sound, depending on the type of snow— packed down trail or fresh snowfall—and coldness of the temperature. A can of drinking water for the school sat at the back of the toboggan. The can had a tight-fitting lid, but it was always a relief when we got to the school without it tipping over. Thankfully, on very cold days Dave would drive us in the heated van.

I had a dozen students, Grades 1 to 9, in most cases two or more per family. Personalities ranged from quiet to rambunctious, serious to fun-loving, but all were pleasant, likeable kids, with nary a real discipline problem in the lot. The Grade 9 students were taking correspondence courses, so I just had to supervise them and give help with anything they didn't understand.

One noon hour, a feisty girl in the middle grades took her horse out of the barn and was showing the other kids how she had trained him to jump a low barricade. A school trustee happened to be driving by at that moment. He put an instant stop to the activity, then came into the school to find me putting the afternoon's tasks on the blackboard. In the interest of safety, we now had a new school rule—no horse out of the barn till you were ready to go home. There were some things Normal School hadn't prepared me for.

There were other things I hadn't expected. I knew I would have to plan, organize and direct the annual Christmas concert, a rural tradition. However, it was a surprise to discover that Shamrock School, and other schools in the area, usually hosted one or more school dances every year, with the proceeds going to a community charity. A school-sponsored dance was unheard of in the district where I grew up.

One Saturday in mid-October the threshing crew arrived at the Tullochs. Doris said she would call me for lunch after the threshers had finished eating. I was surprised, when shortly after I sat down to eat, a man with dusty, chaff-covered work clothes, obviously one of the threshers, walked in and sat down across from me. Doris, introducing us, said he was her brother John. He explained that he was late to eat because he had been doing some maintenance work on the threshing machine. I didn't pay much attention to him. With his thinning hair I thought he was probably a year or two younger than Doris, much too old to interest me.

Later, in conversation with Doris, I learned he was 10 years younger than her and only three years older than me. So, when he came by the next Sunday and asked me to go for a drive, I thought, "Why not." We toured the neighbourhood as he described who lived on every farm, starting with my students' homes. The farms became a blur of houses and barns as he pointed out where he lived with his parents and a sister, his best friend's home, where an aunt and uncle lived, a married cousin's home and every other farm in the neighbourhood it seemed. We drove by Mitchell's Lake where he would swim in the summer and skate in the winter. We explored Stornoway, a small town where he used to haul grain to the elevator, but which was now virtually a ghost town with only two or three families still living there. We ended up in Rhein, the town to which he now hauled his grain. It was a hot day, so we got drippy ice cream cones which we quickly ate in the car. That was our first date.

When he asked me to go to a community dance the next weekend I hesitated because I was an insecure dancer, but I again thought, "Why not."

That was the first of many, many dances we went to. John loved to dance and was such a good dancer that it was easy to follow his lead. When I danced with him, for the first time in my life, I felt like I could dance. And he ended up dancing right into my heart.

We were engaged in May and married in October.

Real life may not be what you dreamed you wanted. It may be better.

First Comes Marriage, Then a Baby Carriage

My teaching career looked to be a short one. When I got engaged in May of my first year as a teacher, with our wedding date set for October, I planned to be a full-time farm wife. In the 50s it was not the normal thing for a woman to continue working after marriage, and especially not a farmer's wife, with all the work to be done on the farm.

But at the end of the third week in September, a phone call from my former school superintendent added a few weeks to my teaching experience. He had an out-of-control school that had already sent two teachers "packing" since the fall term started in September. The last time he had answered a distress call, the kids had hidden the school bell high up in a tree and were running around outside, ignoring the teacher's pleas to get back into the school. With some trepidation, I agreed to "sub" for four weeks to allow time to find a permanent replacement.

Being forewarned, the first day I quickly established who was in control. It was not as relaxed a classroom atmosphere as I would have liked, but it was civilized. When the superintendent visited two weeks into my tenure, he was pleasantly surprised to find all the other students busy at their desks as I worked with one group. His gratitude was more of a reward than the pay cheque at the end of the four weeks.

October 30th, the day after John finished harvesting, we were married. Years later our kids asked us, "Why didn't you get married on the 31st? You could've worn Halloween costumes." Today you can be as original as you like on your wedding day, but back then things were much more formal. For example, John was getting married in a navy suit and white shirt. The two of us purchased a red tie to complete his outfit, but his mother vetoed it—too bright. It didn't seem to matter that I had red roses in my bouquet. She bought a boring brown and beige tie that did not coordinate with navy at all. Easygoing John's attitude was, "Oh well, it's just a tie." I wasn't happy about it, neither the tie nor the interference, but decided it wasn't wise to pick a fight with my future mother-in-law on the eve of our wedding. It turned out none of our wedding guests said, "Ugh, what an ugly tie," at least not in our hearing, and our wedding pictures were black and white, making the tie's colour irrelevant. And John never wore the tie again after the wedding.

When we were dating I would, from time to time, complain about my super-fine straight hair that didn't keep a curl. And John's response was always, "It can't be as bad as Florence's." Florence was his sister, who also lived at home on the farm, helping his mother and sharing in some of the farm work. I thought it was not a fair comparison, as he would see Florence heading to the barn to milk the cows in the early morning, before she had even bothered to brush her hair, whereas he had only seen me after I had sat under a hair dryer, with my hair in rollers, for half an hour. That first morning after our wedding, when we woke up, side-by-side in bed, John looked over at me and the first thing he said was, "Your hair is worse than Florence's."

We borrowed John's folk's car for a two-week honeymoon to Banff. When the gas tank on the car began to leak at a stopover in Calgary, I discovered John was resourceful. He plugged the hole with chewing gum, and it held till we got home. Then John discovered, to his chagrin, that riding in a car lulls me off to sleep, just like rocking a baby in a cradle. Here

we were travelling through these towering mountains for the first time, a wonder he had expected us to experience together, and I was sound asleep beside him, seeing nothing. Exasperated, from time to time he would prod me awake, so I didn't miss all the mountain scenery.

We didn't have money for shopping, so we found Banff underwhelming except for the elk wandering freely about the town. On the other hand, a side-trip to Radium Hot Springs, a natural outdoor pool carved out of the wilderness, exceeded our expectations. There were "ohs" and "ahs" and little screams as we slowly eased ourselves into the water, which felt boiling hot compared to the frosty November air. It was a wonderfully invigorating experience. However, after a week in the Banff Springs Hotel we both felt hemmed in by the mountains and couldn't wait to escape to the prairies.

When we got back to the farm, John's mother, dad and sisters, Florence and Vivian, left for their new home in Winnipeg—in the car. There we were, stranded on the farm without a vehicle and not enough cash to buy one. But it was the middle of November, we had snow and there would soon be much more. We could travel in a warm, wood-heated, horse-drawn van all winter.

As soon as it was cold enough to keep the sheets of ice in the community rink frozen, John and three of his friends began curling once a week in Rhein, our closest town. I discovered that while the men were away, the plan was for the wives to take turns meeting at each other's homes to play canasta. There it was again—cards—my nemesis. I felt marooned, an outsider with the other women who had known one another forever. And I did not have a clue how to play canasta. Everyone was kind, probably feeling as uneasy as I was, wondering how I would fit into their group. They patiently explained the rules of the game till I finally mastered them. When I tried shuffling the cards the way they did, holding half the deck between thumb and fingers in each hand and fanning them to integrate the two halves into one, the cards repeatedly flew everywhere. As they helped me replace the cards, they made good-natured jokes about it—"maybe they should get a clothes basket to try and catch the cards before they hit the floor." Finally, they gave up and suggested I just place all the cards face down on the table, stir them around and, after they were well mixed, gather them up into a deck.

I soon discovered I was living smack-dab in the middle of a close-knit, card-playing community, where neighbours regularly visited back and forth for a night of card games, and of course, before going home, a "lunch" with coffee and baked sweet treats. Over the ensuing years these neighbours became my lifelong friends. I learned to drink coffee and I learned to enjoy playing cards, though I never did become an expert shuffler.

Bringing card-playing John into my family also changed my mother's attitude to cards. My game-loving mother could not resist. She said she was beginning to realize things were not as black and white as her evangelical upbringing had taught, that there were shades of grey, that cards were not necessarily evil, it depended what you did with them. Using cards to gamble was still bad, playing fun family games was okay. My mother soon became an avid card player and we became a card-playing family—and still are, into the next generation. Whenever our kids get together a deck of cards will soon come out.

My family changed John too. We were a noisy bunch, all seven of us teasing and joshing one another. The first summer after our marriage, when we would be driving home after a Sunday visit, John would complain, "Your family is so noisy. They give me a headache." He soon learned to enjoy the camaraderie and join in the fun. We regularly visited my family, including my brothers and sisters as they married. We went on camping and fishing trips together, had backyard hotdog roasts and just "hung out" together. As a result, our kids grew up knowing all their cousins.

With marriage I had taken a step back in time from my parent's home. I was now living on a farm without electricity and the only "running" water was what I ran to the well to fetch. I cooked on a wood-burning kitchen range and used a gas-powered washer for the laundry. In summer our "fridge" was an icehouse situated at the back of the house yard, in the shade of a willow grove. This low, slope-roofed shed was built over a hole in the ground filled with huge chunks of ice in winter, which were then covered with sawdust for insulation. To keep your food cool in summer you would scrape some sawdust away so you could put your container of food right on the ice. Then you would heap sawdust up around the side of the dish. It was kind of messy, but it kept your food safe to eat.

The sun-warmed spring day I learned I was pregnant, we celebrated with a strawberry milkshake at the Dairy Queen. A restaurant meal was far beyond our means.

I immediately set to work doing all the obligatory things you were expected to do in preparation for your baby. I hemmed cloth diapers, and with my sister Lorna's help, used a pattern to make the flannel gowns babies wore in those days before onesies. Having no sewing machine, all the stitching was done by hand. Crocheting with one hook sounded easier than knitting with two, so I bought a book, taught myself to crochet, and then managed to produce the sweater, bonnet and bootee set a well-dressed baby would wear home from the hospital. December 16, 1954, after a lonely 12 hours of on-and-off labour in the Yorkton Hospital (no family allowed to stay with you in those days) our son, Darryl, made such a precipitous entry into the world that he was born on the stretcher before I made it into the delivery room.

Money was in short supply. We borrowed a crib and an old-fashioned wicker carriage from John's sister. It was a big day when we bought an old second-hand treadle sewing machine. The thing was so old that the "head" did not fold down out of the way. Instead, there was a rounded box that you covered it with when you were not using it—but when you treadled, it stitched—which was all that mattered. I made all Darryl's clothes on it, usually from the good parts of discarded clothes my mother gave me. A major accomplishment was a "recycled" parka I made him—dark brown with a cozy, nubby beige lining. It would have shocked my high school home economics teacher who regarded me as the most-inept seamstress she had had the misfortune to meet.

I kept some outfits to hand down as keepsakes to the kids. There are the baby gowns with their tucked and embroidered front panels, and my favourite, a bibbed pair of navy cotton shorts, trimmed with white rickrack and an appliqued white duck with a yellow bill.

Darryl was a very active kid. From the time he was a toddler, keeping track of him when he was playing outside was a major challenge. In 30 minutes, he could be who knew where, but fortunately, always tugging his little red wagon behind him. That wagon was like a flashing beacon, helping me spot him many a time. And he did have some favourite haunts that I learned to check first.

One was the icehouse with its roof that sloped from ground level to about six feet high. I was sick with dread the first time I saw my little boy and his red wagon surveying their world from the highest point of that roof. With frequent repetition of this scene, the dread wore off and it became just one of the first places I looked for him.

The open shed which housed the tractor, the old Model T Ford, and an assortment of tools was another favourite hangout. A major clean-up was needed the day I discovered him happily stirring a five-gallon pail of waste oil with a stick.

If his dad was working on a repair job in the shed Darryl was sure to be there, observing and trying to use the tools. He learned it was okay to hammer nails into boards but never into car or tractor tires. We learned how adept Darryl was with tools the weekend my brother, Bill, was helping John with the field work. Bill had hooked the cultivator up to the tractor and was heading for the field when a wheel came off the cultivator. Upon checking, Bill was mystified to find that nothing was broken but it seemed every nut had been so loose the wheel jiggled off with the motion. John solved the mystery with one word: "Darryl!" Yes, our four-year-old son had used a wrench to loosen those nuts.

Always busy, never still, that was Darryl. It was mid-afternoon. John had helped me carry out the laundry water and dump it in the shallow pit just beyond the house yard, where it would slowly soak away. Now, we were sitting at the kitchen table, relaxing with a cup of coffee. I was sitting facing the kitchen window. John was sitting on the opposite side of the table, his back to the window. As I sipped my coffee, I watched Darryl repeatedly dipping his little sand pail into the water we had just dumped and trotting away with it. I couldn't see where he was going because the car blocked my view. After watching for a few minutes, I said, "I wonder where Darryl is going with the water." John turned around, saw Darryl disappear behind the car with his pail of water, jumped up with an agonized, "No!" and raced for the door. He found what he feared—the gas tank cap unscrewed and Darryl filling the tank with soapy water.

April 4th, 1957, our second son, Lloyd, announced he was on the way. Our driveway was still a sludgy mixture of ice and water and halfway to the road the car got stuck in the mire. John, hands shaking with nervous haste, had to hitch the horses to the front of the car and pull it to the road. This time I barely made it to the hospital in time.

Lloyd, unlike his brother, was not a wanderer. I could plunk him down in the sandpile with his truck and pail and shovel and be confident I would find him there an hour later. However, he did have an inquisitive finger that could get him in trouble. We called him our "button pusher." He discovered that touching the wringer roller on the washing machine was not a good idea when it sucked his arm in up to his armpit, holding him a pained prisoner till I discovered him. With more serious consequences, he got a finger too close to a grain auger belt. That ended in a visit to the emergency department and a very sore, swollen, bandaged finger. The injured finger was the finger he liked to suck when he went to sleep, so it was a sad sleepless night for all of us.

One of my biggest frights came the day I heard Darryl screaming, "Help! Lloyd's eye's stuck!" as he came running toward the house. I dashed out to find Lloyd attached to the gate by a piece of wire that was, indeed, stuck in his eye. I had no idea how long the wire was, if it was straight or crooked—if I pulled it out would I be pulling my son's eyeball out. Slowly, steeled for the worst, I manoeuvered the wire till Lloyd was free of the gate. There was blood, but his eyeball was still in its socket. I began to breathe again. That was another visit to Emergency. This time he ended up with an eye patch and the good news that he wouldn't lose the sight in his eye. And John checked every wire on that gate to make sure it couldn't happen again.

Our first five years on the farm were not easy. Because John's father owned the machinery, we were farming a half-section on half-shares. And then we had a succession of bad crops: frost, rust and hail. In 1958, with Darryl and Lloyd, ages three and one, I began a two-year tenure teaching at Clyde, our local school. We moved into the two-room teacherage on the school grounds so that I would be closer to the boys—able to see them till right before school in the morning, over the noon hour, and as soon as school closed for the day. It was a lesson in "living small." All four of us were squeezed into the one bedroom with a double bed, cot, crib, and dresser. I became an expert in under-bed storage. The other room was our kitchen/dining room/living room combined—very basic accommodation, but we were together—and we had a regular income.

I purchased the boys' first store-bought outfits: flannel-lined jeans with cuffs that turned up to reveal the red plaid lining with plaid shirts to match. High fashion at the time!

At the end of the two years, visibly pregnant, I resigned from the teaching position and we moved back to the farm. Life was easier as the electrical grid had reached us and we now had power, which meant an electric range, fridge and washing machine. John decided to start raising hogs so we wouldn't be totally dependent on the crops for income, and in preparation, we had a cement floor poured in the lean-to off the barn.

And then on September 5th, 1960, very fittingly on the Labour Day holiday Monday, our daughter Lynn was born. I didn't make it into the delivery room with her either as another woman beat me to it, so everyone on the floor heard my excited cries, "It's a girl. It's a girl. It's a girl!"

Unlike the boys, who ate and slept like babies should, Lynn was very colicky, and in retrospect, seemed to cry non-stop for the first month. It didn't matter how you held her—draped over your shoulder, lap or arm—or whether you walked the floor with her or rocked in the rocking chair, she cried. Though all efforts to calm her seemed futile, it was impossible to do nothing so you walked, and you rocked, till her exhaustion would finally give you a brief reprieve. Eventually, she outgrew the colic and ended up a sunny, easygoing toddler.

Another new stage in our family life came that September as Darryl started school. The decision having been made to close our local Clyde School, he, and the other students, were now being bussed to Stornoway.

Over the next three years, watching our young family grow and develop, John and I began seriously thinking about the future. After 10 years, we were not getting ahead renting on half-shares. Would John's folks consider selling the farm to us? We didn't know. It was time to find out.

The Big Decision

"They said, "No.""

"No to what?" I asked.

"No to everything," John said with a tremor in his voice.

I tried to keep the frustration out of my voice. "They won't let us buy the farm?"

"No."

"No father-son agreement?"

"No."

"You mean they expect us to rent on half-shares till they die, and then pay your four sisters for their share of the farm?"

"Yeah," he sighed.

I no longer tried to hide my frustration. "Who knows how old we might be by then. We'd be paying off a mortgage the rest of our lives." Our eyes locked as we sat on opposite sides of the table. "We don't have to stay," I said.

Silence filled the air. Finally, John said, "You mean move to the city?"

"Yes," I said. "If we stay here, we'll be poor all our lives."

Following that conversation, we spent many days weighing the pros and cons of going and staying. I had my teaching certificate but we had three children, the youngest only two years old. John had left school early to run the farm when his father lost the use of his legs. We wondered what skills he had that could be applied to a job in the city. Finally, we sat at the kitchen table and made a list:

Experienced in animal care–zoo attendant

Worked with horses–work at racetrack

Butchered animals for our use–butcher or meat cutter

Drove tractors and combines, took a course in diesel engines–road construction or semi-trailer driver

Helped neighbours build their houses—carpenter

It was not a long list, but after much deliberation we decided an uncertain future, with possibilities, was preferable to continuing the struggle to make a living on half-shares, with the prospect of being saddled with a mortgage in our old age.

Having decided to move the next question was, "Where—Edmonton or Winnipeg?" John had spent six weeks in Edmonton when taking that diesel course and liked the city. However, for both of us, the pull of family bonds was the deciding factor as we chose Winnipeg.

We asked for no advice as we pondered our options, so we were not prepared for all the unsolicited advice, most of it negative, we received when we announced our decision to leave. Nevertheless, we remained steadfast in our decision.

We owned one-quarter section that was mostly pasture land. We sold it, and in spring had an auction sale of all the farm machinery and most of our household goods. While John left in our clunky old car to look for work in Winnipeg, I stayed on the farm with our three children so Darryl could complete his Grade 2 year.

We had a roof over our heads, but because we had sold our bed frames, our range, and our refrigerator, we lived like campers. We slept on mattresses on the floor and I cooked on a gas camping stove. Lunches were non-perishable foods (kudos to the one who invented peanut butter) and supper came from a can. It was a long and lonely two months.

Meanwhile John was living with his parents in Winnipeg as he began his search for employment. First on his list of prospective employers, the construction company in charge of building the St. James overpass.

They were not hiring.

The next day, moving down his list, he visited Burns Meat Packers. They were not hiring.

Then his job-hunting had to be put on hold. The trip to Winnipeg had been too much for our old clunker. It was now burning more oil than gas, belching a black and noxious exhaust. He would have to trade the oil–guzzler for a newer vehicle. During negotiations, the car dealership owner discovered John was a farmer. He immediately offered John a job running a farm he owned up north. I received a phone call. We considered the offer and agreed we did not want to return to farming.

John's search for work resumed. His first stop was a butcher shop the car-dealer said was looking for a meat cutter. This was another dead-end. The shop was closed. However, the next day, when checking the Help Wanted section of the newspaper, he found an ad that would change our lives. The University of Manitoba's Animal Science Department needed a herdsman. It sounded like the perfect job for a former farmer. He arranged an interview and was offered the job with one proviso. His family had to live in the house on the campus and his wife had to be willing to provide room and board for four single agricultural workers.

That night I received another phone call. "I have a job!" John announced, almost yelling into the phone in his excitement and relief. We decided he would come and get us the next day so that I could see the house and agree to the terms of employment. He said nothing about having bought another vehicle. The next morning, when we realized who was behind the wheel of the sleek green vehicle with fins that drove into the yard, there were screams of surprise and delight.

The house on the university campus, a four-bedroom two-story with the four boarders sharing two bedrooms, became our new home.

The herdsman position (a job title that was later changed to the more politically correct "animal attendant") was a perfect fit for John. It allowed him to apply his knowledge and skill in animal care, while working with professors and students from around the world.

When our youngest child started school, I returned to teaching. I taught kindergarten for three years before taking a leave of absence to attend university full-time. After graduating I was employed as a teacher-librarian, and then, as a library consultant.

We continued to live in the house on the campus, without boarders now, as our children progressed from childhood through their teenage years. The campus was their playground, and in some ways not far removed from their life on the farm. After school or on weekends they could spend time in the barns with their dad, helping him measure and mix special feed rations for test animals and watching newborn piglets and lambs as they learned to stand on wobbly legs and search for their mother's teat.

They also had a unique opportunity to observe the veterinarian at work as he tended to sick or injured animals: prescribing medication, giving injections, and performing surgery. A wonderful, caring man, he would explain what he was doing as he worked and patiently answer the kids' questions. Sometimes they even got to participate in a small way, for example, during caesarian surgery on a sow, being handed a slimy wet piglet to be passed on to their dad, who was assisting the vet.

With their friends they spent hours playing in the wooded area south of the university, building forts, riding their bikes on the winding trails they called "monkey trails" and doing whatever kids do when they have the freedom to roam and invent their own activities. Though they were out of sight we never worried about them, believing in safety through numbers. We had just one rule—they had to be home at noon for lunch and 6:00 for supper.

A common after-school job for students was delivering the city's newspapers. Our kids' paper routes, the university students' residences, were the envy of their friends. It was indoors, warm in winter, cool in summer and did not involve trudging along blocks of city streets lugging a heavy bag of papers. They could go from door to door along a hallway and take an elevator to the next floor. In addition, in those pre-credit card days, the paper carriers were responsible for collecting payment, and the university students tipped well.

We used the summer holidays for memorable camping trips from Vancouver Island to Newfoundland and north to the Yukon and Alaska. We made frequent trips back to Saskatchewan to see my family, giving the kids many opportunities to play with their cousins. And, whenever we were in Saskatchewan, we also stayed in touch with the good friends from our farming days, visiting them for rousing games of cards "like in the old days."

John and I felt like we had the best of both worlds: still close to our farming roots but with all the convenience and opportunities offered by life in the city. For the first time in our married life, we were financially stable and able to save for the future. Remembering those 10 lean years on the farm, we vowed we would never complain about paying income tax—and we never did!

As one by one our children became independent, left home, married, and built successful careers, John and I often thought back to that big decision we made so many years before. We were so thankful we had found the courage to face uncertainty in hope of a better future for our children and ourselves. Life was good.

A Long and Twisting Path To
A University Degree

The long and twisting path I travelled to a university degree began in 1959 when I took a first-year English class from the University of Saskatchewan by correspondence. The first assignment was to write an autobiography. I described my "ordinary" life growing up on a prairie farm. My long-distance supervising teacher's comment was, "No life is ordinary. Every life is unique and extraordinary." Since it is never too late to correct a mistake–I have spent the last nine years writing about my extraordinary life after taking courses on "Writing a Memoir" from the University of Winnipeg in 2011 and 2012.

But back in 1959, when I was taking the English correspondence course, I was in my second year of teaching at Clyde School. John and I and our two boys, Darryl and Lloyd, were living in the teacherage. I wrote the final exam in the Yorkton Collegiate Institute where I had attended high school, and the supervising teacher was my former principal. It felt almost like being back in high school, except now I was squeezing a pregnant midriff into the school desk–no separate tables and chairs back then. I also met a few of my former Normal School classmates who were there to write an exam–a sort of mini-reunion on several levels.

I passed the exam with a very good mark and promptly enrolled in a statistics course. I had completed the English course while teaching, and as I would now be home with a new baby, I looked forward to finding the statistics course a breeze. My sunny expectations soon clouded over and ended up being a rainstorm. I did not plan for a continuously crying colicky baby. At the same time, I, who had loved algebra in high school, was finding statistics incomprehensible and boring. There were days when the baby and I cried together, she with tummy pain, me from frustration. I finally gave up and dropped the course.

When we moved to Winnipeg in 1963, there was no more need for correspondence courses. Having an opportunity to teach half-days in a private kindergarten classroom for the 1964-65 school year, I enrolled in a professional course, Kindergarten 1, at the University of Manitoba summer session. This would be the first of six summer sessions I took over the following years. My family made many sacrifices for me to do this, and it would be several years before they could breathe a collective sigh of relief at regaining regular family summer vacations again.

In 1965, kindergarten was not yet a mandated part of the public-school system, but discovering it was being taught in Winnipeg School Division #1, I took a full-time position teaching kindergarten at Weston School the following year. It was a difficult 10 months. The school was in the north end of the city, a long bus ride from the south end where I lived. I had to leave early in the morning and did not get home till after dark in the winter. Fortunately, the next year our local Fort Garry School Division established kindergarten classes for the first time, and I began an enjoyable three-year stint teaching kindergarten at Oakenwald School, completing a Kindergarten 2 summer professional course in 1967.

These professional courses did not have university credits, and realizing teachers were soon going to be required to have an education degree, I decided it was time to pursue that objective. I transferred my University of Saskatchewan credit for English to the University of Manitoba (U of M), and took Introduction to Psychology in the 1968 summer session at the U of M. At the end of the next school year, I resigned from my teaching position at Oakenwald and enrolled in the regular session at the U of M, planning on attending university full-time for a couple of years.

The best of plans doesn't always work out, however. Halfway through the first year of university I began experiencing severe pain in my left leg when walking. X-rays showed that my left hip, damaged by osteomyelitis when I was a kid, was shifting with every step. Surgery to fuse the hip joint was recommended. I managed to suffer through the rest of the academic year, and that summer of 1970 I had the hip surgery.

When the waist-to-ankle cast was finally removed in November, my left leg was a useless, flabby appendage with atrophied muscles. On November 6th, a few days after the cast was removed, my mother and father came to Winnipeg to visit me. My mother's diary records, "Visited Jean in hospital. Can't move leg. No muscle strength." It was a short three-day visit, and after our "goodbyes" and farewell kisses, my mother kept turning around and looking at me as they walked to the door. Six days after they got home, she was admitted to Yorkton Hospital with severe stomach pain. She learned the cancer she had surgery for two years previous was active once more. Now I realize, when she kept turning around to look at me as she was leaving my hospital room, she probably suspected she had a health issue and was wondering if she would see me again.

Regaining muscle strength in my leg was hard work. Lying on my stomach I would struggle for hours trying to lift my foot off the sheet. The first little movement became a half-inch, and then, inch by inch, I worked up to being able to bend my knee a few degrees. As soon as I could manage on crutches, I was transferred to the Rehab Hospital to begin physical therapy, the next step on the long road to independent walking.

In January, my mother was admitted to Yorkton Hospital with terminal cancer. Although still on crutches, I was determined to see her. We decided to take the three kids with us as we knew their grandmother would like to see them, and it would be their last chance to see her. As I was unable to sit for any length of time, I lay on a mattress in the back of the station wagon for the trip to Yorkton. It was a scary ride as we drove into a howling blizzard, but we made it through safely. We found my mother thin and wan, but uncomplaining. After we said our last goodbyes, I was now the one turning back for one last look. My mother died on February 12th, 1971, age 68. Her funeral was the saddest day of my life.

For the next two years I lived with a deep depression brought on, I believe, by a combination of grief at the loss of my mother and stress from the hip surgery. I admitted it to no one, not even John, going through the motions of normal family life, but with no inner joy.

Despite my depression, when I could walk once more without crutches, I resumed my university studies. I enrolled in two classes for the 1971 summer session, the English Novel and Canadian History from 1534. It was a heavy course load. I had never tackled two subjects in a summer session before, and both required a lot of essay writing. I managed a B+ and an A, but I promised myself I would never do that again.

That fall I began my last year of university studies. Deciding on a career change, I enrolled in all the library-related courses offered by the Faculty of Education. Two of the courses, Library Organization and Administration, and Library Informational Materials, were taught by Gerald Brown. This was my introduction to Gerry. He was a master teacher, using a variety of instructional strategies, incorporating group collaboration and peer feedback. He had a vision of the role of the teacher-librarian as a partner with classroom teachers in planning and implementing programs in literature appreciation and independent learning skills development. His mission was to make that vision a reality. Teaching these evening courses after a day of work was one way to achieve that objective, aiming to send a cohort of us, committed to his vision, out into the field. I became one of the committed and it changed the direction of the rest of my professional life.

I began work as a teacher-librarian in 1972, but I still needed two more courses to complete the requirements for a Bachelor of Pedagogy Degree. Remembering my promise to myself to never again take two courses in a summer session, I took English Neoclassical and Romantic Literature in summer 1973 and Canadian History–1760 -1867 in summer 1974.

On October 16th, 1974, I graduated with a Bachelor of Pedagogy Degree, 15 years after I had begun this quest, and I ended up having a wonderful 19-year career in library media services in Winnipeg School Division #1.

Under the direction of Nan Florence, Chief Librarian, and Gerry Brown, Assistant Chief Librarian, the division led the way in school library program development in Manitoba. I spent three years as a teacher-librarian in two schools, Kent Road and Inkster. The next year my time was divided between Kent Road School and working out of the Library Service Centre as a consulting teacher. The following year I moved into a full-time library media consulting teacher position, working with Nan and Gerry till Nan retired in 1978, and then with Gerry, till I retired in 1991.

I had the privilege of working for many years with two of the most dedicated, inspiring, and hard-working educators I have known.

North to The Yukon and Alaska

In July 1969, John and I, and our three children, Darryl (14), Lloyd (12), and Lynn (eight), embarked on a camping trip from Winnipeg to Alaska. No teenager wants to spend a month with only a younger brother and sister, so Darryl's friend, Bruce, was invited to join us.

In preparation for the trip, we procured a homemade camper trailer with a wooden top hinged at one end. When you raised the top and propped it up, you had an A-frame with canvas sides and front. We fitted it with two wooden boxes to hold all the canned and non-perishable food we would need for our trip into the "wilderness." With foam mattresses on the floor, there was sleeping space for John and me, as well as Lynn, while the three boys shared two pup tents.

Because we were inexperienced campers, and because it was an unusually wet spring and summer in the Yukon, it ended up being a trip with many challenges.

The following are excerpts from my trip journal.

Thursday, July 3ʳᵈ

We left home yesterday, stopping at Mum and Dad's for an overnight visit. As we slept in their house on beds last night, our camping adventure really started today.

It was a sunny and hot morning, but we found a lovely, shady picnic spot a few miles past Lanigan for lunch. After lunch the kids stretched their legs by chasing gophers about.

As we scrambled back into the car, we saw dark rain clouds rolling toward us. It poured all afternoon. Miles of highway, under construction, were soft, wet, and slippery—a great combination with a trailer swaying behind! We planned on camping at Saskatoon, but got there early in the afternoon, so decided to go on to North Battleford. However, on the bypass at North Battleford we missed the exit for the campground, so just kept on a-going to Lloydminster. It was 7:30 p.m. by the time we found a campsite. By that time all the picnic tables were taken, so we made do with the station wagon's tailgate. On the plus side, the campground was dry, and it had a playground with lots of space for the kids to run about.

Friday, July 4th

It rained all morning, but fortunately had stopped by noon when we pitched camp at Half Moon Lake near Edmonton. We spent the afternoon at the Alberta Game Farm, which has an impressive number and variety of animals, including zebras, tigers, grizzly bears, giraffes, elephants, rhinoceros, elk, and a peacock that fanned his brilliant tail feathers for us.

Lloyd had the fright of his life when we were looking at a baby elephant in a pen in one of the barns. The elephant stuck his trunk out over the pen wall, and animal-lover Lloyd reached out to pat it. In an eye blink that baby curled his trunk in a vice-like grip around Lloyd's wrist. With strength born from sheer panic, Lloyd managed to wrench himself free. But before he could move out of range, that trunk shot out again and wacked him on the side of the head, knocking him sideways and breaking his sunglasses. His swollen wrist was a potent reminder of a lesson learned.

Before we finished the supper dishes it began to rain, and the downpour continued all night. Fortunately, Darryl and Bruce had their pup tent up before the rain started. John threw a tarp over it and they stayed dry all night. However, we discovered the trailer roof was leaking and my mattress was wet. So, Lloyd and I slept in the back of the station wagon, while Lynn curled up on the front seat and John made a bed on the dry side of the trailer. We were so damp and chilled we all slept in our clothes.

Saturday, July 5*th*

It was still pouring this morning, so we opted for breakfast in an Edmonton restaurant. The potatoes were mushy, the hotcakes doughy, and Lynn, thinking she had picked up the salt shaker, poured sugar on her chips. But we were dry!

At an Esso station outside Whitecourt we decided it would be prudent to have plastic headlight covers installed. We also bought a copy of *The Milepost*, a guide to the Alaska Highway.

We had a trailer tire blowout at noon. While John and Darryl changed the tire, I made sandwiches and we ate lunch by the side of the road.

Continuing to Dawson Creek, we found a lovely camping spot back in the willows. The kids went for a swim in the outdoor pool while John and I dried our wet towels and bedding over the camp fire. They smelled smoky, but they were dry, so no one complained.

While Darryl and I were exploring the creek, a representative of the local Baptist Church stopped by the campsite with leaflets on their Sunday service. Lloyd informed him we were Baptists, and then John had to explain that the kid meant our name, not our church affiliation. The incident put Lloyd and Bruce into hysterics, and they acted like a couple of goofballs, re-enacting the scene the rest of the evening.

Sunday, July 6th

We woke to dense fog. That did not deter Lloyd, who spent an hour and a half starting a campfire. It kept him amused while the rest of us dozed till the fog dissipated. A leisurely breakfast of toast cooked over the coals was gourmet fare compared to yesterday's restaurant meal in Edmonton.

We discovered the trailer frame must have got bent when we had that tire blowout yesterday. While John took it to a garage for repair, the kids and I went for a cold, but refreshing, swim.

Monday, July 7th

Leaving Dawson Creek, we had a tremendous view of the Peace River Valley. We stopped to admire the panorama while the boys climbed part way down the gorge. Across the river we could see the community of Taylor, which is the centre of the natural gas industry in the area.

About 35 miles past Fort St. John the pavement ended. The gravel highway was unbelievably rough—enough to crack your dentures! Sixty miles past Fort St. John—catastrophe! A trailer wheel came off due to a broken axle stub. We had to backtrack 60 miles to Fort St. John for a new stub and to have it welded onto the axle. As insurance we bought a spare stub. John and Darryl reassembled the trailer and we were on our way. Shortly after, we drove into a violent hailstorm. What a morning!

At Trutch Lodge (Mile 200), more trouble! The hub on the trailer wheel broke. As there was no welder in Trutch, we couldn't get the broken hub repaired, so John and Darryl replaced it with an old cracked hub we had with us. Holding our breath, we headed for Fort Nelson and a welder. It was not to be! Twenty miles before Prophet River, and 55 miles from Fort Nelson, the cracked hub gave out and the trailer wheel came off for the third time that day. John managed to pull the trailer onto an outcropping of ground at the edge of the highway. The ground dropped away steeply to a gorge below at that point, and while John was busy stowing the wheel and hub in the station wagon, the kids and I called out, "That's it! We've had enough. It's going over!" and we pretended we were shoving the trailer over the bank. As John shouted a frenzied, "No, no, no!" we dissolved in laughter.

Back in the car, with that blankety-blank wheel and hub, we headed for Prophet River. In Prophet River our luck changed (we hoped) as we were able to buy two steel hubs. So, we now had a spare stub and a spare hub. By the time we got back to the trailer it was 9:30 p.m. While John and Darryl fixed the wheel, I set the gas stove on the ground and cooked hot dogs for our supper. We didn't want to spend the night perched on the edge of the road, so we packed up and headed for Fort Nelson. The kids had withstood the frustrations of the day with amazing fortitude, but they were dog-tired and asleep the moment we hit the road.

It was 1:30 in the morning by the time we found a campground in Fort Nelson. Upon opening the trailer, we discovered the damage that was the result of the bumping each time the wheel came off. The wooden food boxes had sprung apart. Cans were battered. Shattered glass was everywhere. The trailer floor was a sea of ketchup, coffee, sugar, and pickle vinegar. Cans, boxes, and even some of our bedding, were covered in the evil-smelling goo. John pitched a pup tent and we got Lloyd and Bruce bedded down in it. Darryl was so bushed we couldn't rouse him, so he and Lynn slept in the back of the station wagon with their clothes on. John and I scraped the goop out of the middle of the trailer floor. We couldn't begin to do anything else at that time of night, so we flopped onto our mattresses and covered our noses with our blankets, attempting to escape the smell. I went right to sleep but John said he was still awake at 4:00 a.m.

Tuesday, July 8ᵗʰ

When we woke this morning we saw, in the bright daylight, what a dismal trailer court we were in. Dirt and rubbish were all about. Without stopping to make breakfast we packed up and got out of there. We made it the 35 miles to Kledo Creek campground without a breakdown. Amazing! It was a lovely spot beside a swift but shallow river. The boys set up their pup tents on the riverbank so they would be able to sleep to the sound of the bubbling water. Discovering an island they could wade to, they spent most of the day there. John showed Lynn how to cast with just a weight on her fish line and she practised for hours. When she got tired of casting, she walked along the riverbank, with her fishing rod over her shoulder, singing "A fishing we will go."

We could not have wished for a more beautiful setting for the horrendous task of cleaning up the trailer. First, we had to clean the goop off all the cans and boxes. The wooden food cupboards were such a mess we discarded them. I managed to scrape goop and glass off the trailer floor and scrub it without getting any glass in my hands or knees, but it was a wonder. It was a lesson learned—you do not take anything in glass containers on a camping trip. Next, we washed the sheets and hung them to dry. Then came the task of repacking. We shifted the weight from the trailer to the car top carrier by putting the food on top of the car and the clothes in the trailer. Another lesson learned: do not pack a four-week supply of food for six people. There are grocery stores—even along the Alaska Highway.

It was an all-day job and were we filthy by the time we were finished! That evening we all washed our hair and had sponge baths. What a luxury to climb between clean, dry sheets, feeling clean ourselves!

Wednesday, July 9th

At Mile 392, just past Summit Esso, we had more trailer trouble, this time the wheel on the opposite side–a flat tire and another broken axle stub. We had that spare stub we had bought in Fort St. John and they had a welder at Summit Esso, so it didn't take long to make the repair. There was a little blip back at the trailer when John and Darryl were replacing the wheel. While greasing the bearings Darryl dropped one in the gravel, which caused John to have a mild trauma. Fortunately, he had bought two extra bearings in Prophet River, so we did have spares.

Lloyd made up a joke about our asking, "Have you got a welder?" so many times in the last few days. He asked, "Have you got a welder?" and then, in a deep voice, he answered, "Nope. Ain't got no welder here, but sure got lots of welderness." It kept the kids amused the rest of the morning as they took turns playing the two roles and then dissolving in laughter.

At noon, we stopped by the swift Toad River for lunch. After lunch we had a stone skipping competition. Darryl was the champion. He had a stone that skipped to the opposite bank. He then decided to tackle another challenge and climbed to the top of a steep, smooth-surfaced hill made by a slide. He took the easy way down, sitting on his heels and sliding like a human toboggan.

We made it to Liard River without any more breakdowns! A side trail led to a stream trickling down a naturally terraced mountainside. Amazingly, John found fish in a pond up there. After setting up camp, John and the boys tried fishing under the Liard River bridge, without any luck, while Lynn amused herself making sandcastles. Supper was a family favourite–a campfire wiener roast. John, Lloyd, and Lynn then went for a swim in the hot springs. I do not know how they endured the heat. I sat on the pool edge and dipped my feet in and out, but the water was so hot I could not stand to keep them in for more than a few seconds.

Thursday, July 10th

We left Liard River campground rather late in the morning. The light at night is deceiving. We tend to go to bed late and then have trouble waking up in the morning. Our first stop was at Whirlpool Canyon where Darryl gave me a gut-wrenching fright by going right to the edge of the cliff overhanging the whirlpools.

Next, we stopped at Allan's Lookout where we got an impressive view of the Liard River. Legend has it that a band of outlaws took advantage of the sweeping view of the Liard River from this point to attack and rob riverboats of furs and supplies.

The kids were getting restless, but Lloyd saved the day by hamming it up with his French-Canadian accent and his Scottish one, as well as a few others not quite as expert. We stopped at Hyland River for lunch and then the boys fished for an hour or more, again without any luck.

After lunch we drove by burnt out forests where vibrant purple fireweed now blankets the ground. Wildflowers were plentiful–purple, blue, white, and yellow varieties I didn't recognize, as well our familiar wild roses and dandelions.

We made it to Watson Lake campground, and without a breakdown today. The boys set up the trailer while John and I sat and relaxed, and Lynn ran about. Our campsite was another lovely spot beside a swift little stream. The kids amused themselves by crossing the river on a tree laid across from bank to bank. There is nothing like imagined danger to keep them happy!

Friday, July 11th

Today the "fishermen" stopped at every river we crossed to try their luck. They could see the fish follow their spoons and flies, but they just would not hit. By the time we got to Wolf Creek campground, near Whitehorse, we couldn't find a site with a table. But we are getting resourceful. Darryl and Bruce crossed a narrow footbridge to a picnic area on the other side of the creek and floated a table over to our side!

After supper the kids crossed the creek to climb a big hill on the other side. They planned to go back and plant a flag on top of the hill, but halfway through making the flag they abandoned the project.

The evening was the coolest we had yet. I went to bed with my hooded sweatshirt and terry housecoat on over my pyjamas.

Saturday, July 12th

We slept in, and then lingered over a late breakfast of pancakes. As we were breaking camp it began to rain, and it continued all day. We stopped at a service station at Mile 910 to get the trailer axle straightened once more. The mechanic broke our hub while he was trying to fix the axle, so he installed a new steel hub and then charged us only 10 dollars, so we got a steel hub quite cheaply! From here to Whitehorse the road was under construction and so rocky and rough we could only creep along.

Driving around Whitehorse in search of a grocery store, we saw campers lined up in front of the laundromat and parked in front of every tavern we passed. In rainy weather campers either do their laundry or drown their sorrows!

We decided to drive on to Dawson City, hoping for dry weather in Whitehorse on our way home. It was still raining when we stopped at a picnic spot for lunch, so we made and ate lunch while scrunched together in the car. It was too much togetherness for the kids. They snapped at each other and argued most of the day. And Bruce got an acute attack of homesickness. I got to the point I would have loved to gag all four of them.

To make matters worse, the campground where we planned to camp was burned out, so we had to continue to Stewart Crossing Junction, near Mayo. It was 12:30 a.m. by the time we finished our supper of hot soup, but we didn't need a lantern as it was still light outside. You have no idea it is that late till you look at your watch, and then you can hardly believe it.

Sunday, July 13*ᵗʰ*

Today we drove up to Mayo and on to Keno where we explored a couple of old mines. The deserted houses, with furniture, appliances, and dishes still in place, were eerie. The kids collected some Yukon licence plates, miners' hats and hammers, and rocks that looked like they had traces of silver.

On the way back to the campground we had two flat tires. While I made supper, John took the two tires to get repaired. After supper John said, "Darryl, you and Bruce can put the tires back on."

Bruce was incredulous. "You can do that?" he asked Darryl.

"Yeh," Darryl said.

Looking back, I see my diary entries show a pattern—John and Darryl changed the tire, John and Darryl replaced the hub, John and Darryl fixed the wheel. That is just how our family works. I never realized it might be unusual. From a young age, Darryl was interested in anything mechanical and John had the patience to "teach him how" and let him help.

Monday, July 14th

At noon we made camp at Rock Creek just outside Dawson City. It was a lovely treed campground about a mile from the Klondike River. We spent the afternoon washing clothes, using a five-gallon pail and a "plumber's helper." The boys were enthusiastic punchers with the plunger, while Lynn helped with the wringing. We ran out of rope and pegs before we had everything hung to dry, so John and Darryl scraped the bark off a long, dry tree trunk, supported each end on a sturdy living tree, and we draped clothes over it.

Tuesday, July 15th

We spent the day visiting the tourist attractions in Dawson City. First, we toured the Palace Grand Theatre which had been restored to what it was when "Arizona Charlie" opened it in 1899.

While waiting for the Dawson Museum to open, the kids played by the old locomotives used during the early mining operations in the Klondike. John and I, as well as a couple of elderly ladies, waited on a park bench. Lynn frequently skins her knees when she is playing, so John and I were not surprised, or worried, when she came running and crying, with blood trickling down her legs. In fact, we looked at one another, laughed and said, "Oh no, not again!" The two elderly ladies, sharing the bench, looked at us askance.

When the museum finally opened, we found it had an interesting collection of early-day relics. Unfortunately, most of the items were poorly displayed, with dust and clutter being the most pervading impression.

After lunch we boarded the beached sternwheeler, the Keno, which has been meticulously restored. Before touring the boat, we viewed slides of the Yukon–as it is now and during the Gold Rush. Our next stop was the

Gold Room in the Bank of Commerce where, during the Gold Rush, they melted the gold and poured it into bars. At Robert Service's cabin we sat on the ground as Graham Campbell, an actor enacting the spirit of Service, told the story of his life and recited some of his poems. Dawson City is a peculiar mixture of the old and the new, the ugly and the beautiful, such as you would see nowhere else.

Back at the campground, I cooked supper, while the rest went fishing. Lloyd caught a very wee fish, which John cleaned, I cooked, and Lloyd ate in one mouthful.

In the evening we drove back to Dawson City for the Gaslight Follies, a slapstick comedy staged in the renovated theatre.

Wednesday, July 16th

At Bonanza Creek we tried panning for gold before driving on to explore one of the huge gold dredges. The dredges ceased operation at the end of the 1966 season. The Klondike valley is scarred by massive piles of grey rock tailings left by these dredges.

Panning for gold the easy tourist way.

Top left: Darryl
Top right: Lloyd
Bottom picture: John helping Lynn

After an ice cream snack, we drove up to the Midnight Dome where we got a breathtaking view of the Klondike valley, Dawson City, and the Yukon River.

On our way back to the campground we stopped at the Klondike River bridge for the fishers to try their luck. They didn't have any.

Thursday, July 17th

Leaving Dawson City, we crossed the Yukon River on the ferry. Lloyd bought a 28-ounce bottle of orange pop and enjoyed himself acting intoxicated.

The road along the west bank of the Yukon River follows the ridges and domes above the timberline, with magnificent views of the Yukon and Klondike rivers, the Ogilvie Mountains, and the green valleys. The first section of the road, used by the trucks from the asbestos mine at Clinton, is excellent–wide, smooth, and well gravelled, although it is very dusty. The remainder of the road reminds you that it was originally a wagon trail for freighting to the gold mines, being narrow and rough, with steep grades and sharp turns.

About 50 miles before Tetlin Junction we developed brake problems. There were numerous steep grades in the area, and I was petrified with fright, but John kept his cool. No amount of trouble on this trip has fazed him.

Leaving Tetlin Junction, it was bliss to be driving on pavement once again. The old 98ers can have their wagon trails that have been smoothed and widened a bit and called highways. We passed through U.S. Customs at Tok and continued 18 miles to Moon Lake campground.

After supper John tried fixing the brakes himself, but couldn't, so decided to take the car to a garage in Tok in the morning.

Friday, July 18th

While John was in Tok with the car, Lloyd and Lynn decided to go for a swim. The two of them found a raft and began poling it about. That looked like too much fun for Darryl and Bruce to resist, and before you could wink an eye, they were in the water too. The four of them spent the rest of the morning poling around the lake, diving off the raft, swimming, and crawling into the airspace under the raft. They were having so much fun we had to issue a royal command to get them out for lunch. We promised we would stop there on the way home, weather permitting.

After lunch we packed up and left for Fairbanks. The pavement was dippy and wavy, but wonderful after all the rough gravel highway we had travelled over. The comparatively level rolling landscape was also a change, and we were surprised by the number of farmyards and ranches along the way.

Arriving at Fairbanks we camped along the Cheena River, about five miles out of town. After we made camp, the kids played in the kitchen shelter, climbing on, and swinging from, the rafters. We shared the space with Donna, a cute little blond toddler, running around clad in only an undershirt and briefs, with her massive, ugly bulldog, Boozer.

After supper Bruce wrote postcards to his family, John and Darryl played crib, and Lloyd had a great time playing in the sand with a truck shared by a little kid in the park.

We watched the colourful paddlewheel, "The Discovery," as it passed by on the Cheena River several times during the evening.

Saturday, July 19ᵗʰ

Boozer attempted to share breakfast with us, which the kids found highly amusing. That brute is not exactly the shy type as he tried crawling into the pup tent with Darryl and Bruce during the night.

This morning we visited the Eskimo Museum at the Fairbanks University. The towering stuffed brown bear, standing on its hind legs just inside the door, startled us a little as we entered. The museum has an excellent and varied collection covering 10,000 years of Alaska's history. The displays are beautifully arranged, and everything is impeccably clean.

Alaskaland, by contrast, was a huge disappointment, a commercialized tourist trap and a waste of time and money. And that was the extent of our sightseeing in Fairbanks.

Sunday, July 20ᵗʰ

Today we began our return trip, heading back to Moon Lake, as we had promised the kids we would. To our disappointment it rained most of the way. By the time we got to the campground the rain had stopped, but the ground was wet and the air was damp and cold. The chilly temperature did not deter the kids, who played on the raft and went swimming, both before and after supper. We thought they would all end up with pneumonia, but they did not develop as much as a sniffle.

Monday, July 21ˢᵗ

We woke at Moon Lake to rain, and ate breakfast scrunched in the tent trailer. The rain conveniently stopped when it was time to pack up the pup tents and close the trailer, but it rained off and on most of the way to Kluane Lake campground. The view of the St. Elias mountain range was magnificent–high rocky peaks with snow on their summit. And Kluane Lake was beautiful, even on such a grey, cloudy day.

After supper Bruce went to bed in the pup tent with my mystery book. I think he is getting quite homesick. The rest of us played Cheat while basking in the warmth of the campfire.

Tuesday, July 22nd

We woke to rain, said, "What a surprise on this trip!" and went back to sleep till it stopped. When we finally broke camp, the mist still shrouded the mountain tops. At a garage near the campground, we got the trailer hitch welded. Then it was on to Silver City, where we found another mining ghost town to explore. The mine shafts are now walled up and the town is totally deserted.

Pine Creek campground was a lovely tranquil spot for our lunch break. The stream gurgled over rocks in a miniature waterfall. Vibrant green undergrowth covered the banks right to the water's edge and tall straight pines grew solidly along the banks. In the distance the creek curved out of sight, and the pines, following the curve, stood in contrast to towering and snow-capped mountain peaks. It was so beautiful and so peaceful we hated to leave.

About 40 miles after Pine Creek, we stopped to visit an Aboriginal cemetery. The graves were covered with "spirit houses," ranging from elaborate little buildings, complete with doors, windows, and shingles, to simple squares of canvas draped over a pole.

It was about 7:00 p.m. by the time we made it to the campground at Whitehorse, so we had to settle for a campsite without a table. We couldn't find a table to borrow or steal this time.

Wednesday, July 23rd

It was cold, drizzly, windy, and unfit for sightseeing, so we did the "camper thing" and spent the day at the laundromat. I did not feel like cooking supper in the rain, so we bought Kentucky Fried Chicken and ate in the car.

Thursday, July 24th

John was up and had breakfast ready when I crawled out from under my blankets. What luxury!

We spent the morning sightseeing in Whitehorse, except Darryl and Bruce, who have little interest in museums and historical points of interest and wanted to stay at the campground. Our stops included the beached sternwheelers, which are in a sad state of repair compared to the Keno in Dawson City, the Aboriginal cemetery, which is ugly and ill-kept compared to the one at Pine Creek, and the old log church, which we found locked.

While we were waiting for the McBride Museum to open, Lloyd and Lynn played on the old locomotives and wagons that were outside. The museum is far superior to the cluttered one at Dawson City, but cannot be compared to the huge one at Fairbanks University. We also visited a couple of unique log skyscrapers, that are still in use today.

We returned to camp to find no trace of Darryl and Bruce. Lunch was eaten and dishes washed, and still no sign of them. We assumed they must have decided to hike to Miles Canyon as they knew we were planning on driving there in the afternoon. Before leaving for the canyon, we took down the tents, closed the trailer, and packed up ready to go. As we surmised, we met Darryl and Bruce on their way back to the campsite. We gave them a spot of scolding for not leaving a note to tell us where they were going, and then listened to their enthusiastic report on the wonderful time they had hiking along the narrow trails, all the way to the canyon.

The canyon was impressive. High rock walls rise on each side of the rushing Yukon River. Spanning the gorge is a suspension bridge, which the boys assured us was perfectly safe, though it swayed too much for my comfort. It led to a narrow trail that we followed as it wound along the edge of the cliff. It was originally the route of the wooden tramway used to transport miners' goods around the treacherous waters of the canyon and the Whitehorse Rapids. The turbulent waters faced by the Gold Rush prospectors are tamed today by the hydro dam at Whitehorse, but still look mighty treacherous to me. On their hike the boys had discovered a natural spring. We filled our water bottles with the clear, icy water before heading back to the campground where we hitched up the trailer and left for Tagish Bridge.

We took the "loop road" and there was the bridge, just as in the picture—long, narrow, and wooden. Our would-be fishermen were quite encouraged when they saw a fellow carrying a large fish. They went down to the bridge after supper, but it was too late to do any fishing, so they had to be content to wait till the next day.

Friday, July 25ᵗʰ

It rained all night and was still raining at 6:30 a.m. when Lloyd got up to go fishing. I told him he was being silly, but he said, "No. I'm a true fisherman." When we woke at 10:00 Lloyd was still not back from the bridge. John and I found him soaked to the skin, happy and proud, with a mound of about 40 little herring beside him. He had been busy selling them for bait to other fishermen.

It was still raining so we packed up what we needed for breakfast and drove over to the cookhouse to eat. We shared the space with four bachelors cooking their porridge, flavoured with whiskey, in an empty beer can.

While the rest of the family, even Lynn, went fishing despite the rain, I bundled myself in a blanket and spent a leisurely morning in the trailer, reading and eating peanuts.

By 3:00 the fishermen gave up. John had hooked a big one, but it got away. These Yukon fish are cagey! We had a late lunch in the cookhouse, packed up in the rain, and left.

Before Watson Lake we had more trailer trouble–a broken axle and hub. By this time, it was dark and still raining, so we gave up and drove to the nearest motel. They were full because of the wet weather, but they let us sleep in a filthy little trailer.

Saturday, July 26th

By 11:30 a.m. the trailer parts were welded, and we were on our way. Since we got such a late start, we only got as far as Liard River, but that was probably a good thing. The rest of the family took advantage of the hot springs to warm up and get rid of travel grunge, while chicken-me had a sponge bath in the trailer.

More trouble–John broke his glasses when he was at the hot springs.

Sunday, July 27th

What a day! We were up at 6:30, and getting an early start from Liard River, we made Kledo Creek by noon. We found we had a flat trailer tire, so after lunch John and Darryl put on the spare. Then, at Fort Nelson the car had a flat. Darryl and Bruce changed it, while John took the trailer tire to get repaired.

We were hoping to make it to Kiskatinaw River as there are few campgrounds between Fort Nelson and Kiskatinaw. However more rain slowed our progress. By evening the mist hung so low in the valley we felt like we were driving above the clouds. Visibility was poor, but we had to keep going till finally, at 11:30 p.m., we found a campsite at Pink Mountain. It was still raining, so we hastily put up the trailer and ate supper standing in the shelter of a three-sided lean-to that made do as a kitchen. It was too wet to put up the pup tents, so all four kids slept in the station wagon, sardine style.

In addition to being wet, it was bitterly cold. John and I froze while doing dishes in the so-called kitchen. However, we were somewhat distracted from our misery by all the comments painted on the kitchen walls, such as "Camping–when you roast marshmallows and yourself at the same time" and "Keep calm and camp on."

Monday, July 28th

We woke to rain and it continued to drizzle most of the day. It was a dramatic moment when we reached Mile 83–the end of gravel and the beginning of pavement. Throughout the trip, Darryl and Bruce did a good deal of grumbling about the rough gravel roads. At some point they said they would be so happy to see pavement again that they could kiss it. So, at Mile 83, John stopped the car and announced, "Okay boys, We're not moving till you get out and kiss the pavement."

Being good sports, Darryl and Bruce jumped out, and resting on tiptoes and hands, managed to lower their lips to the wet, rain-slicked road without getting their clothes wet.

That seemed to mark the end of the trip for us. We were all anxious to be home and made excellent time, passing through Edmonton before camping for the night.

Tuesday, July 29th

Today we travelled from Edmonton to Churchbridge and my parents' farm. It was a long drive, but no one complained. Staying with Mum and Dad till Saturday, we regaled the family with tales of all the trials and tribulations we survived on our Yukon/Alaskan adventure.

If I were to ask our adult children, "What was our most memorable family holiday?" I am certain they would all say, "The trip to Yukon and Alaska!" That adventure has been relived over and over in "remember when" stories shared around many a campfire or family dining table. Now we laugh as we recall all the problems we encountered and are amazed we did not let them spoil the trip. And we remember all the simple, fun things we did as a family.

That camping trip was the first of many, many years of family camping, with spouses, children, and assorted pets added through the years. Looking back, I realize that more than the trailer was welded as we travelled the Alaska Highway.

Paying It–Backward?

School was not our son Darryl's happy place. From the beginning he struggled with reading, writing, and spelling, his skills far below what could be expected of his intellectual level. This was frustrating for his teachers, many who thought he was just lazy. It was frustrating for us because we knew this kid did not have a lazy bone in his body. Most of all it was frustrating for Darryl, by nature a hard worker, who aimed to excel in all he did.

We now know the cause of his difficulties with language skills is dyslexia, an inherited brain dysfunction, resulting in difficulty translating letters and words to speech sounds. It is most common in males, but while Darryl inherited it from his father, he passed the genes on to his daughter, not his son. There is no cure for dyslexia and you never outgrow it, but you can develop coping skills that help you manage your difficulties with written language. This Darryl did as an adult, first as foreman for a roofing company and then as owner of a successful commercial roofing company, with his wife, Janis, as office manager. But at 16, the legal age to drop out of school, he did just that. Our only proviso was he had to get a job.

He went down to the unemployment office, took the first available job–a bike courier at minimum wage–and became one of the boys pedalling from business to business in downtown Winnipeg.

It was winter and the young couriers would take their warm-up break at the Salsbury House on Garry Street. They saw the restaurant had another regular visitor–a shabbily dressed man, who appeared to be a homeless street person as he always had his big packsack on his back. He would come in, sit down at a table, and one of the staff would bring him a bowl of hot water and a spoon. He would then make himself a bowl of soup by adding ketchup from the bottle sitting on the table. Darryl, who would be going home to a warm meal, was so moved by the sight of this man having to eat ketchup soup that he would regularly order two cups of coffee and take one over to the fellow's table.

In the spring Darryl found work with a construction company. On his last day as a bike courier, he bought the "ketchup soup" gentleman a cup of coffee as usual. "This is the last coffee I can get you," he said. "I've got another job, so I won't be coming here anymore."

"Just a minute," the man said, reaching into his backpack. "Thank you for all the cups of coffee," and he pressed a $50 bill into Darryl's hand.

Everyone Makes Their Own
Lunch On Sunday

Mum never milked a cow or slopped a hog. Farm chores were Dad's domain. Housework, cooking, gardening, and childcare were Mum's responsibility. I do not remember Dad washing a dish or making his own toast or hushing a crying baby. My parents' roles were strictly defined by gender.

I do have one early memory of being held by my Dad though. I had an agonizing earache that day. As I whimpered in pain, Mum filled the hot water bottle and held it to my ear while she rocked me in her chair. Dad eventually took me from Mum and continued to cradle and rock me. I know it was evening because I remember the mellow glow of the kerosene lamp. That's it—just that one memory.

Unwittingly, Dad sowed the first seeds of my feminism. It was a frigid winter day and he had gone to see a neighbour for some reason. Stomping the snow off his boots and hanging his jacket on a peg by the door, he laughed as he described his visit. "I drove into the yard and there was that poor hen-pecked guy bringing the frozen diapers in off the clothesline."

Mum said nothing. I didn't say anything either, but I was scolding inside. "It's not fair," I thought. "Why shouldn't he help his wife? She's got a new baby." As the eldest in the family, I knew how much extra work a baby makes.

I also saw how, in the evening, Dad would sit in his chair listening to the radio or reading *The Western Producer* while Mum was always busy—folding laundry, mending, sewing, knitting, helping us with schoolwork and at the end of our day, reading the never-missed bedtime story as we gathered at her feet. The only time Mum had for reading for herself was after we were in bed and on Sundays.

Fast forward thirty-six years. I am a teacher and taking university courses in the evening to upgrade my qualifications. Our second son, Lloyd, is a teenager. He has just returned from a two-week visit with a former school pal. That kid has a stay-at-home mother who ends up spending all her time waiting on her husband and family. It is noon on Sunday, and I am lying on the sofa reading the newspaper. "What's for lunch?" asks Lloyd.

"Everyone makes their own lunch on Sunday," I remind him. At that moment, my husband walks into the living room and sets a cup of coffee on the side table for me.

As Lloyd stalks out to the kitchen to make his own lunch, he voices his disgust, "Some family. No mother, two fathers."

John and I laughed. Back in 1972 our son's reaction was humorous. But, in the intervening 40 years, society has evolved. Today a response to our son's comment would be, "So what?" Now two women or two men can legally marry and raise children and are entitled to the same social benefits as any heterosexual couple.

Lloyd's attitude has also changed over the years. He is married to a career-woman and perennial university student, who recently earned her doctorate. He is not only supportive and proud of her accomplishments, he shares equally in the housecleaning chores and enjoys preparing gourmet meals for family and friends.

It's nice to know that those first seeds of feminism my father sowed for me years ago—no matter how unwittingly—continue to grow in my son today.

You never know what seeds you sow, where they may fall or how they will grow!

No One Will Play Monopoly With Me

It was January of the year I was in Grade 4. My elation at finally being able to return to Liscard School after an absence of two years was, within a week, tempered by reality. The first science lesson was a review quiz. The question, "What are the five classes of animals?" had me stumped. From September to December there had been nothing in my correspondence lessons about classes of animals. It never entered my young head to answer, "I don't know. I didn't study this yet." Instead, though I knew it could not possibly be correct, I listed what I was most familiar with–five farm animals. As she returned our quizzes the next day, the teacher's frown and tightly pressed lips signalled she was not pleased.

"I see there are people who need to take another look at their textbook," she said, sounding disappointed. Then came a zinger. "Horses, cows, pigs, sheep and chickens are not the five classes of animals." It was my answer, word for word. To my ears she sounded amazed at such a silly answer, even sarcastic. As one of the older kids sniggered, I felt the heat of blood rising in a telltale flood of scarlet from neck to hairline. Sick with shame, I heard none of the teacher's remaining comments on the quiz.

At the end of the school day that science text went home with me and was read cover to cover. Mammals, amphibians, reptiles, birds and fish, and their characteristics, were permanently etched on my brain before I went to bed that night. The remaining subject texts were toted home, one by one, for nightly study till I was confident I could avoid further embarrassment.

This episode did not make me like school less. Rather, I embraced the challenge of proving I was as good a student as any of the other three in my class. In fact, in those long-ago days when students were ranked in order based on an average mark, my goal was to be first in my class by the end of the year.

Report cards were handed out the last day in June. Eager anticipation turned to a bitter pill of disappointment when I saw I was second in class. A quick look over her shoulder told me that Phyllis, who shared the double desk with me, was first in class. Her average was 88 percent. My average was only 87.5 percent. My face obviously revealed my disappointment. "If you are unhappy with your mark, you will just have to work harder," the teacher said, locking eyes with me. That was another zinger. My stomach roiled as disappointment was swallowed in a wave of seething resentment that there was no recognition of how hard I had worked and by a renewed determination to be first.

That was 70 years ago but the memory of these incidents rankles still. Why did the teacher not simply list the chapter to be reviewed for each of the questions answered incorrectly? And why not assuage my disappointment by pointing out that a half a percentage point was not significant. Now I shake my head at how this system of marking may have encouraged an unhealthy competitiveness in me.

With maturity, trying to be the best was replaced by working to be my best. In high school, my personal goal was to achieve at least an average of 85 percent in every subject so I would not have to write any final exams. In Grade 11, I did not achieve my goal in Latin and had to write that exam in June. In Grade 12, we were required to write final exams in every subject and my goal was to get a minimum of 85 percent in every subject. I no longer have a copy of my marks, but, if my memory is correct, I did achieve that goal. Attending university, I strived for an A or A+ on every assignment. B or B+ was a disappointment.

By this time a pattern had been established in my life. If I had a conflict of priorities, intellectual activities invariably won. For example, though married and with a family, my university studies had priority over house-work. I did try for more balance after the day my husband returned from a work-related trip and walked into the kitchen where I was working at the table on an essay due the next day. As he eyed the counters overflowing with three days of food-encrusted dishes, he said in disgust, "You could have at least pushed the button on the dishwasher."

Another wake-up call came after I moved from elementary school teacher-librarian to a consulting position at the divisional level. I had the good fortune to be working with two administrators who imbued me with their vision of the role of cooperative teacher-librarian/classroom teacher programs in education. However, my workday gradually evolved to include two, three or more evenings a week for meetings and planning sessions with my two single, dedicated, workaholic superiors.

Dedicated and workaholic I had no problem with, but single I was not. At first John accepted my evening absences, assuming it would be a short-term settling-into-a-new-job sort of thing. Eventually, the conflict between my drive to do well and his increasing unhappiness with my evening commitments put such a severe strain on our marriage I realized the situation could not continue. My offer to resign and go back to a kindergarten classroom broke the impasse. "No," he said." You don't have to do that. You like your job. I just want you home more." And I found saying, "I'm sorry I can't stay. My family needs me," to more than one evening commitment a week was met with understanding and acceptance. However, compromise and negotiation are two life skills that do not come easily to me.

My attitude to life is also reflected in how I play games. My children and grandchildren know I play to win. And we are a game-playing family. Card or board games are a part of every family get-together, even if it is just a couple coming over for an evening visit. However, we have one board game that sits on a shelf, unused and gathering dust. This has now become a family joke, one of those stories shared around the table when we reminisce.

When playing Monopoly if I were on the verge of bankruptcy and knew I would inevitably lose everything to the bank, I would not make a deal with anyone to sell my property at a discount. To me, selling at a discount was giving up, while getting cleaned out by the bank was simply losing the game. This made sense to me, but my refusal to consider offers for my property from the other players always brought on howls of frustrated protest from everyone else in the game.

Maybe Monopoly is a microcosm for life and calls for a bit of negotiation, because now, no one will play Monopoly with me.

One Surgery–Two Passions

I am a 38-year-old wife and mother. I have walked and danced with joy for many years, but now I am once more on crutches as I recover from surgery to fuse my hip. I am standing at the window in my ward at the hospital, watching the people walking along the street several stories below.

"Do you know how lucky you are?" I would like to ask them. "Are you thinking, 'What a thrill,' as you place one foot after another firmly down on the pavement, propelling yourself forward? Are you rejoicing in the nippy autumn air, hinting of frosts to come as it brushes past your face? Are you savouring the slightly sour smell of the wet leaves, lying in the gutter? I think not. I think it is far more likely that you are just thinking of your destination, oblivious to your good fortune to be walking along this street. How I long to be down there with you, away from this stale, warm, antiseptic-laden air, free of cast and crutches, striding along, swinging my arms, rejoicing with each step!"

I am discharged from the hospital while still in a cast. After six weeks at home, I return to Grace Hospital to have the cast removed. I am then transferred from the Grace to the Rehab Hospital, the next stage in my recovery from the surgery. Today the hospital social worker has come to talk to me.

"They tell me you are refusing to go to Occupational Therapy," she says.

"It's a waste of time."

"A waste of time?" she says, sounding surprised.

"They have me standing with my crutches and tying knots in some macramé hanging. The next day my work has been ripped out and someone else's correctly tied knots are in front of me. It's a totally mindless activity. If I wanted to learn to tie knots, I'd have joined the Girl Guides."

Despite my struggle to maintain self-control, tears of frustration well up in my eyes, my voice quavers, and the words spill out. "I go to physical therapy every day. It makes sense. I need to get my muscles strong again. I don't need occupational therapy to give me something to do. If they want me to stand for an hour, I can do that right here by my bed while I'm reading a book."

She eyes the stack of books on my bedside table. It is a tall stack. The titles indicate that they are all books on architecture and house design. She looks at me with a little smile of amusement and says, "I see."

I hear nothing more about attending occupational therapy.

I was using the enforced downtime while recovering from hip surgery to study house design because I had a dream. For all 17 years of our marriage, we had lived in a rented house, first on a farm we rented from John's family, and then in a house in Winnipeg that came with his job. I wanted a house of our own–a house designed for convenience and efficiency that would meet the needs of everyone in the family.

Using a list I had compiled in advance, John kept me supplied with books from the local library. My study project helped the weeks in the hospital pass more quickly.

It is seven months before I experience independent walking again, but walk I do, promising myself I will never take this wondrous gift for granted.

Walking is now a passion. Every morning my alarm rings at 5:00 a.m. so I can fit in an hour of exercise–walking on my treadmill, running up and down the basement stairs, and lifting weights before leaving for work. Every evening, after supper dishes are done, John and I walk for an hour in Kings Park, a lovely treed neighbourhood park nestled in a curve of the Red River. On weekend walking excursions with our family we explore other Winnipeg parks, the Assiniboine Forest, and Fort Whyte, and make many day trips to provincial parks.

Walking was not my only passion following the surgery. By the time I returned home I was convinced I could design our "dream home." I haunted the house building sections of the city's bookstores, creating a personal library on house design. Energy-efficient construction was becoming a hot topic. I attended workshops and bought books to learn more. I analyzed the floor plans in books and magazines for traffic flow, storage, efficient use of space, and furniture placement, assessing how well they suited my family's lifestyle.

I began reproducing plans from my books onto graph paper and then trying to adapt them to include all the features we wanted. How could I add a mudroom, a ground-floor laundry, a pantry in the kitchen, or improve the efficiency of the water lines? The revisions were always unsatisfactory in some way, seeming awkward or tacked on.

I began to work on creating my own perfect floor plan. Then I would read a book, gain a new insight, and start again. Family needs, university classes, and my teaching responsibilities were a priority, but I could occasionally find time to work on my latest creation. Then, completely absorbed, I was oblivious to our teenagers' rock-and-roll music thumping up from the basement. My cup of coffee was forgotten till it was too cold to drink. I would lose track of the time till my husband or one of the kids would poke a head around my study door with a plaintive, "Hey, when are we eating?"

Each change in family dynamics changed our housing priorities and required a new or revised plan. Teenagers did not want a family room adjacent to the kitchen. They wanted a place to hang out with their friends as far from the adults in their life as possible–and "Oh yes, big enough to hold a pool table." I found the kitchen table worked fine as a desk when the kids were young and early to bed, but with the comings and goings of boisterous teens I wanted a study with a door I could shut as I planned lessons, studied, and worked on assignments.

The years flew by. One by one the children left home and married. My husband and I were shocked when we realized we had been talking about and planning for our dream home for 12 years!

Deciding we wanted to move out of the city, we began the search for an acreage. On a sunny day in late March with the promise of spring in the air, we finally found what we were looking for: 20 acres about 50 miles southeast of Winnipeg that called out, "Buy me!" After a fun-filled hour of tramping through snow up to our knees we decided it would be perfect. An open area facing the road was backed by a stand of poplars covering the remaining two-thirds of the property. We would be able to cut hiking trails through the woods for our daily walks. And our house could be tucked into an open space in the poplar grove, invisible from the road. We purchased the property immediately.

Spring arrived. The snow melted. In June we decided to take our little house trailer out to our property. We would live in it while we spent the summer building a rail fence to mark our boundaries. As we drove onto our open meadow that fronted the poplar grove, we felt our wheels begin to sink. Within moments our vehicles were mired in mud up to their hubcaps. Getting out of the car to survey our predicament, I wailed, "We've bought a bog and a bush." Although our land was not really a bog, it did have a high water table. But there we had it—the name for our new home—the "Bog 'n Bush."

Neighbours soon helped us get unstuck. We spent the summer hard at work erecting a rustic rail fence to enclose our property. And we began work on cutting a network of hiking trails through the trees.

Now it was back to the drawing board because we needed a plan to suit the site where we had decided the house would go. After much discussion and several revisions, I thought I had the "perfect" plan for the cedar and stone house of our dreams–open space before it was fashionable–so I wouldn't be separated from my husband or from visiting family, whether I was cooking in the kitchen or working at my desk. A wall of windows, wrap-around deck, and screen porch would let us enjoy the natural world at our doorstep. Our bedroom would be a balcony overlooking the living room, with a dressing room and a walk-in closet. A large multi-purpose area could be an activity room for the grandchildren during the day, and with mattresses on the floor, a dormitory at night. Moveable dividers would let us make separate spaces if we wished. And the plan included the essentials identified years before–a mudroom, ground-floor laundry, pantry in the kitchen, and loads of storage.

My attempts to construct a 3-D model convinced me it was now time for a professional. With a firm picture in our minds of what we wanted we engaged an architect to produce the blueprints. He suggested a few changes that we agreed improved on our perfection! In a couple of weeks, we had the blueprints in our hands. He had done it–here was our "dream" floor plan transformed into a "dream" building. The architect, however, did not seem to share our enthusiasm for our rather unconventional plan, for he also brought the blueprints for another house for us to consider. To our amusement, it was the complete antithesis to our vision, with closed rooms and my study secluded at the back of the house–the kind of house that would have suited us just fine when we had teenagers living at home! It was our plan we took to a contractor.

Our new home fulfilled our expectations. It proved to be convenient, adaptable, and energy efficient. And it was beautiful with its high cathedral ceilings, the combination of cedar and stone, and interesting vistas in every direction. It became the centre of family life for our children and grandchildren, a frequent weekend retreat for the Winnipeg families, and a holiday destination for the Saskatoon family. We celebrated 22 Christmases, countless birthdays, and many a fun-filled gathering of family and friends in that house.

Then, John had quadruple bypass surgery. Arthritis in my knees and spine began to make walking difficult. I could no longer navigate our rough, root-laced trails. I was reduced to walking up and down our long, winding driveway for an hour. I tried to see something new on each repetition, breathing in the beauty of the white drifts of blooming high-cranberry bushes in spring, the changing kaleidoscope of wildflowers in summer, the vibrant gold, red, and brown of autumn leaves, and the long blue shadows of the leafless poplar trees etched on the white snow of winter.

After two years of this we began to question the wisdom of living on 20 acres when 15 of them were no longer accessible. When our health issues convinced us it was time to sell our beloved Bog 'n Bush and move back to the city, our children and grandchildren mourned the impending loss of the family "homestead." In fact, it would be more accurate to say the grandchildren were devastated. Grandpa, Grandma, and the Bog 'n Bush were inseparable in their experience.

This was where they hiked with us, skied, snow-shoed, and snowmobiled. This was where they carried the stones to help build the patio, netted tadpoles in the pond, and laughed at the playful antics of the deer that came to steal the sunflower seeds from the birdfeeders. This was where they slept together, played dress-up and air-band. It was where they played countless games of cards with us, in the screen porch in summer and by the wood-burning stove in winter. This was where they spent every Christmas, when at five o'clock in the morning they would tiptoe down the stairs and huddle in the under-stair nook, whispering and giggling as they explored the contents in their Christmas stockings. This was their childhood being left behind.

It was the grandchildren who kissed walls and shed tears that last day, when all our family gathered to say farewell to our country home. For me, it was the bittersweet ending of a dream that had begun so many years ago.

The Bog 'n' Bush in 2 seasons

We celebrated 22 Christmases in this house

The first Christmas

Many Christmases later

Kim, Marlo and Kyle with their gingerbread mansion

The grandkids helping to build the patio

Above–Jason and Laura
Below–John and Kyle

I'm working on some of my 50-60 pots and boxes I planted every year

Where Marlo learned to climb the stairs

And Kyle learned to play Othello

Laura, Marlo, Kim, Jason, Kyle

Laura showing the cousins you don't need to be afraid of snakes

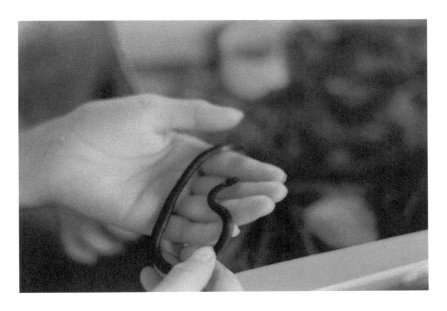

Playing by the pond

Sharing a story

We played card games in the screen porch in the summer and by the stove in the winter

Watching the wildlife right outside our living room windows

Playing in the snow
Kim, Kyle–and Johns arms!

Darryl taking the grandkids for a ride

Jordon playing in the snow

Kim
The final goodbyes
Kyle, Laura, Marlo, Jason

We completed a circle when we bought a house in Winnipeg where we are making new family memories. It is close to Kings Park, the city park where we walked so many years before. It has paved paths that I walked with the aid of a cane, then two canes, and now, a walker. Although my daily walks have morphed from pleasure jaunts to a painful challenge, I have not forgotten how I felt as I looked down from that hospital window. I still feel the wonder of walking and rejoice with each step I make.

PART 5
On This And That

Generation Gap

As a child, I strongly disliked apples, but in adulthood they became a favourite fruit. In fact, when I was pregnant with Lynn, I devoured so many apples while I was doing my teaching "homework" that I would joke that this baby was going to want applesauce in its formula, have rosy apple cheeks, and be the apple of my eye.

Back then, in the 50s and 60s, apples came in what were called "handipacks," very sturdy, shallow cardboard boxes with hand grips at each end. Being strong, with convenient hand-holds, and not too heavy to lift, even if full of books, these boxes were definitely "keepers." As I had eaten a heap of apples, I still had a pile of these boxes stored in our basement many years later. So, I was completely mystified the day I sent eight-year-old granddaughter Kim to the basement to fetch an apple box and she came back up and said she couldn't find one. "There's oodles," I said. "Under the worktable."

Kim dutifully returned to the basement, and once more came back up empty-handed. "I can't find any," she said.

"Okay," I said. "I'll come show you." Down we went, I picked an apple box off the pile and handed it to Kim.

"Oh," she said. "I was looking for an Apple computer box."

Crafty Kid

Brodie and Braydon, ages seven and five, were visiting their grandparents, Lorne and Pat (our nephew and his wife). One morning the kids were being especially rambunctious, rough-housing and chasing one another about. Finally, their grandmother's tolerance was stretched to its limit. Herding them outside, she decided to redirect their energy to helping her rake the yard. The seven-year-old pitched right in and went to work with a will. The five-year-old not so much. He dillied and he dallied till finally his exasperated grandmother warned him, "Shape up and get to work–or else."

"Fire me, Grandma," he said, hopefully.

Memorable Hikes

Over the years our family has camped and hiked in every province in Canada, plus the Yukon and Alaska.

There are wonderous gruelling hikes I will never forget. One is in the Whiteshell Provincial Park, at the edge of the Great Canadian Shield. John and I clamber over huge boulders I could not have scaled without his help, then slip and slide down sharp cuts in the terrain. When we come out onto a barren rocky plateau, with no more painted trees to mark our way, we wonder "What now?" till we spy small piles of rocks obviously made by human hands and realize these are now our trail markers.

Another challenging hike was one we made with our daughter, Lynn, when camping at Blue Lake in Ontario. This is a self-guided trail through a densely forested area. The faded paint on the blazed trees and the tangled mess of deadfall blocking our way tells us this is a trail laid out many years before, not maintained, and little used. After a strenuous morning climbing over and scrambling under fallen trees, we reach the trailhead at the edge of the lake. As we sit there eating our lunch, our exhausted teenager says, "If a boat came along right now and offered me a ride back to the campground, I'd take it."

"Not me," I say. "I'm walking back if it kills me."

"Mum!"

"Speaking metaphorically," I say.

No imagined boat appears, and we all make it back to the campground, weary to the bone but exhilarated by achievement, a feeling never to be forgotten.

Not all challenging hikes are in wild, untamed areas. Heading to Burlington after a visit to Niagara Falls and Niagara-On-The-Lake, we stop for lunch in a grassy area by the roadside at Queenston Heights atop the Niagara Escarpment. After our lunch we spot a sign pointing the way to Brock's Monument. The trail, descending steeply as it winds through the trees, beckons us to follow. We have no idea where it is going, or how far it goes, but it is irresistible—we must follow. In several places the trail is so steep that wooden steps and a railing have been installed to aid the explorer. At the end of the trail, we "discover" an imposing 56-metre-tall monument to Sir Isaac Brock. Atop a column stands a 4.8 metre stone statue of Brock in a heroic pose. A plaque informs us that Sir Isaac Brock was killed in Queenston in the War of 1812, waged against the invading Americans, and his remains are buried at the base of the monument.

Following the trail down to this piece of Canadian history had been adventuresome, going back up was just tough. I'm not sure if I would have made it without John and Lynn giving me a helping hand in places.

There are other hikes that have introduced us to natural wonders or presented vistas of nature's beauty that took our breath away.

One of those wonders wrought by the forces of nature is Hopewell Cape in New Brunswick, where we spent two fun-filled hours exploring the "Rocks."

The high shoreline of soft red, gravelly, clay-like rock has been eroded by the tides, leaving countless cave-like crevices we climb into, as well as towering, giant "doughnut rings" and "flower pots" we view with awe. Seaweed, clinging in thick, slimy green mounds to rocks along the shoreline is treacherous underfoot while the slowly advancing tide whooshes in menacing waves and catches us by surprise as it grabs at our feet.

Although it is 43 years since our family camping trip to the Yukon and Alaska, I can still see Miles Canyon when I shut my eyes. Rugged rock walls, grey and brown with splotches of orange and white, tower over turquoise green water circling in swift whirlpools. We cross the canyon on a swaying suspension bridge, high above that swirling maelstrom, and follow a narrow footpath winding along the cliffs. We discover a spring and fill our water bottles with the icy, crystal clear liquid before heading back to camp.

On a trip from Winnipeg to Qualicum beach on Vancouver Island with daughter, Lynn, her husband, Neville, and their three kids, Kim, Kyle, and Marlo, we have many opportunities for hiking and exploring natural wonders.

The first of those hikes was in the "Badlands" in Horseshoe Canyon, located just southwest of Drumheller, Alberta. It is an alien landscape carved out of the surrounding flat or gently rolling terrain by long-ago glaciers.

The buttes, canyons, coulees, ravines, and cone-shaped hoodoos gouged in the sedimentary rock by water erosion are a "treasure chest" of prehistoric fossils, having yielded complete dinosaur skeletons. We have great fun clambering down rough rock walls to the bottom of the canyon, then climbing to the tops of some of the hoodoos. It is a lot of climbing. Every time we climb up, we need to climb down, and then, finally, at the end of the afternoon we must summon the energy to climb out of the canyon if we don't want to join those dinosaur skeletons.

In Banff National Park we climb Tunnel Mountain to its flat rocky summit. It isn't as arduous as it sounds. We don't scale up a steep rocky incline with crampons and grapple hooks. There is a well-maintained 4.5-kilometre hiking trail up the forested side of the mountain that eases the 300-metre elevation gain with numerous switchbacks, some steep enough that we do get a good leg workout. By the time we reach the summit we are ready to stop for a rest and enjoy the panoramic view of the Banff town site, Bow River valley, and Mount Rundle. It is a good tiring three-hour hike by the time we get back to our starting point. Our assessment of our performance: John–most rest stops; Lynn–most brave act, going off-trail to rescue Neville's sunglasses; Neville–most athletic, doing push-ups at the summit; Kim–speediest, running ahead up the trail with Sparky, their dog; Kyle–most adventuresome and most cuts and bruises (not a good idea to try running up a sheer rock face edging the trail); Marlo–most water drank; and me–most in need of a bathroom!

Between Hope and Vancouver, we make a stop to see the Bridal Veil Falls. It is a steep climb, but the unique sight is worth the effort. The falls begin their descent far above the viewing platform, cascading down the terraced mountain side in an ever-widening sheet of white water–looking, indeed, like a giant bridal veil. As Lynn and I are standing at the back of the viewing platform taking pictures, six-year-old Marlo assumes we are too scared to move closer to the falls. She comes back, takes our hands and urges us to be brave and come up to the front rail. This site was also a first for Kyle–he made it both up and down a steep hike without a scrape or a bruise!

No climbing is needed for a hike in the Cathedral Grove in Macmillan Park on Vancouver Island. A trail leads us through a stand of huge old cedars that tower high above us. We are amazed at the girth of the largest tree in the park, said to be 800 years old. It would have been 300 years old when Columbus first came to America. One of the most amazing phenomena is the trees on stilts. They have grown out of a huge log, which has rotted away, leaving the exposed roots. There is also a living stump which has no leaves but gets its nourishment from the roots of a nearby tree. This meandering trail, at one point following a little stream through the trees, was an easy but awe-inspiring hike, leaving us with a heightened awareness of the short and transitory nature of human life.

These are only some of the many hikes we made together as a family, especially memorable for how they tested our physical endurance or reminded us of nature's wonders, and often did both.

The Long Road to Racial Equality

In 2003 our daughter Lynn and son-in-law Neville invited John and me to accompany them and their two younger children, Kyle and Marlo, on a four-week trip to South Africa. Also joining the group were Neville's younger brother Willie and his son Will, making eight of us in all. It was Neville and Willie's first trip back to the country of their birth since leaving many years before.

Their father William (Bill) Rhoda, a school principal, and mother, Gwen Rhoda, a teacher, had raised their family in South Africa during apartheid, and were politically active in the anti-apartheid movement as members of The Teachers' League of South Africa. The authorities were not pleased. Their house was raided several times and books confiscated. Would arrest and prison come next? Neville had already been detained twice, for sins as deadly as sitting on a bench for "whites" and insubordination. Wanting a better future for their family, Bill and Gwen decided in 1967 to emigrate to Canada with their four youngest children. The two older boys would follow—Neville, after he finished his final year of high school, and Stan, his second year at university. The government would not issue passports for the family, so they left with only exit visas, which meant, under apartheid, they could never return to South Africa.

Now, Neville and Willie were looking forward to seeing a country that has undergone many changes in the intervening years with the abolishment of apartheid and the release from prison of revered leaders in the struggle for racial equality, such as Nelson Mandela.

The following are excerpts from my trip diary as I explore what I learned from this trip—about South African culture and cautions for Canada.

Thursday, July 24

We landed in Johannesburg at 7:30 this morning, our first day in South Africa. We were met by Stewart and Ivor and whisked to Stewart and Estelle's home for a sumptuous brunch, our first experience of South Africa's amazing hospitality.

We spent the afternoon in the Soweto district, which was the scene of the Soweto uprising, a pivotal event in the fight to end apartheid. As we toured Mandela's house, we were fortunate to have a knowledgeable guide who gave us a passionate and moving introduction to the struggle. The pictures of ANC (African National Congress) freedom fighters included pictures of Mandela and O. R. Tambo, both of whom attended Fort Hare University with Bill Rhoda. Though Mandela was two years ahead of Bill, they played rugby together and Bill and Tambo were classmates.

We also visited the Hector Pieterson Museum, named in memory of the first black person killed in the Soweto uprising. Through pictures and film, the museum presented the history of the fight to abolish apartheid. An enclosed courtyard, with a brick placed for each child killed in the uprising, helped us realize the scope of the tragedy. The afternoon was a sobering experience that gave us a historical perspective for the rest of our trip.

Our first day in South Africa has also given us some insight into the contradictions in the culture of the country. Estelle and Stewart's home, where John and I are staying, is a large L-shaped house with an attached three-car garage and maid's quarters. All the main rooms have French doors opening onto the landscaped backyard with brick patio, pool, palm trees, shrubs, and flowers. It sounds perfect, but it isn't.

The whole property is surrounded by a high brick fence topped by several strands of razor wire. Further protection is provided by an electronic gate and a security camera. Despite this protection, Stuart was held up at gunpoint about a year and a half ago. And shortly before our visit, Estelle had been stripped of her wedding rings, handbag, and cell phone before she could close the security gate. As Sales Manager at Dell Computers, Stuart travels frequently, leaving Estelle and the two children alone. So now they are selling their "perfect" home and moving into a house in a gated community, with a 24-hour guard at the gate.

Ivor and Zandy's home, where Neville, Lynn, and the kids are staying, is much more modest, but its yard is also protected by a fence and gate, though not nearly as high as Estelle and Stewart's, and sans razor wire or electronic surveillance. In fact, on the drive from the airport this morning, we had been surprised by the high fences and steel gates surrounding most of the houses in both the affluent and middle-class areas we passed by. It is such a contrast to the open front yards we take for granted in Canada.

Another surprise—we were not prepared for the frequent use of the terms "black", "coloured," and "white" in casual conversation. Knowing how open-minded and accepting of differences Neville, Willie, and their parents are, I was surprised by the racist comments, aimed at blacks, made by some of their relatives and friends, members of the so-called coloured group who, under apartheid, suffered racial prejudice themselves.

With the end of apartheid, and the ANC Party winning the subsequent election, blacks and members of the coloured group moved into positions of power and influence in the government and institutions. Those who were coloured still felt the sting of discrimination however, with blacks getting the best positions despite many having less education and qualifications. This could explain some of the anti-black comments we heard.

Years of racial stratification enforced by government policy has made change hard and ever so slow. All the relatives we have met so far have "black" maids and gardeners. It is "blacks" who live in the many shanty towns scattered throughout the city. It is "blacks" who walk between the vehicles at every major stoplight, trying to sell their wares. It is "blacks" who work the parking lots, competing with one another to direct a driver to one of their parking spots. It is "blacks," including children, who drum and dance on the sidewalks, hoping for donations. It is mostly "blacks" who are begging in the streets and parking lots, though we did see some poor "whites" begging for handouts at stop signs. The gulf between the "haves" and "have-nots" seems huge. Education is free for all, but with unemployment at 50 percent, and even higher among young adult blacks, it does not seem possible for education, alone, to solve South Africa's social and economic inequalities.

Friday, July 25

Today we made the seven-hour bus trip from Johannesburg to Kimberley, home town to Neville and Willie. A plateau region with cultivated fields and sheep pastures gave way to the wide horizons of endless veldt.

This arid, semi-desert area is dotted by doring trees, a South African hardwood, towering anthills, and low, shrubby, thorn trees.

Again, we were met and warmly welcomed with hugs and kisses by numerous relatives at the bus station. During the buffet meal at Auntie Helen's, and late into the evening, there was much sharing of memories from the days when Neville and Willie lived in Kimberley, and catching up on what has happened since, including an animated debate about the future of their country. It was the optimistic versus the pessimistic view, with no clear winner. As we listened, everyone in our Canadian group hoped the optimists were right.

Saturday, July 26

We began the day with a huge breakfast of eggs, bacon, sausages, buttered toast, and honey kooksistas, a deep-fried confection like a yeast doughnut. Stepping outside to pick oranges and lemons from the trees in Auntie Helen's front yard, we were stunned by the intense blue of the crystal-clear sapphire sky, not a wisp of cloud in sight.

However, all was not beautiful. When we turned our eyes to the north, we could see the shanty town in the open field at the end of the street.

Later, driving to downtown Kimberley, we stopped to visit the area where the Rhodas (Neville and Willie's family) and their relatives lived, before being forced to leave to make way for "whites." The area is now completely commercial. I realized a parallel displacement happened in Winnipeg in the late 1950s, when residents in the Metis settlement known as Rooster Town, were forced to move to make way for suburban development, including the Grant Park Shopping Mall.

In the evening, cousin Ian took us to a karaoke nightclub where we met Shuttie and his wife Bella. They are a most unusual couple. Bella's striking appearance—short black and blonde streaked hair, smart black outfit dripping with gold necklaces and bracelets—matches her vibrant personality. She is a party girl who enjoys dancing, drinking, and smoking. Shuttie is a Muslim who does not dance, drink, or smoke. He came to the bar tonight, for the first time, to invite us for lunch with his family, including his father, who was Neville's favourite teacher. Shuttie and Bella seem to be able to accommodate each other's differences without rancour or resentment. There is a lesson there for each of us, a lesson the countries of the world would do well to heed.

Sunday, July 27

Today we visited the "Big Hole," the diamond mine that produced 14.5 million carats of diamonds before it was closed in 1941. It is the largest hand-dug excavation in the world—215 metres deep, with a perimeter of 1.6 kilometres—dug by blacks wielding picks and shovels.

This has been another day of over-the-top South African hospitality. Lunch at Poppy and Keith's included chicken, a curry dish, pasta, potato salad, steamed pumpkin, rice, bread pudding, and spice cake.

Arriving at Auntie Millie's for dinner, we were urged to come sit at the table for some "snacks" before dinner—scones with a savoury topping, scones with jam and whipped cream, and three kinds of tarts. All this, and we were still full after our huge lunch at Poppy's! The "snacks" were followed by the dinner meal–chicken pot pie, curry, roti, rice, and salad, which was followed by chicken, sliced roasts, oven-fried potatoes, and more rice. When you knew you could not eat another mouthful, along came the desserts–jello crammed full of fruit, chocolate cake, white cake, hasty pudding, tapioca pudding, and ice cream. Through it all, 86-year-old Auntie Millie was watching like a hawk, noting what you had not tried and urging, "Eat! Eat!"

Auntie Millie is living in Neville and Willie's childhood home. Neville said the wallpaper is the same as when he left 34 years ago. However, he discovered he was not the same when he found he was too big to hide behind the door he used to hide behind as a kid!

Family storytelling followed dinner. We heard about the day Auntie Millie and daughter-in-law, Thora, went to a funeral and had to get a boost from the hearse, and the time they forgot to pay for their gas and were afraid the police were after them. Cousin Joey described the day Mandela came to his house for tea and couldn't convince his bodyguards he was visiting a friend, and they didn't need to supervise the tea making to ensure he wasn't in danger of being poisoned. They didn't realize that Doctor Joe looked after many ANC members who couldn't afford to pay and was viewed as a friend to many of the poor. There was the story of the priest that revived as he was being given the last rites, a tale about the woman Joey gave a wild ride in her wheelchair... and on and on and on. It was 10:30 p.m. before we left, still laughing—and still full!

Tuesday, July 29

We visited Neville's good friend Zakie and family today and were served another multi-course lunch. Inevitably the conversation turned to politics, and I think for the first time since we arrived in South Africa, all present seemed optimistic about the country's future.

One of the first things we noticed about Zakie's house was that it was unfenced and ungated even though it stood alone, far from other homes, except for the shanty town in the open field nearby. The openness of his home seemed to reflect Zakie's stated attitude toward racial openness and interaction. He acknowledged social change was slow, though he was convinced things would improve as the next generation took over. We all shared his hopefulness, but unfortunately, we did experience a couple of incidents that day that dramatized the depth of the country's racial rifts.

For example, after lunch, Zakie's daughter took Marlo with her to pick up a younger sister from school. During the drive she asked Marlo if she would ever marry a black man. Marlo said, "Yes, if I loved him."

"Not me," was the response.

"Why?" asked Marlo.

"Because they're lower class and I would lose status," was the reply.

When Marlo shared this experience with us, it was disappointing considering Zakie's optimism about the next generation.

Another contradiction between words and deeds was apparent when we visited Zakie's brick factory. The workers all lived in the nearby shanty town, and scrawled messages on a billboard in the factory indicated unhappiness with both wages and working conditions. However, the presence of the message board suggested an openness to change.

In the afternoon we time-travelled, stopping at the sport field where Neville and Willie played rugby in their youth. We also visited Prescot High School where Bill Rhoda was principal, and where Neville went to school. We have already met several people who have fond memories of Mr. Rhoda's tenure at the school.

Wednesday, July 30

Today we drove through flat veldt, with its scattering of short rounded trees, to Riverton Park. Along the way we were surprised by a waterway pink with flamingos, and we had our first sighting of ostriches in the wild. Standing on the bank of the Vaal River in the park, Neville observed that we were on what had been the "white" side in his boyhood—the side where he was not allowed to go.

Thursday, July 31

Before leaving on the train to Cape Town this evening, we visited all the Kimberley relatives for a last farewell and to thank them for their hospitality. At every stop we were given food to take on our trip!

*Saying goodbye to Auntie Helen
and Aunty Millie*

On the train we had two compartments that were quite roomy and reasonably comfortable. However, our decision not to rent bedding was a grievous error as the night was cool. At first, I used my fleecy for a pillow, but the cold made wearing it a priority over having a pillow. The chilly temperature, the very firm, plastic-covered bunk, and no pillow, were not conducive to a sound sleep.

Friday, August 1

When John and Lynn woke up, I looked so cold they dug into our suitcases and got out John's heavy terry housecoat and our beach towels and covered me snugly. The unexpected warmth felt wonderful! However, I got no more sleep as they kept talking about what they were seeing out the window, and my curiosity forced me to sit up too.

We watched low mist-covered mountains flit by. Then came a stretch of dry hilly terrain that reminded us of the area around Swift Current. As we sped along, we travelled through rocky mountains with vineyards in the valleys. Gradually, as we neared Cape Town, the landscape became greener and lusher.

The train was late getting into Cape Town. The local folks said it is always late, so why don't they change the schedule and then it will be on time? We were met by Jeannette and Claude, and Geoff and Lillian. It was hugs and kisses with each introduction, which we are getting accustomed to now.

Another warm welcome awaited us at Auntie Esme's where we had a four-course supper–soup, followed by curry, roti, and rice, followed by lamb, chicken, and oven-fried potatoes, followed by trifle for dessert.

Saturday, August 2

John and I woke to the happy sound of Aunt Esme's singing. Shortly there came a knock at the bedroom door, and in came Aunt Esme bearing a tray with fresh coffee, sugar, and cream.

We spent the morning exploring the Cape Peninsula with Claude and Jeannette. The palm trees lining the streets in Simon Town are quite a contrast to the arid veldt we just left in Kimberley. We drove by a line of colourful bathing houses at St. James Bay before stopping at a flea market. I watched, bemused, as Jeannette negotiated the price of a tablecloth I was buying to R200 from R350. Lesson learned—never pay what vendors are asking—they expect you to negotiate.

At Boulder's Beach we mingled with the shy little African Penguins, or "jackass penguins" as they are called due to their donkey-like braying, that nest just above the beaches along this section of the coast.

However, at Cape Point the bossy baboons wandering freely in the parking lot—around, over, and on top of the cars—were not as much fun. One snatched a sandwich from a tourist dining at an outdoor table, while another made a swipe at Will's ice cream cone, knocking it to the ground.

Making the steep climb to the top of Table Mountain, we were rewarded with sweeping vistas of foaming surf, rocky cliffs, and rugged mountains. The ant-sized vehicles in the parking lot below made us realize how high we were.

Leaving the parking lot, we drove down the mountain side through the Cape of Good Hope Nature Reserve where fynbos, aloe, and protea were in bloom.

The morning ended with lunch at the fishing village, Haut Bay: good old-fashioned newspaper-wrapped fish and chips.

Dinner at the African Restaurant, hosted by Lorraine and Colin, was a unique experience: original bead-trimmed menus, a myriad of food choices in tiny dishes, many tasty non-alcoholic drinks, an African dance performed by the waiters, and what really impressed the kids, the elaborate bead-trimmed toilet lids and seats.

Sunday, August 3

This afternoon we took the ferry to Robben Island, where Mandela was imprisoned for so many years. During our visit to the prison, a former revolutionary gave us a detailed description of the events leading to Mandela's arrest, as well as the realities of prison life. Later, standing outside Mandela's small, spare cell, I wondered how anyone could keep his sanity, let alone his humanity, after years of solitary confinement in this space.

Monday, August 4

Canal Walk Mall is so huge it is a "shop till you drop" experience. John will be celebrating his birthday before we leave South Africa, so we got him a jigsaw puzzle and a couple of shirts. Then, leaving John resting on a bench, I secretly purchased a velvety-soft fleece vest, which I hid inside my jacket until I could smuggle it into one of Kyle's bags. Buying it secretly turned out to be a mistake. I should have had him try it on. The shirts we bought were L as the XL (his usual size) was too big. So, assuming all South African sizes were larger, I got an L vest too. When he opened his "surprise" gift on his birthday and tried it on, it was much too small, and by then we were in Johannesburg, far from the Cape Town Mall. So, Kyle was the beneficiary of the vest he had carried around for me in his shopping bag.

Tuesday, August 5

Today we toured the District 6 Museum, which honours the memory of the black and coloured residents of District 6 who were evicted to make room for an all-white enclave. It was the story of a close-knit community destroyed as its residents were dispersed to various "coloured" districts. The pictures and stories of the displaced were laden with pathos, summed up in this prominently displayed poem, printed in bold red on a white background:

HOLD FAST
    TO DREAMS
FOR IF DREAMS DIE
  LIFE IS A
    BROKEN-WINGED BIRD
    THAT
    CANNOT FLY

Dinner tonight was at Geoff and Lillian's. The house was literally packed with people. I lost count long before we had been introduced to everyone. I have never been hugged and kissed by so many people in one evening–and probably never will be again.

As we gathered around the long dining table, Lillian organized the seating, making sure a Canadian and a South African were alternated. Impossible as it seems, this dinner was more lavish than anything we had yet experienced. A soup course was followed by rice, roti, and a variety of curries. Our plates were removed and replaced with clean ones. Then came a potato and meat course with chunky fried potatoes, roast beef, roast lamb, fried chicken, meatballs, sausages, and a meat pie. Once more our plates were removed and replaced with clean ones. The next course was a salad one, including potato, pasta, and noodle mixtures. All this was followed by an array of trifle, pudding, and pastry desserts. The dessert plates were removed and replaced with clean ones. What else could be coming? Cakes and cookies of course! Groan!

Our Canadian hospitality is certainly restrained compared to South African standards. Even our special occasion meals such as Thanksgiving or Christmas are simple affairs, by comparison.

After the meal, the Canadians were invited to share their impressions of South Africa. I was proud of how well our young ones, Kyle, Marlo, and Will, were able to give "off the cuff" gracious little speeches. They showed far more maturity than our generation had at their age.

Wednesday, August 6

We are leaving for Jeffrey's Bay early tomorrow, so I did two loads of laundry this morning, hanging them out on the line. It seems few people in South Africa have a clothes dryer. The temperate climate does not make them the necessity we think they are in Canada.

Relaxing on the patio in the afternoon, I kept a close eye on my laundry, getting it in and folded before Aunt Esme could get at it with her iron. We had come home a previous day to find our laundry, including no-iron shirts and blouses, T-shirts, my panties, and John's undershorts, all smoothly ironed. I do not want our underwear spoiled and expecting ironing when we get home.

Thursday, August 7

We left early this morning for the all-day drive to Jeffrey's Bay, Jeannette and Claude's country home. It was our first experience of South African driving. We were pulling the trailer with all our luggage, and as I watched the speedometer needle it hit 155 km an hour on straightaways, while it stayed between 100 and 120 km an hour as the road curved back and forth around the rolling hills and higher mountains. Claude drives like the marathon biker he is, just leaning into the curves.

Willie, who was following with the rest of our group in our rented van, proved to have nerves of steel. He managed to keep us within sight, while coping with driving on the left side of the road.

Friday, August 8

The planned development where Jeannette and Claude have their home consists of two islands surrounded by a man-made waterway. Colourful houses, lush lawns, and extensive landscape plantings contribute to the tropical atmosphere. Security is assured with access to the development controlled by a barricade at the guardhouse, which is staffed 24 hours a day.

The house, no "cottage by the lake," is a large architect-designed two-story home. The open floor plan permits an easy flow of traffic and communication, from the "dream" kitchen to the living-dining area, to the glassed-in patio. The main floor also has a self-contained guest suite. The second story includes a master suite, guest bedrooms, a large study/entertainment area, and a balcony with a wide-angle view of the neighbourhood. For the first time all eight of us were able to stay in the same home.

We spent the morning enjoying the water, first with boat rides, and then at the beach being tossed about by the pounding surf.

In the afternoon we visited the Kouga Cultural Centre, which serves as a museum illustrating the culture of the Kouga region, as well as providing an outlet for the sale of arts and crafts from the region.

I tried to buy a painting of a woman in a shanty town hanging up her laundry, but they would not take a credit card, and I didn't want to pay cash as I was afraid we would run out of Rand. Now I am mentally kicking myself as we came home with R1000, which we lost money on when we converted it to Canadian dollars. That original painting (framed) that I loved cost a mere R450. And back home, we have spent $400 (equivalent to R2000) to frame four "banana leaf" pictures for which we paid R100 ($20 Canadian). Hindsight is a wonderful thing!

Saturday, August 9

Today's excursion was to Port Elizabeth where we shopped at the mall and visited the casino, where the excellent buffet featured a section with a made-to-order stir fry with your choice of meat, vegetables, and sauce. Marlo tried it, asking the chef's advice for choice of sauce, and said it was delicious. We ended the day with some extremely competitive bumper car races before heading back to Jeffrey's Bay.

Sunday, August 10

This was a more leisurely day. In the afternoon we drove to St. Francis Bay, a unique settlement of upscale houses with traditional thatched roofs. By the time we left the rocky beach, each one of us had a treasure trove of interesting shells washed clean by the pounding surf.

Jeannette, with Willie's assistance, has been preparing gourmet meals since we came to Jeffrey's Bay. Tonight's lobster with a rice pilaf, followed by bananas wrapped in crepes, was the ultimate.

Our suitcases are packed for our early departure tomorrow. Marlo and Will spent this last evening baking chocolate chip cookies for our bus trip.

Monday, August 11

At 6:55 a.m. we began the 14½ hour bus trip to Durban, riding in a double-decker bus. The bus did not stop for breakfast, and all they gave us to eat were two biscotti biscuits and a cup of coffee. Even augmented by four of Marlo and Will's chocolate chip cookies, it was an unsatisfying breakfast.

It was after 10:00 p.m. by the time we got to Winona and Andrew's for supper and a short visit, and 12:30 a.m. when we settled into our rooms at the Beach Hotel. It was so warm and humid we slept with our windows open, the pounding surf providing an all-night lullaby.

Tuesday, August 12

This was another bus day, but this time we were fortified with a bountiful free breakfast at our hotel. As we travelled through the Kwazulu/Natal province the landscape was extremely varied, mountains and orange groves gradually giving way to undulating hills and almost treeless veldt. Open markets with brightly coloured wares lined the streets of the Zulu towns we passed through. In the rural areas, shanty towns were widely scattered on the hills and veldt. Even in these wide-open spaces the modern scourge of plastic bags was evident in the rubbish caught on the scrubby brush and dry grass.

We spent the night in the main house at Zakie's brick factory compound near Standerton. I packed one small suitcase with necessities for the trip to Kruger Park, as we would be leaving the rest of our luggage at Standerton until we returned.

Wednesday, August 13

Taking two cars, with Zakie and Willie doing the driving, this was another day of travel through changing landscapes as we passed from veldt to mountains to orange groves. Arriving at Kruger Park, we settled into two chalets just outside the park gates, and we had our first experience with Kruger animals—monkeys roaming freely about the grounds.

Supper required no cooking as we dined on the food Zakie had brought—samosas, meatballs, and buttered bread—and the fruit and nuts Neville had bought along the way.

Thursday August 14

At 6:00 a.m. we met our guide for a pre-dawn "animal drive" in an open safari van. It was cool and windy, so we were grateful for the blankets we found on every seat. Our first sighting was a mother and baby elephant, barely visible in the dim light. We spotted some deer-like animals, a herd of Cape buffalo, and several birds that Willie was able to photograph, and that was it. We found the excursion somewhat disappointing as our driver had a thick accent, which made his explanations hard to understand, and we had expected to see more animals.

Lunch back at the chalet was the food left over from the previous night. We then spent the rest of the day driving through the park on our own, seeing more animals than we had in the morning.

Large baboons swung from branch to branch overhead. Several herds of Cape buffalo grazed among the scrubby trees. These big and burly animals, one of South Africa's "Big Five," (lion, rhinoceros, leopard, elephant) have upward curving horns that meet in a horny mass on their forehead. We had close-up views of dainty impalas with delicate legs, chestnut backs, and white bellies. The males are easily identified by their ringed horns which curve backward and then up. Male kudus with their distinctive white body stripes, fringe of long hair at the throat, spine fringe, and long twisted horns were a spectacular sight. We encountered gentle zebra that stay together in large groups as their mass of black and white stripes confuses predators who find it difficult to pick out individuals to attack. Mean looking wart hogs used their long bone-hard snouts to dig for roots and tubers. They are ugly and tough animals that can ward off cheetahs, leopards, lions, and wild dogs with their head. Giraffes, further back in the trees, fed on the topmost leaves. Camouflaged by their colouring, even the one closest to us was virtually invisible.

The most exciting event of the afternoon was our "up-close" encounter with elephants. As we stopped to admire a group grazing beside the road, the huge bull elephant decided to cross the road, immediately in front of our car, to graze on the other side.

We sat transfixed, aware he could topple our car like a toy if he chose to. As he paid us no attention, we continued to watch as he gathered a bunch of grass with his trunk, shook it to get rid of dust, and then lifted it to his mouth. Later, we watched a large herd of elephants drinking and showering themselves at a watering hole.

Supper was a braai, a South African barbecue, with Zakie's lamb chops cooked to spicy perfection, accompanied by two South African staples, rice and curry.

Friday, August 15

Breakfast was the rest of our cereal and bread, and the leftover curry and rice from supper.

A long "driving day" was ahead—another exposure to wild South African speeders as the road twisted in and out and around the mountains. I was sitting in the front passenger seat beside Willie as we followed Zakie. On relatively straight stretches of road we travelled at 145-160 km an hour, while S curves were manoeuvred at a mere 100-120 km an hour! There were times when I thought it would be wiser to just close my eyes.

At noon we stopped at Neiser, where Zakie went to a mosque for his Friday prayers, while the rest of us had lunch at a Greek restaurant. Their Greek salad was excellent, the pizza so-so.

At Standerton, Zakie's sister had supper ready for us. Packing all our luggage into the car and truck, we then headed for Johannesburg, with Zakie and his son Omar doing the driving. Arriving back at Estelle and Stewart's felt like coming home.

Saturday, August 16

Today was John's birthday and I forgot it till Estelle said, "Happy birthday," at breakfast.

We spent the morning at Gold Reef City, a combined historical centre, amusement park, and arts and crafts shopping centre. The kids headed for the "thrill" rides while we adults intended to go on the underground gold mine tour. That plan was nixed when they would not let anyone physically disabled (meaning me) into the mine. I tried to convince them I was physically fit, and having a limp did not make me disabled, but to no avail. And then I tried, in vain, to convince the rest of the group to go without me. So, we ended up exploring the 25 shops that invited browsing—and spending.

Dinner at Estelle and Stewart's included Ivor and Zandy and family, and Winkeye—known as the Biltong man for the South African dried meat snack similar to jerky that he makes—and his two daughters. Unfortunately, the after-dinner conversation descended into an anti-black diatribe. Winkeye's wife had been shot twice during robberies, the second time fatally, so his bitter venting was understandable, though hard to listen to.

Sunday, August 17

Our excursion today was to a private Rhino and Lion Nature Reserve. As we drove along the trails in this fenced park, we watched lions, cheetahs, and wild dogs tearing at dead carcasses.

In a more peaceful area several "deer-like" animals grazed, ignored by both the massive rhinoceros and the long-necked ostriches nearby. There were gemsbok with distinctive black markings and long straight horns pointing backwards, and blue wildebeest with what looks like dark paint drips on their sides, upright manes, and under-chin fringe. The crocodile pool gave us a close-up view of these creatures we had viewed from afar when on the bridge by our chalet in Kruger Park.

We were invited to enter an enclosure with a young lion, accompanied by a trainer, but Will and Marlo were the only ones courageous/daring/reckless enough to venture in. They ended up petting and kissing the apparently sleeping animal, who lifted his head as soon as they started to walk away.

Meanwhile, back at the braai hut, Stuart, Ivor, Estelle, and Zandy were busy cooking and unpacking a hearty picnic meal. After lunch, an impromptu rugby game–boys against men–provided our first afternoon entertainment. Then, testosterone still coursing through their veins, Neville, Willie, Kyle, and Will became entangled in a wrestling match.

A young impala, wandering by, thought it looked like a great game. Facing them with his sharp little horns, he circled the group on the ground, trying to join in the fun, until he saw his opportunity and jumped on Neville's back. That put a sudden end to the wrestling, but not to our fun. The impala would not leave despite our efforts to shoo him away. Nature lover Willie offered the impala his hand to lick. It must have been tasty–maybe traces of the braai–because that impala was not going to leave that hand. A worker tried to herd him away, even threatening to braai him, but with no success. Then he got a bottle of milk to lure the animal away. That still did not work. The impala kept circling back to Willie's hand. Finally, the worker, in desperation, said to Willie, "Walk with us." That worked. The impala followed Willie to the enclosure, periodically trying to "jump" him along the way. A laughter-filled end to our picnic.

Monday, August 18

Today a rented van and driver took us, and all the relatives, to the Sun City Resort. Along the way we stopped at Magaliesberg to explore a huge flea market where the sellers aggressively pushed their wares. They sold Lynn and Neville a metal duck for John for his birthday and a batch of batiks.

Arriving at Sun City we experienced the fake volcano on the bridge and played in the technological wave pool, which was not equal to nature's surf at Jeffrey's Bay. Then Neville, Lynn, and the kids had screaming good fun at the water slide. We could hear them on their way down before they came into sight around the last bend, heading down a steep slope to splash into the pool.

We ate supper at the food court and then the gamblers went to the casino, while the kids played video games and I wandered around the shops. Before leaving we returned to the bridge to experience that volcano in the dark. Still fake!

The drive back to Johannesburg in the dark seemed longer than it had this morning. At one point a freak wind blew grass and garbage through the air, almost obstructing the driver's vision. The flames from numerous grass fires flickered in the dark but could not keep us from dozing from time to time.

Tuesday, August 19

This morning we went to the Indian Market with Estelle and Zandy. It was a day with lots of walking and little buying. We lunched on samosas bought at a stand and then visited the Museum Africa. The vast museum, on three levels, included geological, rock art, and photography collections, a history of apartheid, and the story of Johannesburg from the Stone and Iron Ages to the days of gold mining and the present. The gift shops had many handmade African crafts for sale.

In the evening, we went to the casino for dinner with our Johannesburg hosts, Stuart and Estelle and Ivor and Zandy, with their families. The buffet was the largest we have ever seen, and probably ever will. It had separate sections for various ethnic groups and for different kinds of meat, including a "wild life" section, not for me, but John tried it. The dessert selections were just as extensive with puddings, pastries, cakes, ice cream, and toppings.

Everyone was "gambled out" from last night, so we did not stay at the casino very long after supper.

Wednesday, August 20

This was our last day in South Africa, as we are leaving for Frankfurt on the 7:10 p.m. flight. Stuart took the men golfing in the morning. Then we all gathered at Ivor and Zandy's for a lunch of curry, rice, and ostrich neck stew, followed by a selection of desserts. I sampled each one, promising myself they were the last sweets I would eat till Christmas–a promise not kept!

After lunch Olivia, one of the young ones, lit up a bubbly-bubbly (hookah pipe) and demonstrated how it worked. Will and Willie gave it a try. I don't know what it tasted like, but it smelled dreadful.

Then it was off to the airport with Stuart and Estelle, each driving a car with passengers, while Ivor took his car piled high with the luggage that wouldn't fit in the two car trunks. It was fortunate we had allowed plenty of time to get to the airport as Estelle drove over something sharp on the road and got a flat tire. Kyle observed it was a case of "too many cooks," as all the males pitched in to make the tire change, but we were soon back on the road.

At the airport there was another little blip when Stuart's last-minute gift to Neville and Lynn, a bottle of South African brandy, broke in their suitcase, drenching some of their new purchases, including all of Marlo's purses and her banana leaf pictures.

Then it was time to say final farewells to our Johannesburg hosts. Amid the confusion of all the "goodbye" hugs and kisses, Kyle planted a big one on his mother too.

We left South Africa amazed by the generous hospitality of all the hosting families. Also, it had been heartwarming to watch Neville and Willie reconnect with their roots, and to listen to the sharing of family memories and stories.

At the same time, we were looking forward to getting home to Winnipeg, where we do not feel the need to protect our homes with razor wire, or to live in gated, guarded communities, and where our social safety nets preclude the rampant begging, even by children, we experienced on the streets of South Africa.

We also left disappointed and saddened by the racial prejudice that is still so much a part of the country. But, on reflection, how different is it from our own country?

The shanty towns, with their make-shift buildings, sitting on open fields that separate them from houses on nearby streets, are more visible than our poor and underprivileged populations, largely Indigenous peoples or new immigrants. Our city zoning by-laws do not allow substandard housing to spring up within sight of middle-class neighbourhoods, where the mood is NIMB—not in my backyard. Instead, we corral it all in one area "on the other side of the tracks," where it is out of sight, out of mind.

The displacement of the residents in District 6 in Cape Town is like the experience of many of our Indigenous peoples, when they were moved to more remote areas when we wanted their land for expanding cities or hydro dams. It is to our shame that, to justify establishing the black townships that were a part of apartheid, members of the South African government came to Canada and visited our reservations for Indigenous peoples.

Racism exists in our society too, sometimes overt, but also a systemic part of our child welfare and justice systems. In Manitoba, 90 percent of children in care are Indigenous. Federally, 5 percent of our population is Indigenous, while over 30 percent of inmates in Canada's prisons are Indigenous. In Manitoba, 65 percent of men, 90 percent of women, and 80 percent of minors incarcerated are Indigenous.

South Africa has a long road to travel to establish true racial equality. We do too.

POSTSCRIPT

It is now 17 years after our trip to South Africa. I feel sad and disheartened as racism continues to be rampant in North America.

In Canada, in the intervening years, we have had the *Report of the Truth and Reconciliation Commission of Canada* on the Indian residential school system and its legacy. The report, published in 2015, had 94 calls to action, including the adoption and implementation of the "United Nations

Declaration on the Rights of Indigenous Peoples." Five years later many of the key recommendations, including the implementation of the UN Declaration, remain just "calls to action." In June 2019, the *National Inquiry Into Missing and Murdered Indigenous Women and Girls* released its final report. One year later no national action plan has been announced.

In 2015, *Maclean's* magazine named Winnipeg the most racist city in Canada, citing, among other problems, the "fraught relationship" between police and the Indigenous population. Despite efforts by the mayor, the city council, and the police service to improve the situation, Indigenous people continue to report being subject to racial profiling. In the year 2019, Winnipeg police shot and killed seven people. Of the four who were identified, three were Indigenous. In the first four months of 2020, they have fatally shot four people, with three identified as Indigenous—two men and a 16-year-old girl—being killed in three separate incidents in a 10-day span.

In May 2020, George Floyd, a black man in the United States of America, died as a police officer knelt on his neck for almost nine minutes as he lay handcuffed and face down on the pavement, saying he couldn't breathe. The horrific video, photos, and media reports of Floyd's death have sparked massive anti-racist demonstrations in the United States, Canada, and worldwide. On June 5, 15,000 peaceful protesters gathered outside the Manitoba Legislative Building for a "Black Lives Matter" rally. In the wake of the demonstrations, stories of injuries to Indigenous people and racial minorities during arrests by Canadian police are now surfacing. There are petitions calling for increased funding for social services and mental health supports.

Will these demonstrations be a catalyst for significant, lasting change? On a personal level, each one of us who cares needs to speak up and counter racism whenever, and wherever, it rears its ugly head.

Really Letting Go This Summer

After pulling a muscle in my back this spring and spending six weeks in pain and therapy, I have commenced what I see as a new phase in my life—really letting go.

The last few years I have hired a university student to mow and rake the lawn and help with the planting and weeding in the perennial beds. However, I still managed the watering and fertilizing, the planting and care of the annuals in the raised flower boxes around the deck, and the daily sweeping up of the tree litter on the patio and flagstone paths in the backyard.

This summer a lawn care company is looking after the grass and a real gardener, not a student helper, is doing the rest of the yard work. I have learned it is possible to enjoy flowers I have not personally selected, purchased, and planted, and living with a few days tree litter lying in the backyard will not kill me. In fact, it has been surprisingly enjoyable to spend summer relaxing in a deck chair instead of attached to the end of a hose or a broom.

Also, for the first time in my life I have hired a housecleaner. I found that hard to do and I am not sure why. Was it an invasion of my privacy? Or was it because I did not trust someone else to meet my standards? In three hours, the young woman does what would take me two days at my current speed. And I still get to give the rooms my personal touch. When dusting she does not have an "eye" for replacing accessories on shelves or tables, so after she has finished and left, I go round and set things right. Now, when I think of all the hours of cleaning that could have been spent reading or writing, I wish I had followed my family's advice and hired household help years ago.

A daily walk—combining exercise, enjoyment of the outdoors, and a time for quiet contemplation—has been my passion for many, many years. However, this summer I have had to accept that it is not the best form of exercise for my arthritic knees, hip, and back. By nature a rather solitary person, I am not a "joiner" and have never relished the idea of group exercising, but this summer I have taken the plunge and enrolled in a water exercise class designed for people with arthritis that is offered at our local pool. These twice-a- week sessions will replace two of my daily walks. To my surprise, I am looking forward to the starting date in October.

By far the most important "letting go" has been in relation to my husband's dementia. It has been a "trickle, drop-by-drop" process to gradually erode my resistance to outside help.

John's erratic behaviour after hand surgery resulted in our introduction to the Manitoba Home Care Program. To give me a break from caregiving, our caseworker arranged for John to attend a day program for people with dementia at Deer Lodge Hospital. However, he did not like the long van ride and after a few weeks refused to go. This elicited another visit from our Home Care contact. She did not mince words. I had been careful to present the day program as a chance for John to get out of the house and enjoy new activities, but she told him straight out I needed a break. Since he was not attending the day program, we would need a Home Care worker to stay with him one afternoon a week so I could go out. Fortunately, she made a compatible match and he likes his worker.

About a month later she phoned and said there was an opening in another day program closer to home, and I should convince John to try it. She also said I must stay firm and not allow him to withdraw. It was wise counsel, as again, after attending the program for a few weeks, he said he was not going anymore. With new resolve I said, "Yes you are. If you don't get up, I will phone Home Care and ask them to send a man to drag you out of bed."

He got out of bed by himself.

After this scenario was repeated a couple of times there were no more refusals, and now he looks forward to his day out.

His day out is my day at home, relishing the peace and quiet of being alone for a few hours. The afternoons when the caregiver stays with him are an opportunity to shop or meet with friends. I had not realized how much I needed the relaxation and renewal of those two half-day breaks.

Then in June, during a short trip to Churchbridge for a family event, John became so disoriented at night, relieving himself anywhere but the bathroom, that I realized overnight visits were no longer possible. It felt like walking smack, face-first, into a plate glass door that I knew was there but did not realize was so close. It meant no weekends at Lloyd and Karen's cottage at Whytewold–day trips only. It meant no trips to Saskatoon. By the middle of July, I found I was aching for a week at the cottage at Big River with Darryl, Janis, and their families–going boating during the day and relaxing by campfires in the evening. I felt frustrated, trapped, and cheated of a normal life.

It was then that a friend gave me a copy of *Caring for a Husband with Dementia: The Ultimate Survival Guide*, written by Angela Gentile, a specialist in aging, living here in Winnipeg. I found it helpful in learning to identify situations I could control and recognizing when to "let it go," in improving communication to maintain peace, and in dealing with some of John's difficult behaviours. Particularly timely was her concept of "mini-vacations," stolen moments alone. Realizing I was having many mini-vacations this summer—morning tea and the newspaper in the gazebo, writing at the computer, even the snippets of time I spent solving crossword puzzles in the bathroom—helped improve my state of mind.

Then in August, three daytrips in one week to Bird's Hill Park, where Lynn and Neville were camping, became our summer vacation. I had my time in the water with Lynn while John was content to sit under the umbrella on the beach. Later, as we ate a barbecued supper and sat around the campfire it was like reliving our camping days for a few hours, only, like Cinderella, we knew we had a curfew—leave before sundown.

Finally, attending an Alzheimer Association meeting for the first time, hearing of other's experiences, sharing my frustration, and having my feelings validated, helped me realize that I needed to consider respite care for John. As a baby step on the way to regular respite—a two-week stay in a personal care home—granddaughter Kim is coming to care for John for a week in October. I have my airline tickets for Saskatoon, but as John would be devastated if he knew I was going to see our son's family without him, we will be using what Angela Gentile called "therapeutic reasoning" and saying I am visiting my sister in Ontario.

That week-long holiday with the Saskatoon families will be like the pot of gold at the end of my rainbow—and the end of my summer journey of "letting go."

Christmas–2013

The temperature may have had the bite of a polar vortex, but it was a Christmas week wrapped in the warmth of family love and togetherness. The week was bittersweet happy, for as we hugged, kissed, reminisced, and played card and board games, we all realized that this might be the last time that all the family would be together for Christmas. There are age and health issues. John is 84, I am 81 and, our oldest son Darryl, 59, is gradually recovering his speech after a second stroke. In addition, we share our children and grandchildren with in-laws, and increasingly there will be the magnetic pull of the grandchildren's careers that may take them afar.

It's a good thing there was lots of love because there was also lots of "togetherness." After Darryl and Janis and their children with their spouses and kids arrived from Saskatoon, there were 15 of us tucked snugly into our beds every night. During the day and evening our Winnipeg children and grandchildren, partners and in-laws swelled the number within our elastic walls to 28 at times. With that many people, six of them ages one to six, the house was in a perpetual state of chaos.

In the past, even though overjoyed at having all the family here, I found the inevitable litter of keys and cameras, phones and iPads, crayons and paper, games and puzzles, and baby paraphernalia bothersome. In my need for organization, a place for everything and everything in its place, I would toss stuff left lying around into a big basket and everyone knew to look there for a missing item. The system worked fine when there were only the grandchildren, but became unmanageable as the family increased in number. This year I nixed the basket, turned a blind eye to all the untidiness and kept "top-of-mind" how lucky I was to have all the family home to make a mess.

Perhaps it was Darryl's stroke in August that changed my priorities. There was a lump of emotion in my throat as I watched Darryl's little grandkids nestle in beside him when he was sitting on the sofa, or I saw him down on the floor with seven-year-old Connor as they created a Lego original. Now he might talk only in words, not sentences, but he was still their beloved Poppa.

What a difference my change in mindset made! When I sat down to watch the kids at play, hold the babies, join in a card game, or just listen to the good-natured family teasing and joshing there was now no niggling inner voice whispering that I really should be tidying up. As a result, it was the most enjoyable and relaxed Christmas of my life.

Also, I had many helping hands. Loads of towels and linens were magically laundered and folded and the dishwasher repeatedly loaded and unloaded, while the grandchildren served as my sous-chefs—slicing, dicing, and grating as required.

Like always, it was a memory-making Christmas. Every morning we would wake to the sound of the baby-babble and bubbling laughter of Jason and Carrie's one-year-old twins as they trotted about the house. That happy music was irresistible. It pulled us out of bed with a smile, even after laughter-filled evenings of "remember when" stories and card or board games stretched to 3:30 a.m.

Listening to the twins brought back memories of Christmases past. "Remember when the grandchildren used to get up at five and huddle in the nook under the stairs to open their stockings—and their excited whispers and giggles?" I asked John, giving him a nudge. "Yeh," said John, and then, sadly, I realized his dementia had likely erased the memory and he didn't really remember.

The young generation has added a new Christmas tradition. We were introduced to Pickles, Santa's magic elf, who flew down from the North Pole to watch and listen to the children during the day, and then flew back to the North Pole at night to report to Santa Claus. Each night, with the help of our grandson Jason, this little stuffed toy found a new place in the house to perch. Spotting the elf in the morning was the great-grandkids' delight. A mischievous little imp was Pickles, because on Christmas Eve morning we woke to find the elf balancing on a branch of the Christmas tree, which was now decorated with garlands of toilet tissue! That night, after all the children were in bed, Pickles flew back to the North Pole until next year, fortunately trailing a jet stream of toilet paper!

Now that we have little people in the family again, Christmas has regained a special magic. On Christmas Eve, when the children were each given one present to open, there were excited cries of delight as layers of wrapping paper were torn back to reveal new pyjamas. This was followed by spontaneous disrobing, the donning of the new night-time attire, dancing and prancing about as they admired the logos on their tops, and finally settling down, sort of, for a group picture before heading off to bed to wait for Santa Claus. Even in this day of lavish gift giving, the simplest things delight.

On Christmas morning the grandchildren piled into Grandma and Poppa's bedroom to wish them a "Merry Christmas." It was three-year-old Rowyn who thought, "What about Great-Grandma and Great-Grandpa?" She padded down the hall to our bedroom and pushed open the door, which was slightly ajar. The room was dark, but she saw a sliver of light coming from the bathroom door, which wasn't quite shut. I turned quickly as I sensed the movement of the door. I saw a little hand and then Rowyn's upturned face. "Merry Christmas, Great-Grandma," she said in the sweetest loving voice. "Merry Christmas, Rowyn," I said and bent to give her a kiss. It didn't bother her one bit that her great-grandma was standing there stark naked!

There was no time to struggle into day clothes if I wanted to watch the excitement as the kids delved into their bulging stockings, so I quickly pulled on my Christmas pyjamas and joined the circle in the living room. "Love your pants, Grandma," was the reaction to my red jammies peppered with white polar bears.

First, the stockings revealed their secrets to cries of surprise and pleasure. I smiled inwardly as I watched Laura's kids' reaction to the hobby horses she had tucked under the tree. Emilee eyed hers with puzzlement for a moment and then, jumping to her feet, she attempted to twirl it behind her back and over her head like a majorettes' baton, a feat made difficult by the weight of the stuffed head on one end. Connor and Zachary immediately began sparring with theirs as if they were two swords! "Hey, those are hobby horses. You ride them," said Laura. Emilee obediently put the stick between her legs and did a few rabbit-like hops before abandoning it, while the boys simply dropped theirs and went back to exploring what was hidden in the depths of their stockings.

Time folded in on itself as I remembered my sister and I puzzling over why our children didn't play with their fancy hobby horses, with stuffed fabric heads and flowing yarn manes, when our plain stick horses had given us so many hours of fun. We finally concluded it was because horses were not a part of our children's daily lives as they were for us. And now, horses are even farther removed from our grandkids' and great-grandkids' experience. Times change, and I think it is time the manufacturers of hobby horses "rode a different horse!" Maybe they could learn from the makers of doctor's kits, as that toy was an instant hit with its stethoscope and ear thermometer. Having visited the doctor many times the kids knew exactly what to do with each instrument. Every day for the rest of their visit I would frequently come upon them, especially Emilee and Rowyn, huddled in a corner of the hallway, playing a doctor/patient game.

After the stockings had been emptied, the gifts under the tree were distributed. As that growing pile of torn wrapping paper and discarded boxes was accompanied by an appreciative "Oh" or "Ah," or "Thank you," I realized there may be many more gifts now than in years past, but the love that's in each gift given and received is just as strong.

When the "rip and tear" ritual was finished I had to get the hash brown and egg casserole for brunch into the oven. All the Saskatoon family were due to leave at 2:00 for Christmas dinner with the other grandma and grandpa, so while they showered and got dressed in their Christmas finery I was on my own in the kitchen. When all were ready to eat, I was still in my pj's. "Oh well, no time to dress now."

Brunch over and cleared away, there was the time pressure of getting the 22 lb. turkey on to cook while there were still strong young muscles in the house to get it up from the basement refrigerator and into the roaster. As the last person was out of the door at 2:00, I realized that in only three hours the stuffing, potatoes, Brussel sprouts, yams and carrots had to be ready to go in the oven for Christmas dinner for the Winnipeg families. Food prep had to take priority over donning day clothes.

Horrors! When the doorbell rang I was still peeling carrots and still sporting my polar bears. Horror was followed by relief when I opened the door to find it was the young adult grandchildren, who had decided to come an hour before their elders in case I needed their help. It reminded me of all the times they were my eager "helpers" in the kitchen when they were kids. Did I need their help now? Indeed, I did!

As the crew were removing their outdoor clothes I stared in surprise, and then erupted in laughter. The fun-loving four had made a pre-Christmas pact and were all wearing fleece onesies. "Well," I said, "If you young ones can wear fleece onsies, this oldie can stay in her flannel twosies." And I did. Now that is what I would call a "very" relaxed Christmas—and maybe the start of a new Christmas tradition!

Doggone It

Nestled in a curve of the Red River in Fort Richmond, King's Park has been part of our life for many years. Now back living in Winnipeg, John and I are again walking its trails daily.

An urban oasis for dog owners, bicycle riders, joggers, and walkers, it was created on the site of a former market garden. The park has a huge off-leash dog park, trails that follow gently sloping hills and valleys, a man-made pond, and a stream meandering under two arched footbridges. The hills are now too steep for our arthritic joints, but there is also a paved, wheelchair-friendly trail that traverses the perimeter of the park. This trail, edged by the tree-lined riverbank on one side, meanders through groves of elm, ash, and poplar interspersed by open areas giving panoramic views of the hills, pond, and bridges.

Bikers, joggers, and walkers are not the only ones to use the paved trails, however. Some dog owners seem to prefer the hard surface trails to the grass of the off-leash park. A sign in the parking lot says, "Dogs must be on a leash at all times on the trails and walkways." In addition, there are signs at every trailhead stating in red capital letters "WARNING TO PET OWNERS" and then in black lower-case "Pets must be on a leash." Apparently, a few dog owners in Fort Richmond cannot read.

When I was walking with a cane, any unleashed dog bounding down the trail ahead of its owner aroused mixed emotions of fear and irritation–fear of being tripped, and irritation with the irresponsible owner. Stopping to steady myself was not a wise move as a dog might see that as an invitation to come check me out, so I would always continue walking while keeping a wary eye on the beast.

Only once did a dog brush against my leg and though I stumbled, I did manage not to fall. For the first time I rebuked a recalcitrant owner. "Your dog should be on a leash," I said.

"Then he would pull me over," said a quavery voice. For the first time I raised my eyes from the big black dog to its owner. The old man approaching had an unsteady shuffling gait.

Now feeling a touch of contrition, mixed with sympathy, I said, "Then, you should really have him trained to heel."

Now that I use a walker, I no longer have the same fear of unleashed canines, but I still feel disgust at their caregivers' lack of respect for the rights of others. I still do not really look up at what is coming my way though. This became apparent one day this summer when I had an unforgettable encounter with a pair of dogs on a leash.

John and I, both with our walkers, were on the last half of our daily one-hour jaunt in the park, making our way along a section of the path edged by trees on both sides. I was in the lead with John following a short distance behind. As I was approaching a sharp curve in the path two large dogs on a leash came around the corner and immediately raced straight towards me while, unbelievably, their owner made no attempt to restrain them. I resolutely continued moving forward and at the last minute they veered and ran on by me. As they raced past, I caught a glimpse of their owner's rust pants and sandal-clad feet with painted toenails. "Stupid dogs and stupid woman," I was fuming internally.

And then I heard John say, "Hi big fella."

"I don't believe it," I thought as I continued walking. "He's actually talking to those stupid dogs and that stupid woman."

"Jean, come here," John called.

Now I was incredulous. "He expects me to talk to that stupid woman!" As I reluctantly turned around, I heard a familiar voice say, "Hi Mum."

"Lynn," I said in shock as I raised my eyes to see my laughing daughter standing there with her pair of friendly and well-trained dogs.

Recognizing me, of course they had wanted to run up and say "Hello," dog-fashion, and Lynn had sped along with them, expecting me to know the dogs, see her, and stop, happily surprised by her unexpected visit.

In the retelling of this event there have been many laughs at my expense.

But to me it is more than just a funny family story. It has made me ponder the question, why didn't I recognize those dogs I know so well? After all, dog-lover John did immediately. If I have lumped all dogs into one feared group—what other prejudices do I have that skew my perception?

Finding Humour In Dementia

Yesterday Lynn said, "Mum, you're laughing more. That's good to see." And I realized she was right. I am learning to live with John's dementia. It has become part of our daily routine for him to repeatedly ask me, "What day is it today?" or "What's up today?" or "What time is *Heartland* coming on?"

John has always liked horses. He enjoyed the challenge of training a horse to accept a rider. And when he began working with his father on the farm, horses were still used to do all the field work. So it is not surprising *Heartland*, which follows the adventures of an Alberta family raising horses on their ranch, is his favourite TV show. He can no longer follow the storyline, but there are horses and hay, and occasionally even the cleaning out of a stall.

And now, we may have horses standing on the city street outside our living room windows. Sometimes they even manage to get inside and stand at the foot of John's bed. At first I would deny their existence, which led to an angry rebut that they were "right there." Now I have learned to accept John's reality. As you ask for specifics—what are they doing, what colour are they, do they have halters, are they work horses or light horses—the phantoms gradually dissipate.

Images on the TV are also confused with reality. There are times, especially with ads where the speaker is looking directly at the camera, that John thinks the person is looking at him. In the evening, if there is a crowd scene such as a demonstration or a rally, he will say, "We can't lock up till all the people have gone." You turn off the TV and say, "There, they've all gone home," and he believes they have.

Dementia does not understand logic. From one angle the image on the TV screen in the living room can be seen in the dresser mirror in the bedroom. If John sees people in the reflected image in the mirror, he is convinced that the neighbours on the other side of that wall are looking into the bedroom. You can turn the TV off and on to show it is just a reflection. You can get him to feel the solid wall behind the mirror. It makes no difference. If the reflection is there, he still thinks he is being watched by people on the other side of that wall. So now the mirror is covered with paper.

Dreams can also progress to wide-awake hallucinations. The other morning John called out to me in some distress and I found him up and rubbing the top of his head. "What are we going to do about the dirt on the roof?" he said. "Oh, we'll get it cleaned off," I said. "But now you have to come have a shower." While I got him into his housecoat and down the hall to the bathroom he was still worrying about the dirt on the roof. Standing in front of the shower and rubbing the top of his head again he said, "Will the water go on the roof?"

"Yes," I said. "It will take off all the dirt." By the time he got out of the shower the top of his head was clean—and no longer a roof!

The rule is you never accuse dementia of anything. But walking into John's bedroom last Wednesday morning, I was so shocked I burst out, "John, what were you doing?" as I surveyed the mess.

"I didn't do it," he said.

"Well then, it's a mystery," I said.

What had once been a seniors' pull-up brief for incontinence was lying beside his bed, only now all its padding had been plucked out in bits and pieces, and what wasn't scattered about his bathroom and bedroom was lying in a little heap of white cotton tufts on top of the empty casing.

Fortunately, our son Darryl was visiting for the week. Hearing my startled outburst, he came to investigate and then helped in the clean-up. Later, with John safely out of earshot, I said, "Two wild dogs couldn't have done a better job." Darryl and I looked at one another, shook our heads in disbelief and collapsed in quiet laughter.

For months John has been complaining of a pain in his head. He has been scanned and x-rayed and had his eyes and ears tested and no physical problem, other than a bit of arthritis in his neck, can be detected. Two regular Tylenol, morning and night, were prescribed for the pain, but he continues to complain of the "rocks in his head," especially if we have visitors and he has a new audience. From time to time he will demand that I give him more pills, and when I explain that I cannot, he will become quite angry. When this happened one day last week, he demanded to talk to Lloyd. I dialled Lloyd's number, handed John the phone, and then listened on the phone in the computer room. John complained. Lloyd said, "Dad, Mum can't give you any more pills." John said he could not stand the pain. Lloyd said, "Well Dad, you have two choices, we can get an ambulance to take you to the hospital or I can email you."

"Email you!" I was amazed at our son's inventiveness and laughed silently as I continued to eavesdrop on their conversation. John complained again. Lloyd gave him the two choices: go to the hospital or let me email you. This scenario was repeated several times till John said, "All right, email me."

"Okay Dad, I'll go do that right now," Lloyd said. And that was the end of the pain for that day—a pain that I believe is as much a phantom as those horses on our street!

There *is* humour in dementia if you look for it. Yes, it is sad-funny, if you didn't laugh, you'd cry, but I *am* learning to laugh.

Never Again

"Never," I said. "I am never having bone surgery again."

In the 48 years since I had surgery to fuse my left hip, I have repeated this vow many times to family and friends. It wasn't because the surgery had not been successful. It was very successful, as that hip has been pain-free ever since.

It was the pain almost immediately after the surgery that has been branded onto my brain. When I was moved from the operating theatre to the recovery ward and then to my hospital bed, my lower body was immobile, encased in a plaster cast from my waist to my knees. Unfortunately, the cast had not been made large enough to allow for my after-surgery swelling, and as the hours passed, the pressure on my internal organs slowly increased, literally squeezing the life out of me. All I wanted was release from this crushing agony. "If I die," I thought, "It will stop hurting."

In a semi-delirious state, I was too confused to call for help, but fortunately, I had a roommate who realized I was in difficulty and shouted for a nurse. A nurse came, assessed the situation and disappeared, to return a short time later with the doctor. As they sawed the cast open down the front and the two sides sprang apart to accommodate my swollen body–what a sense of immense relief!

It was years after the experience before I was able to talk about my "death wish." Was it shock, shame or fear of the family reaction? Probably a combination of all three. When Lynn, who would have been 10 at the time of the surgery, heard the full story of that painful episode for the first time, her reaction echoed my own hidden feelings.

"Mum, how could you?" she said, shocked and hurt. "I was at home. I needed you."

"I don't know," I said. I tried to explain it didn't mean I didn't love her or the rest of the family. I was shocked, too, that I had had such a thought. But unbearable pain can drive everything else from your mind. I now understand why torture victims would confess to anything to stop their torment.

The new cast was more comfortable, but I was still in for another kind of pain. To prevent bed sores, it was necessary to flip me over regularly to lie on my stomach for a time. The first flip in the new cast made me cry out at the sharp stabs of pain. It didn't stop till they flipped me back onto my back. The nurses tried turning me onto my stomach once more and again the same sharp pain. At that point they gave up, awaiting consultation with the doctor. By the next morning the left side of the cast was stained red.

I was immediately sent for an x-ray. After checking the x-ray, the doctor assured me my hip looked fine. The conclusion was that a stitch had caught in the dressing and flipping me over had pulled a small part of the wound open, causing the bleeding. All the shifting about seemed to have loosened the errant stitch as, thankfully, I could now be flipped over without pain or additional bleeding. Eventually I was casted for the third time and sent home. This was September 1970–four years before Home Care was established in Winnipeg. There I was in a cast from waist to hips and all the way down my left leg, and we were on our own for the next six weeks. John juggled his job, caring for three kids, ages 10, 13 and 15, and being my nurse. Fortunately, we lived on the university campus, so he was able to come home at noon to make lunch and help me with my personal needs. Mornings and afternoons, I was on my own–flat on my back in bed. It was like going back to my childhood days, only now, instead of a chamber pot under the bed, it was a bedpan.

Darryl got home from school an hour before the other kids. This became our time for playing chess, or more accurately, for Darryl to try and teach me how to play chess. I would lie crosswise on the bed, on my stomach, so my head and shoulders extended beyond the mattress. An upturned cardboard box placed beside the bed held the chess board, while Darryl sat cross-legged on the floor, opposite me. Patiently, he explained the rules, day after day, but I never internalized the strategy well enough to ever win a game. I have never played chess since, but I loved spending all those hours alone with my son, trying to learn.

The weeks passed, my hip bone fused, and I was back in the hospital to have the cast removed. My body emerged white, flabby and muscle-less. Then began weeks of physical therapy to begin to regain muscle tone. At first, while lying on my stomach, I would struggle till I perspired just to lift my toes off the bed. Half-inch by half-inch and inch by inch I progressed until I could bend my knee up to a 90 degree angle and I was home again, still on crutches till I could walk independently once more.

That was then. This is now.

In the ensuing 48 years my legs have carried me hundreds of miles on my daily walks and holiday hikes. My right knee, on the longer and weight-bearing leg, has taken a beating. The cartilage in the knee joint has completely worn away and it is now painful bone-grinding-on-bone when I take a step with my walker. I wear a brace which can only stabilize the knee to a certain extent. I manage to make my own meals by sitting at a table to do all the chopping and preparation, but I can no longer shop on my own for groceries. When the family takes me out, it is in a wheelchair. If I do nothing, I know it is only a matter of time before I will end up in a wheelchair full time.

So, I have seen an orthopedic surgeon and I am scheduled for knee-replacement surgery in eight months. It will be a painful eight months, and I am hoping for a cancellation so my date for bone surgery will move up the wait list.

Never say, "Never."

My Summer That Wasn't

July 12th–after walking in excruciating pain for two years, the date of my knee-replacement and leg straightening surgery at Grace Hospital. August 1st–after a two-hour operation and three weeks at Grace Hospital, transfer by bumpy stretcher van to the Rehab Program at Deer Lodge Hospital. Then: seven weeks of stretching, strength and knee-bending exercises three times daily, plus an hour-long physiotherapy session to relearn how to walk. As I regained strength and balance I progressed from a high, platform walker to a two-wheeled walker, and finally, my own trusted and familiar four-wheeled walker.

If one must spend seven weeks in a hospital, I cannot imagine a better place than Deer Lodge. The staff were caring, encouraging, and friendly. Except for the soggy breakfast toast, the meal choices ranged from good to excellent. And there was always a choice. For example, two soups were offered at lunch–a cream soup and one with a broth base. In addition, you had a choice of two main dishes, and if you wanted something lighter, two sandwiches were on offer as well as a salad. Supper options included two main dishes with a choice of potatoes or pasta, two vegetables and a salad. And there was always a choice of at least two desserts, even at breakfast, which I found exceedingly odd. I would rather have been offered a banana at the beginning of my breakfast so I could have sliced it on my cereal.

Neither Jan, the physiotherapist nor Sara, the occupational therapist was enthusiastic about my moving back to my house to live alone, and suggested I might want to consider an assisted living option. When I was adamant that I could manage on my own, on the morning of September 20th Jan and Sara brought me home in a taxi for a trial run. They wanted to see if I could get in and out of a regular taxi, get up the step at the back of the house, unlock the door, let myself in, and get up to the main floor.

Then they put me through my paces—it was on and off the toilet, and then, barefoot, in and out of the shower. Moving on to the kitchen I had to demonstrate how I could carry things with a tray on my walker and retrieve items from the refrigerator and cupboards. Surprised to discover a map attached to the freezer, they realized I really did have frozen meals for at least three months. Then, it was on to the dining room. For the past year I had been sitting on my walker for meals as I was unable to push myself up from my armless dining chairs. This was something they did not allow at Deer Lodge. Fortunately, in preparation for the surgery, I had purchased some dining chairs with arms, but I had to satisfy them that I could get in and out of the chairs in both the dining room and the computer room. They also wanted to see how I managed the laundry, so it was down to the basement on the chairlift.

My bedroom was the last stop. I had already requested a hospital bed to assist in getting in and out of bed. They concurred and said they would order one from Home Care immediately. "That means I've passed?" I asked. Their verdict: I had done a good job of thinking ahead and preparing for life after surgery, and as soon as the hospital bed was delivered, I could come home.

Then things moved quickly. The home visit had taken place on Thursday morning, and Home Care delivered the bed the following Monday morning. Monday afternoon, I was discharged from the hospital and home at last. The date was September 24th, 10 weeks from the date of my surgery.

Three days later, Kyle and Charity arrived from Vancouver with four-week-old Forrest. The next morning I was cradling my eighth great-grandchild in my arms. Then two days later there was a "meet the baby" party at my house for all the Rhoda side of the family: 25 adults, two babies and a dog. Lynn and Neville, the proud grandparents, were hosts, and all I had to do was enjoy visiting with folks.

Four days later all the Saskatoon families arrived for Thanksgiving. With seven kids from four to eleven years of age the house was a hubbub of activity. To accommodate various sides of the family we were having our Thanksgiving dinner on Friday. Lloyd was contributing meatballs and cabbage rolls, Marlo was bringing pumpkin pies, and Lynn was in charge of the rest of the turkey dinner. The meal was extremely organized, thanks to the electric turkey roaster and having all the food brought over the day before. Lynn arrived early Friday morning to visit with the Saskatoon gang before commencing her cooking chores.

Then, in the middle of the morning the lights suddenly went out. "Oh no," I thought. "What time is it?" I asked.

"Ten o'clock," the family chorused.

"Is this Friday, October 5th?" I asked.

"Yes," was the answer I did not want to hear.

It was confession time. "I came home to a letter in my mail box informing me Hydro would be shutting off our power from 10:00 to 5:00 on Friday, October 5th to check the underground line," I said. "Lloyd was here with me and I read the letter to him. I guess he never thought about it being this Friday either."

Granddaughter Laura went out to ask the crew working on our bay how long the power would be off. They said it was a long line and it could possibly be off till 5:00. Lynn stayed amazingly calm, saying if the power wasn't back on by noon she'd take everything home and do the cooking there. At 12:00 Laura checked with the crew again. We could tell by her big smile as she came running back to the house that it was good news. "We will have power in half an hour." The huge lump of guilt that had been sitting in the pit of my stomach all morning began to dissolve.

In the end it was a wonderful Thanksgiving dinner "with all the fixings" as my mother would have said. And I felt very thankful, indeed, to be home and surrounded with the love of family.

On Monday, after all the family had left and I was alone in a quiet house I looked out at the backyard—the trees were a mass of golden leaves while under their canopy the flower planters sat bare and barren, all the limp and frost-killed annuals now yard waste.

I realized it was autumn. For me, the summer of 2018 was the summer that wasn't.

I Still Like to Cook

"No, I couldn't have," I think with dismay and disbelief as I spit out my first mouthful of chocolate cake topped with vanilla pudding sauce. What should have been a sweet and creamy sauce tasted like paste–creamy paste, but paste, nevertheless. That is what vanilla pudding sauce tastes like when the cook forgets the sugar.

I had just served this dessert to a crew of woodcutters who were now back at work, the saw screeching as the assembly-line of men shoved a tree, at even intervals, into the path of razor-sharp teeth. What were they thinking as they sat there and ate this stuff without a word of complaint? Why hadn't John said anything?

At the end of the day when I asked John that question he said, "I remembered the coffee."

Ah, yes, the coffee. I was a new bride serving coffee to our neighbours for the first time. We were living in the house where John grew up and these neighbours had been his best friends since childhood. However, they were virtual strangers to me. I was feeling insecure, an outsider in this tight-knit group. When I was bringing the coffee pot around for the second time, and came to John, he said, "Pretty weak coffee."

"Oh," I said, "you like strong coffee." I went out to the kitchen and half-filled the pot with coffee granules. When I returned, pot in hand, everyone watched silently as the thick brown liquid flowed like molasses into John's cup. "I hope that's strong enough," I said. Later, when we were alone, I wailed, "Why'd you criticize my coffee in front of your friends? You could've waited till they went home."

After these folks had become my best friends too, we shared many a laugh with the retelling of this story which, I swear, did get exaggerated over time, as stories do. But it was obviously a lesson John had learned well!

There was another coffee story that had many laughs at my expense. By then I had learned to make respectably strong coffee. As I circled the room with the coffee pot everyone was accepting refills. After filling Leonard's cup, I realized my pot was empty and I still had Bob to go. I decided to "wing" it. "Coffee Bob?" I said, knowing Bob never took a second cup.

"Yeh, I will," Bob said holding out his cup.

"You always say, 'No,'" I said, tipping my empty pot over his empty cup.

My cooking mishaps have been gist for stories since I was a teenager. My sister Lorna likes to tease me with this sad tale. Lorna and I were home alone. She was recovering from the red measles and I had volunteered to stay home with her while the rest of the family went to Saltcoats' July 1st Sports Day. They would be cheering for the Churchbridge ball team while no doubt snacking on Cracker Jack popcorn and triple-scoop ice cream cones. When the family were not home by milking time, as promised, the two of us fetched the cows in from the pasture. Still no family, so I offered to help Lorna do the milking. I had never milked a cow but surely it could not be that hard to do. After three cows, much teat pulling and not a drop of milk I gave up. I left my sister with the cows and went to the house to make supper, promising Lorna a special dessert. I had made countless perfect cornstarch puddings over the years and decided to use the same technique to transform a jar of canned peaches into a peach pudding. Lorna takes great pleasure in pointing out that even the dog rejected my glutinous concoction.

I have learned to take care when substituting ingredients. It was arranged that my mother and dad, who were on a fishing trip, would meet John's family on a Sunday at Madge Lake. John and I would be driving up to join them. It would be the first time the in-laws-to-be would be sampling my cooking and I aimed to impress. I would bake some apple pies. I had never baked a pie before–that was my mother's domain–but I had her recipe. It called for shortening, but only the best ingredients would do for this momentous occasion, so I decided to substitute butter. Picture an extremely hot day at the beach and my sad pies weeping greasy tears. Despite the advertising slogan, butter is not always best.

I did learn to make decent pastry but never on a par with any of my in-laws. Whenever we had a family gathering and they asked what they could bring, I always said, "How about pie?" They never refused.

My initial attempt at making bread was not much better than my first pies. I must have had the water too hot, killing the yeast. Of course, this would be the day that some of John's friends would decide to stop by. They soon found a use for the leaden loaves sitting on the cupboard, cutting off chunks which they took outside and threw at one another like missiles. They left laughing and giving John their sympathy. In time, I did conquer bread-making too, my mother even requesting my recipe for rolls.

My folks never raised fowl on our farm, so John had to teach me how to gut and dismember a chicken. It took a while before I could remove a bird's innards without a tea towel tied over nose and mouth. Slipping the knife between the bones at the joints looked easy when John did it—not so easy the first time I attempted it by myself. As my knife kept ramming into bone again and again, I gave up, went out to the woodpile, got the hatchet, and hacked that bird apart. Several gashes in the cupboard's tin counter top were evidence of my occasional application of excessive force. There was delicious oven-braised chicken for supper–you just had to watch out for bone splinters.

My three Winnipeg grandchildren have a favourite "Grandma goof-up" story. I was measuring the ingredients for a barbecued chicken casserole. Waiting to help stir the sauce and pour it over the chicken, the three youngsters watched my every move. I emptied a can of tomato sauce into a bowl and threw the can into the sink. I measured a ½ cup of ketchup, added it to the tomato sauce, and tossed the measuring cup into the sink. As I added brown sugar, cider vinegar, Dijon mustard, and chili powder I had a rhythm going–measure ingredient, add it to bowl, throw measuring cup or spoon into sink. But then I missed a beat. Carefully I poured Worcestershire sauce, the final ingredient, into a tablespoon–and tossed the tablespoon into the sink. Three shocked voices cried, "Grandma!" as the brown sauce flew in every direction. We now have four words guaranteed to get a laugh–*Remember the Worcestershire sauce?*

It was Christmas Day. An involuntary grunt/groan escaped, the sound competitive weight lifters make, as I heaved the 19.8 lb. turkey up and over the side of the electric roaster. "I can't do this anymore," I thought as I plunked the bird down onto the preheated rack. If this was going to be the last family turkey I cooked, I wanted it to be perfect. I reset the time and temperature controls just to be sure everything was correct. To free up counter space in the kitchen, the turkey roaster had been set up on the table in the computer room. It needed no tending. In three and a half hours, with no peeking and no basting, there would be a golden-brown turkey ready to remove from the oven.

In the kitchen, the cabbage rolls Lynn had dropped off in the morning were bubbling in the slow cooker. It was time for me to get the rest of the dinner ready to pop into the oven–savoury bread stuffing, bacon and cheese potatoes, Brussels sprouts in an oil and mustard seed dressing and sweet potato and carrot puree.

The family arrived right on schedule–Lloyd bearing his contribution to the holiday meal–meatballs in a mushroom sauce and pumpkin pies. When it was time to get the turkey out of the oven I recruited Lloyd to do the heavy lifting. As I removed the lid from the roaster, we both stared in disbelief. "Mum, it's not brown," Lloyd said.

"It's not cooked," I said, poking the slightly warm, pallid, yellowish-white turkey with a finger. "It will be full of deadly bacteria by now."

"It will be fine when it's cooked," Lloyd said, resetting the roaster dials–correctly this time.

No one was willing to wait for the turkey, so our Christmas dinner was meatballs in a mushroom sauce, cabbage rolls, cold sliced ham, and the side dishes I had prepared.

The last Christmas turkey I cooked may not have been perfect–but it was certainly memorable. On Boxing Day, it made great hot turkey sandwiches smothered in gravy–and no one got sick.

Multitasking–drying my hair while cooking

Making bread in the bread maker

Comfort Foods

"Remember Mum's scones?" my brother Bill asked on one of the rare occasions we get to see each other these days.

"Oh, yes!" I answered.

"No one makes scones like hers," he said wistfully. "Everyone else's are light and fluffy."

I knew exactly what he meant. Our mother made wonderfully light and flaky baking powder biscuits. Her scones, made from a recipe with no butter or lard, were the opposite–flat and dense triangles–baked till both tops and bottoms were a deep golden brown. Slice them open while still warm and you had two crusty triangles, not at all like a biscuit, to spread with melting butter and honey, jam or jelly.

"Her cinnamon buns," Bill went on. "And bread pudding. Nobody makes bread pudding anymore." He made these comments while we were enjoying a late lunch in the Boston Pizza in Yorkton. Lynn, Neville, and I were on our way home to Winnipeg after a weekend with the Saskatoon families, and had stopped in Yorkton for a short visit with Bill and Vel. As their house has steps I can't navigate, we had elected to meet in the restaurant.

I don't know what prompted Bill's reminiscing about food from our childhood. None of us were eating anything remotely related. Lynn and Neville were sharing a platter of nachos, I had chicken quesadillas, Vel had a salad, and Bill was tackling a king-sized hamburger. Maybe it was just having someone sitting beside him, who could share his childhood memories. As our numbers dwindle, three of the seven of us claimed by cancer, and the remaining four separated by many miles, I sense we are becoming more nostalgic when we get together.

I do know, after Bill's comments, that the remaining four-and-a-half hour drive that day past snow-streaked fields and quiet towns, was warmed for me by images of the comfort foods of my childhood.

Unlike her thrifty no-fat scones, Mum's cinnamon buns were a high-fat gooey extravagance, unequalled by any others I have tasted since. "The secret to good cinnamon buns," she said as I watched her lather butter on the rectangle of bread dough, "is being generous with the butter and brown sugar." And my, was she generous!

Oven toast was another high-fat, but less extravagant treat. Lard or bacon fat was spread on slices of bread which were then sprinkled liberally with salt and pepper and baked in the oven till golden. Topped with honey it was one of our special breakfasts.

A couple of times lately, I was delighted to find bread pudding on a restaurant dessert menu, only to be bitterly disappointed each time by the dense, cake-like slice I was served. It bore no resemblance to the soft and custardy bread pudding of my memory. I suspect we don't make it anymore because, with freezers in our homes, stale bread is no longer an issue to be dealt with. This was borne out when I checked my updated versions *of Betty Crocker* and *Better Homes and Gardens* cookbooks. Both had a recipe for bread pudding, and both had instructions on how to dry your bread!

Another soul-satisfying dessert on a cold winter day was our mother's baked rice pudding studded with raisins and spiced with cinnamon. Cooked at low heat in the oven for hours, it was checked every 30 minutes or so, when the brown crust which had begun to form on top would be stirred back into the rich and creamy mixture. No quickie stove-top, saucepan rice pudding comes close to its slow-baked goodness.

Economical pudding was another oven-baked dessert staple, but unlike rice pudding it could be table-ready in 40 minutes. Economical in every sense of the word, the batter used no fat or eggs, you baked it in the same dish you mixed it in so there was only one bowl to wash, and the pudding formed its own brown sugar sauce as it baked. We ate it with a splash of thick pure cream to cut the sweetness.

Butchering day brought two special treats. One was "crackles"–pieces of pig skin baked till crackly crisp. The other was spareribs–the long, uncut curved rack of pork ribs, seasoned with salt and pepper, baked till a crispy dark brown and served just like that–wonderfully crunchy, with no sauce to detract from the marvelous flavour of the meat. The first time I ordered a rack of ribs in a restaurant I was not expecting the strip of short-cut ribs, slathered in barbecue sauce, that I was served. I have learned to enjoy, even love them, but they are not the ribs of my memory.

No chickens were raised on our farm, but every year our mother would buy chickens from family or neighbours. In those pre-freezer days she home-canned jars of chicken, which were then stored on shelves in the cool earthen cellar below the kitchen. You can buy nothing like it today–succulent pieces of chicken encased in their own pale, shimmering jelly. On a hot summer day biting into that cold chicken, with droplets of its jelly still clinging to it, was a delectable and refreshing relief from the heat.

As I was writing this I wondered, "Do my kids have favourite foods from their childhood?" I asked each one separately, so they wouldn't be influenced by one another's choices.

The first response I got from two of the three was, "fried bologna."

I was dismayed. "Was that the most memorable thing I fed my kids?"

Fried bologna was part of my childhood and I liked it. In fact, I liked it a lot, and, yes, it did appear on my family's dinner plates from time to time, till the kids were in their early teens. That was when a diagnosis of high cholesterol changed my cooking and eating habits, and by extension, the family's. Fried bologna was banished, never to appear at our family table again. "That's it," I thought. "Its absence is what's made it a nostalgic memory."

Their other choices were healthier, though Klik, mustard, and lettuce sandwiches only marginally so. Baked beans and scrambled eggs made the list. So too did several oven-baked main dishes–meatloaf, chicken and rice casserole, porkchops with Spanish rice, and shepherd's pie–not surprising as I made a lot of oven meals. By using an automatic oven timer, I could come home from work to a table-ready hot meal. My adult children continue to enjoy these dishes in their own homes now.

I was surprised when only Lynn mentioned sweets. "Marshmallows," she said. "When I got my allowance, I would buy a bag of marshmallows." She's 57 years old and still likes marshmallows. If I have a bag in the pantry when she comes to visit, she is sure to snitch a few. "Butterscotch cookies,"

Lynn continued. "And butterscotch bars and the chocolate muffins I would get out of the freezer after school." For years these high-fat treats have been relegated to Christmas baking, replaced by low-fat, high-fibre options such as oatmeal cookies and bran muffins.

I was not prepared for my gut reaction to my children's choices. It was as if every less than healthy food was an indictment of me as a mother. In each instance I was quick to come to my defence, describing how I had changed. Conversely, every healthy selection felt like a vindication.

I didn't evaluate my mother in terms of the rich, high-fat, high-salt food she served her family, so why was I measuring myself by a different standard?

My conclusion: Diets are, for the most part, a reflection of the society of their time. In the relatively unmechanized 1930s and 40s, folks lived more active lives and easily burned the calories in the high-fat food they consumed. With increasingly sedentary lifestyles, by the 70s we were becoming more cognizant of the relationship between diet and health outcomes. This was also a period when women were joining the workforce in larger numbers. We can see both these societal changes reflected in our changing family food choices and cooking and baking strategies.

I wonder if 20 years hence, when my children's childhoods are more distant, will their favourite food choices be the same? And even more interesting to contemplate: What societal changes will impact the food choices of my grandchildren and great-grandchildren?

Already, I see the impact of globalization. A quesadilla anyone?

Bread Pudding

Combine: ½ loaf of stale bread cut into bite-size cubes,
½ c white sugar and ¾ c raisins
Beat together and add to above dry ingredients:
4 c milk, 4 eggs and ½ t vanilla
Sprinkle top with 1 t nutmeg or cinnamon
Bake 300° F for 50 to 60 minutes or till knife inserted comes out clean.
Serve with cream or whipped cream. Serves 6-8.

Two Weddings–Two Stories

The following stories were presentations I made at the weddings of two of my grandchildren–Kyle and Marlo.

To the Dude and Dudess

This happened long ago, so long ago that Kyle was only five years old. He was spending the weekend with us at the "Bog 'n Bush," our country acreage, and the two of us had walked out to our garden. Although it was a pleasantly warm morning Kyle was wearing his beloved red and black, imitation leather jacket, that originally belonged to his much-admired, older cousin, Jason.

We were now on our way back to the house. The path was a narrow swath mowed through the tall grass so we were walking single file, with me in front, when I heard, "Cool dude, eh Grandma?"

I turned to look and there was Kyle strutting along, his jacket off, flung behind his shoulder and suspended from two fingers. "Cool dude, indeed," I said, managing to suppress my smile till I turned back up the path.

That was 24 years ago, but the memory always makes me smile as I see it as if it were yesterday, that proud little five-year-old, adopting a teenage nonchalance far beyond his years.

Now that little boy is 29 years old and a cool dude, indeed, in ways that truly matter–kind, generous, loving, and fun-loving, family-centred, and industrious.

Today, I didn't try to hide my smile as I watched my cool-dude grandson embark along this new path in his life, making new memories. And as he pledged his love to Charity what I clearly heard him say was, "Cool Dudess, eh Grandma?"

Kyle and Charity–February 18, 2014

A Recipe For Happiness

On a pleasantly warm day this July, Marlo and I were preparing to have lunch out on the deck. As Marlo was wiping the dust off the table with a damp cloth, a little black bug was scurrying across the tabletop, trying to escape that swiping cloth. It needn't have worried. Marlo picked it up and placed it gently down on the deck, and then proceeded to finish cleaning the table.

Now, I admit that I am not overly fond of bugs crawling on my table. "How come you didn't kill that bug?" I asked.

"He wasn't hurting anybody," Marlo said. And with those words she flashed me back in time 25 years.

I was caring for Kyle and Marlo before and after school and at noon. We had just finished lunch when I raised my eyes higher than usual, and for the first time noticed a huge spider web stretched across a corner of the room at ceiling level. "Oh, my goodness," I said. "That's the biggest spider web I ever saw!" I left the table, went out to the kitchen, and came back with a broom.

"Gramma, why you got the broom?" Marlo asked.

"I'm going to get rid of that spider web," I said.

A six-year-old dynamo leaped in front of me, barring my way. "Gramma, you can't do that," Marlo said. "That's the spider's home!" Eyeing my horrified granddaughter, I lowered my broom and meekly returned it to the kitchen.

Over the years I have watched Marlo mature into a kind, loving adult– one who will still stand up for what she thinks is right. And in the last few years I have watched as she fell in love with Eric, and then, as their mutual love deepened and grew stronger. Having witnessed the two of them working on several projects, solving problems together with never an argument, I know how compatible a couple they are. Two kind and loving people coming together in marriage–a recipe for happiness.

And Eric, if you should accidently bug your wife–and this happens occasionally in the best of marriages, I assure you–do not worry. Marlo *likes* bugs and will still *love* a bug-a-boo!

Marlo and Eric–August 19, 2017

PART 6
In Memory

1971
Back Row: Leslie, Denis, Dad, Bill
Front Row: Me, Lorna, Leila, Mary

1999
Back Row: Denis, Mary, Bill, Leslie
Front Row: Lorna, Me, Leila

Dear Mum:

It is 48 years since you died, and I miss you still.

There were family milestones I wished you had been here to share–my university graduation, our kids' marriages, the building of our "dream" retirement home, the births of our grandchildren and great-grandchildren (your great and great-great). There are still so many times I think, "I wish Mum could see this." They are simple things I know you would have taken great joy in: my pots overflowing with flowers in riotous bloom, the Amur maple flaunting leaves of red, blue shadows of leafless tree branches traced on drifts of snow, irregular mounds of white clouds silhouetted against an azure sky.

You taught us there were stories everywhere, even in the sky. Sitting two-deep in the back seat of the Model T Ford on our way to town on a Saturday night, there would inevitably be some quibbling between us older kids and the younger ones sitting on our knees. You would divert our attention to the clouds in the sky, describing what one looked like to you, and then asking us what we thought it might be doing. Our fussing evaporated as we studied the sky and made up "cloud stories" the rest of the way to town.

Your storytelling was a gift you shared with us. I remember one miserable, rainy, autumn afternoon when we came home from school to find you sitting at the sewing machine, busy with the weekly mending. Unable to play outside because of the weather, we kids were "goosing around" till you began to describe how you were once caught in a torrential rain on the way home from school, and dripping water on the mat inside your back door, had to strip, sheltered by a towel, before being allowed to step further into the house. You had us hooked. We were soon sitting on the floor around your sewing machine listening to more of your real-life stories. Rainy day tales progressed to sunny berry-picking excursions with horse and buggy, to teenage tricks played on college roommates, to people met and places seen in your teaching days.

Our aversion to doing supper dishes evaporated when you began to use that time to retell, chapter by chapter, a favourite novel. When Anne of Green Gables, Pollyanna, Heidi, Robinson Crusoe, or Gulliver, among many other storybook friends, joined us in that kitchen, they transported us to another time and place. The dishwasher never complained about the piles of dishes to be washed, not even if an eagle-eyed dish-dryer returned a not-quite-clean dish to be rewashed. Dishes were replaced on cupboard shelves without clatter so we would not miss a crucial part of the story. We were sure to turn up on time the next day as you always stopped the story at a suspenseful spot that left us eager to hear the next installment.

You were a bit of a "ham" and did love to show off your phenomenal memory by reciting–maybe emoting would be more accurate–long "story poems." Our all-time favourites were those two tales of love, betrayal, and revenge–*The Highwayman* by Alfred Noyes, and Robert Service's *The Shooting of Dan McGrew*. Another of our frequent requests was Service's "over-the-top" reaction to the Arctic cold–*The Cremation of Sam McGee*.

We grew up with stories. As far back as I can remember, bedtime meant story-time. You would always read two stories, the first a children's version of a Bible story. We would gather at your feet and one of us would get our back rubbed while you were reading. I can still feel the wonderful warmth of your rough, work-worn hand inside my pyjama top, moving slowly up and down my back on the nights when it was my turn.

When we were very young, the second story was a nursery rhyme–and its rhyme and rhythm was our introduction to poetry. We were very proud of ourselves when we could recite all the verses of longer nursery rhymes such as *Jack and Jill* or *Mary Had a Little Lamb*. Then you introduced us to fairy tales and folktales. *The Three Little Pigs, Goldilocks, Little Red Riding Hood, Cinderella, The Ugly Duckling*, and many more fuelled our imagination and were fodder for play-acting games. When we were older, we suffered with Black Beauty and Beautiful Joe, lolled on a raft with Tom Sawyer and Huckleberry Finn, fell down the rabbit hole with Alice, and were blown into the world of Oz with Dorothy. I cannot remember the bedtime story ever being missed because you were too busy or too tired. And that bedtime ritual continued long after we were all independent readers, I think because you enjoyed it as much as we did.

Starting school meant one thing to me–I was going to learn to read stories, just like you.

I remember the first library book I brought home from school. I arrived home to find you hanging clothes on the line after a busy laundry day. Excitedly, I showed you my book and began to read it aloud, walking beside you as you moved along the clothesline. This was an easy-to-read book, but it was still far above my limited reading ability. Whenever I came to a word that stumped me, you provided it so readily that I felt like I was reading the book by myself. Only now, when I look back on the incident, do I realize how I must have slowed down your clothes-hanging task. How easy it would have been for you to say, "Not now Jean. Wait till I get the washing on the line." But by giving me your time and attention, you were showing me you shared my excitement at learning to read.

By the time we left home, we all had personal libraries built from our Christmas books, our birthday books, our books for keeping our garden patches weed-free, and for any other excuse you could find for giving us a book. We three girls each had our favourite titles. Lorna liked the Oz books, and Mary the Pollyanna series, while my heroines were feisty Anne of Green Gables and Emily of New Moon. Today, just like you, reading is one of my favourite recreational activities. I am never lonely if I have a book. And over the past eight years I have been exploring the other side of "story," going back in time and mining my memories as I work on writing a memoir for my family.

Thank you for nurturing my love of literature in so many ways. In fact, you raised a brood of avid readers. What a life-enriching legacy to leave your children.

Thank you, too, for the hours you spent coaching me through Grades 3 and 4 by correspondence when I was home-bound recovering from osteomyelitis. You were the kindest, most caring teacher I ever had. Over those years, despite my demands on your time, you never, ever, made me feel that I was a burden. You made sure I was never bored, keeping me supplied with books and activities like paper dolls that I could play with while flat on my back. You also shaped my attitude to the disease, assuring anyone who tried to "poor Jean" me that I was "just fine." It is a belief that has sustained me through some other rough patches in life. In addition, after I graduated to a wheelchair, you found ways to make me feel I was contributing to family life—I could watch baby Leila in her carriage while you went out to the garden, and I could peel the carrots or shell the peas you brought back.

You planted rows and rows of peas, for eating fresh out of the garden in summer and to can for the barren months of winter. On pea-canning days you would be up extra early to pick the pods while they were still cool and crisp. A morning's picking could yield one or two big tubs of peas to be shelled, and then, many bowls of shelled peas destined for the canning jars.

Shelling those big pickings became a family activity. We would work in the shade, not for our comfort, but because we didn't want any sun shining on those picked peas. You would sit on your stool, your speckled blue enamel colander on your lap, and we kids would sit on old backless chairs in a circle around you, shelling our peas into plain bowls on our laps. It was repetitive work: split a pod open with your thumb and then pull the row of exposed pea babies into your bowl–again and again and again, hundreds of times till those tubs of pods were empty. It sounds tedious and boring, but it wasn't because as we worked you told stories, or we played word games.

From time to time, you would leave to go into the house–to make a meal or to start putting peas into sealers. As you left you would give your colander to one of us, and we could shell into it until you came back. By the time the last pod was shelled, we would each have had a turn with the colander.

After you died and Dad asked each of us what we would like to have as a remembrance, I chose your colander. It represented so many things–your ability to transform mundane tasks into memorable family times, your love of sharing stories, and your conferring of special status, equally, to all of us. And today, with chipped enamel and bent rim, rusted in spots and one handle loose, it sits on an open display shelf in my kitchen, bringing you close in memory.

You loved picking berries and your enthusiasm was so infectious I learned to love it too. Sometimes some of the other kids would come along if Dad did not have a job for them, but usually it was just the two of us.

Together, we braved scratchy wild raspberry canes to fill our pails with the nubby red fruit, sweeter than any tame raspberries. We helped one another clamber over deadfall to reach Saskatoon trees, their branches heavy with grape-like bunches of indigo blue berries. "Pick clean," was your dogma. In your Scottish, depression-trained mind it was scandalous to leave ripe fruit behind to go to waste. It was a lesson I learned well. "Pick clean," I reminded "grazing" John so frequently when we were picking berries that at the word "pick," he would echo "clean" before I could say it.

With your treadle sewing machine you epitomized thrift. Flour sacks, bleached to remove the red and blue brand names stamped on their front, were transformed into bloomers, slips, and bed sheets. Once, lacking a mattress when one youngster had outgrown the crib, or was being pushed out by an impending arrival, you stitched several of those sturdy flour sacks together to make a huge bag which we older kids "helped" you stuff with straw to make a tick mattress. Patching and mending clothes was a weekly ritual. Adult clothes worn past repairing at armholes, collars, and cuffs were recycled into dresses, blouses, shirts, and jackets for the kids. Nothing was wasted. All the fabric scraps were saved and used for hooked rugs or stitched into "crazy" patchwork quilts. As a little kid I loved a quilt, made with a heavier tweedy fabric, that made its way to my bed. Tucked in for the night, I would rub the rough textured fabric with my fingers till I fell asleep.

The school Christmas concert was a special event as it was the occasion for a new dress made with new fabric. My favourite was the year you made three identical beauties for Mary, Lorna, and me, differing only in size. They were made of slightly textured navy crepe with smooth and silky red satin bodices. The navy boleros were trimmed with six shiny gold buttons, three on each side. The finishing touch was a navy band that crossed the red bodice as it joined the two sides of the bolero. Your reward was our cries of delight as we tried them on.

You were not as creative about the dresses you sewed for yourself. They were practical and easy to sew–collarless round necks, short sleeves, and gathered skirts. They differed only in the printed material you chose. I remember admiring a dress Auntie Lucille often wore on Sunday visits–navy with white polka dots and a white lace collar and puffed sleeves trimmed with lace–and wishing you had a pretty dress like that. In pictures taken before your marriage you are wearing fashionable flapper-style dresses. I wonder what caused your change in attitude to style. Was it a lack of time and money, combined with your weight gain as the babies kept coming?

As a rural schoolteacher, with classes of up to 40 students in Grades 1 to 8, you had to be organized. You applied those organizational skills to your housekeeping chores. "You should be able to reach into any drawer or cupboard in the dark and find what you are looking for," you maintained. Each day of the week had its allotted task, Monday–laundry, Tuesday–ironing. You never said you hated ironing, but I know you did, because as the last item came off the ironing board you always sang, "Praise God from whom all blessings flow." You were dumbfounded when you learned a sister-in-law ironed tea towels, underwear and sheets. Your rule was, "It gets ironed only if it shows." On Wednesdays we frequently heard the maxim, "A stich in time saves nine," as it was the day for mending. Thursday and Friday were reserved for sewing and baking. On Saturday the bedsheets were changed, kitchen cupboards washed, linoleum floors scrubbed and waxed, and furniture dusted. As soon as we were able, you involved us three girls in helping with the Saturday cleaning. You divided the work into three areas–bedrooms, living area, and kitchen–and we each had responsibility for one area each week, in rotating turns. Once our work was done, we were free the rest of the day to do whatever we wished. Along the way we learned not only basic housekeeping skills, but also that work comes before play.

In addition to the weekly tasks, you also fitted in there somewhere all the seasonal jobs. In summer the garden was planted and weeded, and the produce picked and processed. Jams and jellies were made from all those wild berries we picked. In spring and fall there was a thorough housecleaning with no spot left untouched. Winter days were spent sewing clothes, stitching and assembling quilts, knitting mitts and scarves, hooking rugs, and crocheting or tatting lace and doilies. You used to say, "A man works from dawn to dusk. A woman's work is never done." I saw how true it was. After supper Dad would sit in his special chair, listening to the radio while you were always busy–folding laundry, mending, sewing, knitting, helping us with schoolwork, and at the end of our day, reading that never-missed bedtime story. Sunday was your day of rest–your day to read a book for pleasure.

In later years, after we kids were grown and gone, you had time for other interests. You and Dad joined the Agricultural Society and over the years won many prizes for the yard and garden. Flowers took over more of your garden patch, and you planted a rose garden that you could enjoy from the kitchen window, winning many flower show awards for your gladiolus, lilies, and roses.

You never were afraid to tackle something new. When Grandpa was spending the winter with us after his crippling fall, you seized the moment. With a hammer and handsaw, and supervision from Grandpa, you constructed a long-wanted closet and bank of drawers in the upstairs hallway. Later, with new confidence, you transformed my very small bedroom with built-in furniture, including a bed, closet, dresser, and desk.

From the time we were young we admired your independent spirit, listening to your stories about your Model T Ford and how you learned to crank it till it started, and later, fix tires and broken wires.

In the early 1940s, a special meeting was held at our school. A survey was being conducted to identify wartime supports that were available in the country. On the line that asked you to identify your preferred job in support of the war, you wrote "airplane mechanic"–no traditional job such as a Red Cross nurse, or even a factory line-worker for you. Afterwards you laughed at the absurdity of the exercise, as you had a family of six by then, but you couldn't hide your satisfaction with your unorthodox response–another spark of that independent spirit.

John loved to tell the story of his first visit to meet my family. After introductions, Dad retired to his chair, newspaper, and radio, while you made coffee and brought out a freshly baked cake. "My first sponge cake. Now watch this," you said, repeatedly pressing down on a piece of cake (fortunately not iced!) with your hand. "See, it pops back up just like a sponge. Isn't that amazing?" John was stunned, scarcely believing his eyes, as he watched you having so much fun with a piece of cake. He would learn to appreciate the enjoyment you took in living, whether it was your latest baking craze, your vegetable garden, a shrub rose in full bloom, a vase of gladiola stems, a crossword puzzle, or a new board game. You loved games, particularly word games. As adults, whenever we visited, we would end up playing a board game or a card game after supper dishes were done. After you received your terminal cancer diagnosis, until you were so weak you had to go to the hospital, you spent almost every morning playing Scrabble with a friend. It was that amazing zest for living that made your untimely death seem so unfair.

In early November 1970, a little over three months before you died, you and Dad visited me when I was in the hospital in Winnipeg for the second stage of my hip surgery–the removal of the cast. Your diary entry reads, "Saw Jean in hospital. Cast off. Can't move, leg muscles weak." As you were leaving on your last visit before going home, you kept turning around and looking back at me again and again as if you did not want to go. It would be the end of the month before you learned your cancer was active once more and surgery was not possible, but I think you already suspected something was wrong, and that you might not see me again.

We did meet once more, after we drove through a blinding January blizzard to visit you when you were the one in the hospital. You were looking thin and frail, but had not a word of complaint, instead focusing on what everyone in the family was doing. I have one especially sad memory of that visit. John and the kids had left to get some snacks, and we were alone in the room. You were lying on your side, facing me, your one hand lying, wrinkled and veined, against the white hospital bedspread. I was sitting in a chair by your bed, but because of my fused hip, unable to lean forward to take your hand. When the others returned, you rolled onto your back, and in the ensuing conversation the moment was lost. Hugging you as I was leaving, I whispered in your ear my thanks for everything you had done for me. It seemed so inadequate. As we left, I was now the one looking back again and again, knowing I would not see you again.

I found the family viewing the night before your funeral difficult and disorienting. The person lying in the coffin did not look like you–cheeks puffed out to remove the wrinkles, face powdered and artfully touched with blush to have a healthy glow–the reality of age and illness denied. It was many months before I could replace that false image with a real-life memory picture of you. That experience motivated my search, later, for a funeral home willing to forgo all chemical and cosmetic preparation after death.

For two years following your death I lived in a deep, dark fog of depression. While I moved through the routines of daily life, I felt no joy. I think it was a result of stress overload, mourning your death, while also coping with the many months of recovery from hip surgery and its effect on the family, and also resuming university classes full-time. I resisted medication, focusing on exercise and a healthy diet, and gradually the fog dissipated as the sunshine of a "feeling" life returned.

I feel so fortunate that fate has given me so many more years than you were granted. I have tried, and am trying, to use them well.

This letter is the thank you that I didn't express fully enough when you were still here. Thank you for the treasure trove of good memories you have left me. Thank you for the model of a life well-lived.

You were the most important person in my life, the most important influence in shaping who I am today. Thank you for being you.

Love you forever,

Jean

Vera Margaret (Fraser) Putland

April 03, 1902–February 12, 1971

Dear Dad:

I want to thank you for the good memories and the life lessons I have learned from you. And I want to air some of the things which I would never have been able to tell you, face to face, but which have been lurking like dark shadows in the corners of my memory.

I have two favourite memory snapshots of you. On any Sunday morning in summer, when I woke up and looked out my bedroom window, I knew what I would see. There you would be, attacking the weeds in the shelterbelt south of the house. As I watched the rhythmic motion of your arms, I could imagine the scritch, scritch of the hoe as it sliced through the weeds. I knew if I kept watching I would see you reach into your pocket, take out the chocolate bar you had bought in town last night, peel back the wrapping, take a bite, and then carefully rewrap and return it to your pocket as you resumed hoeing. I knew if I got close enough, I would see a little smile tug at the corners of your mouth at some thought that pleased you.

It would be the same smile I had sometimes spied when I was at the well by the hog barn, fetching milk for supper from the can suspended in the cold water, and you were carrying pails of water back and forth from the well to the pig troughs. When I asked what you were smiling at you would never tell me, so I stopped asking.

Why are those two mind-pictures my favourites? I think because they reveal the father I want to remember—the person who could find pure pleasure in work and the act of growing things, like it was nourishment for the soul. You told me once that if the time came that you could no longer grow things, life wouldn't be worth living.

The hundreds of trees you planted transformed our home from a bleak house perched on a bare hill to a place of shelter and beauty. The sunlight dancing on the leaves of the ash and maple groves was a daytime delight.

The rhythmic sighing of the wind passing through the spruce boughs was my night-time lullaby. Those trees, as well as all the trees you planted along the streets in Churchbridge after you and Mum retired from the farm, will be a living legacy for generations to come.

Our yard was a model of tidiness. No cut-off board ends, coils of leftover wire, or rusted and leaky pails were left lying around. There was a junk pile in an out-of-the-way spot and all junk went into that pile. The tools in your workshop were returned to their designated spot after use. I would not have wanted to be the kid who left a screwdriver or pliers lying on the workbench.

Our playhouses in the bush north of the house did not match your standards. They were an "eye-sore" you said, and you wanted to banish us from the bush. Mum, who valued creative play over tidiness, came to our defence and the playhouses stayed.

I think you were proud of your success as a farmer. I think Mum was proud of your success too and projected that pride so that we children shared it. I know I was proud of all your "firsts." Quick to adopt new technologies, you and your two brothers jointly owned one of the first tractors in the district, a green monster with huge steel wheels with protruding lugs. Later, you were one of the first in our area to replace your binder and threshing machine with a swather and combine.

Your innovation was not restricted to your farming, however. You surprised and delighted Mum with a gas-powered washing machine when washing clothes by hand was the norm. Years before the power grid was a reality on the prairies, you used a wind turbine and a bank of batteries in the basement to provide our own power. I can still feel the wonder of that first day we had electric lights. I was leaving for Winnipeg with Mum the next day for surgery to straighten my hip, and I went through the whole house turning every light on and off. I felt like a fairy godmother. Pulling a cord and getting light was akin to waving a wand and, "Presto," magic.

You also watched marketing trends and used them to plan your farming strategy. The time to increase your hog operation, you maintained, was when the price of pork was low and other farmers were getting rid of their breeding sows. Then, when prices rose, as they would, you would be ready with an expanded, market-ready herd.

There was the year that, anticipating a rise in the price of flax, you reduced your wheat acreage and planted flax. That flax crop was the first time you and Mum had "extra money." I remember the expression on Mum's face, a combination of bemusement and pride, as she exited the bank after depositing that $3,000 cheque. "I can't believe what just happened," she said. "The *bank manager* held the door open for me."

While your life demonstrated the value of hard work and innovation, it was also a lesson in thrift and living within your means. The depression may have forced you to be thrifty, but it was a virtue you practiced the rest of your life. Reminiscing about your life for your eulogy, we recalled how anything that could possibly be useful was never thrown out. Denis described the pails for old nuts, bolts, washers, and nails that you kept in your workshop. We all laughed fondly at the memory when he said, "I grew up thinking new nails came bent and rusty." "Remember his old boat motor?" Leslie said. "He took it with him when he moved to BC. It was literally glued and patched together, but he kept it running for many years."

There was nothing broken that you weren't convinced you could fix. Flat tires were repeatedly patched, and boots and shoes were resoled again and again. Chairs were re-glued, and when glue would no longer hold them together, wire stretched from leg to leg did the trick. Replacements for broken handles on shovels, forks, rakes, and hoes were as close as the nearest bush.

There was more laughter as we recalled your oft-repaired lounge chair, which collapsed under Neville, on his first visit to your retirement home in BC. "You didn't sit on it right," you snorted, and carted it off to your workshop to repair. All offers to replace it were refused with, "Why would you want to do that? There's nothing wrong with it. It just needs to be fixed." We shook our heads in disbelief when that lounge chair came with you when you left Qualicum Beach many years later, to spend your last years of life with us.

You were not a demonstrative father, but maybe you were just in step with your times, a world away from today when hugging and air-kissing virtual strangers is the norm. Though the words were never spoken, we knew you loved us and would be there for us if we needed you. I know you had to borrow money to pay my medical bills in the days before Medicare, but I never ever heard a word of complaint about the increased financial hardship in those depression years. Though you had to leave school at Grade 5 to help on the family farm, you, as well as Mum, valued education, and ensured all four of us girls, as well as Leslie, were trained in careers of our choice. You supported Bill and Denis in their decision to become farmers, and when Mary and Gordon had an opportunity to buy the local grocery store, you were there with the financial help they needed.

However, I often felt getting your approval was dependent on meeting your expectations–that there was one right way–your way.

I think that mindset explains your relationship with Bill. I remember how excited you were when he was born–your first son after three girls. You went to town that day and came back with a present for Mum. That glossy wooden plaque, with its blue and green mountain view, hung on the living room wall for many, many years. The picture never changed, but with the passage of time, your feelings toward Bill seemed to. He was a free spirit with an independent mind and a stubborn streak that seemed to rub you the wrong way. Mum observed that you "ordered" Bill, while you "asked" Denis. The rest of us, including Mum, were teary-eyed when you used your belt and laid a licking on him. That he was tough, and able to hold back the tears, just increased your anger. Unfortunately, the uneasy relationship between you and Bill continued into his adulthood. You were free with verbal criticism when he didn't conform to your standards in some area, while ignoring his many accomplishments. And when we visited you in BC, Bill resented your expectation that we camp in your yard, rather than a lovely treed park a few miles away, but he never told you how he felt.

I felt your disapproval when I was able to walk again after my bout with osteomyelitis. You kept telling me I didn't need to limp; it was just a habit. Eventually proved wrong, when a doctor insisted that my left leg was considerably shorter due to the destruction of the hip bone, you took my shoes to a local shoemaker and had the left heel built up. You never discussed it with me. It was simply, "Now you won't limp so much." I hated those shoes, but I wore them. Complaining or refusing was an option I never considered. Many years later, when I was attending Normal School in Moose Jaw and I took my shoe to a city shoemaker to have a strap repaired, the fellow took one look at my footwear and said, "What amateur did this?"

I promptly bought new shoes for this shoemaker to work on. By building up both sole and heel he made them more balanced and comfortable than the shoes I had been wearing.

In my late 30s, after surgery to fuse my hip, I asked the orthopaedic surgeon if I should get my shoes built up. He said it was up to me. I promptly threw away all my ugly built-up shoes and bought an all-new fashionable shoe wardrobe.

In my old age, because of the arthritis in my knee and spine, I am wearing built-up shoes again, this time prescribed by an orthopaedic doctor. He says I should have been wearing them all those years when I wasn't, as the years of limping have caused the problems with my back. So, you were more correct than I want to admit. But your reason for doing what you did still rankles. It was not to make it easier for me to walk. It was so I didn't have such an obvious limp. I interpreted that to mean you were ashamed of my physical disability.

Lying awake in bed one night I overheard a bedtime conversation between you and Mum that I wish I had never heard. I don't know what preceded this comment, but my ears perked up when I heard Mum say, "We do have good looking kids."

"Except Jean," you said.

I was stunned and hurt by your response. I expected you were then going to say, "Because of her limp." But you said, "Her lips stick out too far." The next morning I studied my reflection in the mirror. My lips looked fine to me. Nevertheless, I walked around for a day or two with my lips pressed tightly together till someone at school told me I looked silly. It is amazing the way scratchy little burrs of memory stick.

You were not a person to give praise. I cannot remember a single incident where you said, "Good job" or "Well done." You expected nothing less. On the other hand, if we didn't measure up, we heard about it.

Adulthood did not exempt us from your criticism, but then your negative comments were frequently not to our face. Rather, you voiced them to others in the family. Now I wonder why I never said, "Stop Dad, I don't want to hear about it. You should tell *them* how you feel." I wonder if, in some secret buried recess of my mind or heart, there lurked a speck of sibling rivalry, and I felt reaffirmed or endorsed by hearing you find fault with one of the others. I had to know that when I was absent, I would be the one being criticized.

A few years ago, I learned that after your first visit to our "dream" home, you told others in the family we would never be able to pay for it. With its soaring ceilings I know it was unlike any house you had seen, but it is too bad you didn't talk to me about your concern, as I could have set your mind at rest. In fact, I learned your lessons on thrift so well the house was paid for as it was being built. If you had known, perhaps you wouldn't have spent the last few months of your life under the delusion we were caring for you because we wanted your last few thousand dollars. At the time that accusation was a stone striking my heart.

I realize the family was not the only recipient of your criticism. I can recall many times over the years when, in the privacy of your home, you often ridiculed and were cuttingly critical of others whose farming practices or political beliefs differed from yours. Unfortunately, as you aged, and your health declined, this part of your personality became more pronounced, sometimes resulting in face-to-face rudeness.

After Mum died, and you remarried, you were often insensitive to our stepmother's feelings. You joined her in her house in BC where she had lived as a widow for many years. It would have been only common courtesy to discuss with her any changes you wanted to make to her yard. She was devastated the day she came home from shopping and found that you had decided to enlarge the garden and had taken a chain saw to the row of trees outside the bedroom window. You, of all people, someone who had planted and nurtured so many trees, should have had more empathy. She loved those trees. For 15 years she had opened her eyes to the shifting shades of their greenery. She said that every time she looked out that unsheltered window to the lane behind the house, she felt a mix of anger and hurt.

You had been married more than 25 years when your cuttingly unkind words about her one remaining sister were the breaking point, and our stepmother suggested you should go back to the prairies. That was when you phoned and asked us to come and get you. Later you admitted that twice before you had made her so angry that she had asked you to leave, and you had said if she ever did it again you were going. It was an unhappy end to a long second marriage.

The last two years of your life, when you lived with us, ended up being stressful for both of us. I did not expect it to be that way. I was happy to take you into my home. I knew how much you dreaded the thought of ending up in a nursing home after you saw your sister, May, restrained against her will, in a wheelchair. I was determined that it would not happen to you. Also, I had seen how caring and patient Mum had been with her father when he stayed with us, and I wanted to do the same for you, while realizing Grandpa may have been easier to live with than you would be.

I knew you had been unhappy and depressed the last few years in BC as your health declined after two heart attacks. You were also living with Parkinson's disease, impaired vision due to glaucoma and macular degeneration, and increasing deafness. However, you seemed excited about moving back to the prairies and being closer to your family. Everything went well for the first three months. The turning point came one afternoon in November when you announced life wasn't worth living and you were going to get up in the middle of the night and go lie in a snowbank.

I was not about to let you commit suicide on my watch. My frantic and teary visit to the doctor resulted in a prescription for anti-depressants, but it was downhill from there.

Your criticism of my cooking became constant. I should not have been surprised because, in the years when I helped Mum in the house, she would never let me try a new recipe because she said you wouldn't like it. And I knew your second wife found cooking for you very frustrating. You were a meat and potatoes man and scathingly described our favourite casseroles and stir-fries as "Jean's mixtures."

When, in desperation, I offered to cook separate meals for you, planning your menus with you a week in advance, the rest of the family told me I was making a huge mistake. "Now he knows he has you," they cautioned. They were right. You wanted ribs. Then they "weren't baby back ribs." When they were baby back ribs, they "didn't have enough sauce." The next time they had "too much sauce." The steak was "hard to chew." Pounding the steak to make it more tender "destroyed its flavour." Hamburgers "weren't brown enough" or "overcooked." Cooking porridge properly was apparently beyond me. I learned I didn't even slice dill pickles the right way!

As I write this, it all sounds so silly, I wonder why I couldn't laugh it off at the time. But I couldn't. Cooking, which had always been a pleasurable activity for me, became a source of daily stress. I should have said, "Okay Dad, I've tried to make meals to please you. No matter how hard I try I can't do it. So, I give up. From now on I'm making one meal for all of us. You have a choice. You can continue to live with us, or you can decide to move."

That is what I should have said, but I didn't. I refused to give up. I kept on trying to please you and became more and more frustrated, and resentful, with each passing day. Thinking about this over the years I have finally come to realize I am just as stubborn as you. It was really a battle of wills and neither one of us won. We both lost a lot that could have been.

Taking your medication was another contentious issue. When you were in the nursing home for a week of respite while we visited family, they discovered you were pocketing your pills. My reaction to this information was hurt, shame, and anger. Hurt–because I had been trying so hard to give you good care; shame–because I hadn't been aware of your trickery, so obviously was not doing a good job; and anger–that you hadn't been upfront and told me what you were doing.

As soon as I brought you home, I told you how I felt, and explained that when you flushed your pills down the toilet, you were wasting taxpayers' money as our provincial Pharmacare paid for your medication. I should have waited till I cooled down before I talked to you because I know frustration and anger were in my voice. Your response was, "You're just as bad as that BC bunch." I guess you tried the same trick there and got the same reaction.

Many months later, when you again decided not to take your meds, you did tell me you didn't want them. In the meantime, I had come to realize you had the right to refuse if you wanted to. So, we both did learn something from our confrontation.

However, when it came down to the wire, you were not as ready to die as you thought you were. There came the day when you felt so ill you asked for an ambulance to take you to the hospital. Then, when I walked into the hospital with your walker and other necessities, you shouted, "Do you see her? That's my daughter and she put me in this place. Some daughter she is." I knew you were delusional, but that really, really hurt. I cried all the way home.

Back on your medication and discharged from the hospital, you said how wonderful it was to be back in your own bed. The euphoria lasted two days before you began swearing at me when I tried to follow the drug regimen I had been given by the hospital. I realized I was the proverbial cat that gets kicked at the end of a bad day, but it still hurt all the same.

For the last few months of your life, when we were physically no longer able to care for you at home, you did end up in a nursing home. I will forever feel guilty that you died in the middle of the night, no family by your side.

Before you died, I wish I would have had the courage to ask you to explain what I overheard in 1942. I was still confined to bed and sleeping downstairs when I heard whispered conversations that included a woman's name. Later, in the kitchen, behind closed doors, there was a meeting of several hushed voices with a church minister. With a child's intuition, I suspected you had done something bad involving this woman. We never again visited that family.

It was years later before I learned Mary, Lorna, and Bill, although sleeping upstairs, had all heard enough to know something was wrong. We had each, secretly, been trying to bury this ghost.

Reading Mom's diaries seems to confirm our suspicions. In the appropriate time there is an entry that says simply, "I got a terrible blow. Rest of day wasted." The next two days record that she is "thinking my own thoughts" and "slept little last night." The meeting that we know took place is never mentioned.

I now marvel at Mom's strength of character. Life seemed to return to normal. With six children, the youngest a baby, and the oldest bedridden, her options were limited. But by facial expression, actions, or words, she never revealed a hint of hurt, stress, or animosity. I think she was determined to protect us kids.

We suspect that was not your only betrayal. That is the trouble with ghosts, impossible to keep confined, they keep creeping back to cloud our perceptions. After we read Mom's diary, Mary shared a concern she had been carrying secretly for years. There was a day she had walked into the barn and found you and the hired girl alone – and the girl was crying. And now, we wonder about the necessity many years later for all those trips with your snowplane to help a certain widow.

The possibility of your sexual impropriety, or worse, infidelity, is still incomprehensible to me. But there it is—the amorphous ghost floating among all the other memories. You should have had an opportunity to give your side of the story. Now it is too late.

I wish we would have had a happier relationship during your last years. I know that I was not as empathetic as I should have been. That learning helped me care for John as his dementia changed our lives many years later. Thank you for all the life lessons you taught me by example. Yes, some were cautions, showing me what I did not want to emulate, but they led to positive learning too.

And I will forever treasure those wonderful memory snapshots I have of you—so happy to be growing things and enjoying your work.

You were my dad and I loved you, and I love you still.

Your daughter,

Jean

Edward John Putland

July 9, 1907 – August 7, 1999

Dear Mary:

We were only 13 months apart in age, but we were quite different in personality and interests. You made decisions based on emotion; I am ruled by reason. Your decorating style was traditional and frilly; I opt for modern and cubic. You had a weekly appointment with your hair stylist; I get my hair cut every five weeks. You took great care of your complexion with numerous preparations; I wash my face once a day; You chose your stylish outfits with care; I wear whatever isn't in the laundry that day.

Those differences were evident from an early age. Our playhouses in the bush were very distinctive. You marked your boundaries with pink and blue tie-dyed curtains. I used rough twine tied from tree to tree. Your mud pies were artfully decorated with berries and leaves. I might stir some berries into mine. You always loved clothes, and as an adult could recall every Christmas dress Mum had made for you. I can remember only one special Christmas dress—the year Mum made identical dresses for Lorna, you and me. Writing a "Memories" piece, you recalled your first store-bought outfits: "Mine was a red crepe with a red velvet bodice. It was gorgeous and I felt like a queen! Alas, all too soon I outgrew it and Lorna had the dubious pleasure of my hand-me-downs. Another one that sticks in my memory is a navy crepe with a square neckline and a peplum trimmed with lime green. It was very smart and trendy." I draw a blank here, having no memory of a first store-bought dress.

Our sibling rivalry must have started at an early age. Mum said when we were little and got into a scrap, she would tie the two of us to the rails at the foot of their bed, just far enough apart that we couldn't touch one another, till we promised not to fight. No doubt I was a bossy older sister. In the earliest family pictures, I am standing with my legs firmly planted, staring straight at the camera while you are usually looking down more shyly. Many years later, when we were both middle-aged, you said you always envied my self-confidence.

It didn't help our relationship that we started school the same year, when I was six and you were five. I loved school and embraced reading. You struggled and wanted to quit but didn't dare say so because you had begged and begged Mum to let you go too. In that "Memories" piece you said, "Jean was an excellent and willing scholar and I walked in her shadow as a mediocre student. But, once, just once, I not only beat the rest of my class, but Jean as well, in a spelling bee!" You opted out of the last year of high school, choosing to take a secretarial course instead. When I saw the shorthand that secretaries had to learn back then, it looked harder to me than my studies. There are different kinds of learning, but I never told you that.

I was very happy to have you and Lorna join me in Yorkton for my Grade 12 year as I had been very lonely the year before. While we did have lots of good times together, you did find living with me a trial. I was not the tidiest of teenagers. Schoolwork always came first, and when I was working on an essay the floor would be littered with discarded pieces of paper notes. It didn't bother me if the pile accumulated for two or three days, but it drove you wild. Did I care enough about how you felt to clean it up? I'm sorry to say I didn't. No wonder, with your first paycheck you moved out into a place of your own with nary a piece of paper on the floor.

It seemed there were always three girls in any grade we were in from Grade 1 through high school. You always formed a close "best-female-friend" relationship with the other girl and I was left out. Although I never admitted it, I envied the ease with which you made friends, but I know I would never have been a "close" friend like you, confiding your innermost thoughts to another person. Your "best friend" changed with the years, but all your life you always had someone who was a bosom pal.

Throughout our childhood and teenage years, we both had a talent for aggravating the other person in many subtle ways, while convinced of our own innocence or right to be aggrieved. Instead of being upfront with one another, Lorna said we would complain to her individually, and after she listened to our grievances, we would get on with living together. Your tone of voice could turn "I see you changed your hairdo" or "Where did you buy that skirt?" into a criticism. And me, I used joking, which you didn't appreciate, to needle you or to present my "right way," or I simply ignored what you wanted me to do.

Casting back in memory, I realize Bill and Denis never teased and made fun of you the way they did me. When they were young you probably would have bonked them on the head, and when they were older, I think they realized you didn't share the same sense of humour.

Thank goodness as adults we did finally learn to accommodate our differences and embrace our sisterhood. Shared experiences of marriage, children and running a household no doubt helped. And we each knew that we could count on the other if we needed help. For example, when I was pregnant with Lynn, and we were preparing to move back to the farmhouse after two years at the school teacherage, you helped John hang new wallpaper. Many years later, when you came to Winnipeg for hip replacement surgeries, you asked me to go to all your appointments with you and take notes.

My favourite memory of our adult interactions was a day in our mid-40s when I was visiting you for the weekend. I was jokingly pointing out the differences between us when you got the last word with an hilarious come-back. I was sitting on your bed watching you get ready to go out for dinner. As you were artfully applying foundation and blush, I said, "When I realized John took less time than I did to get ready for work because he didn't have to put on make-up, I threw all my cosmetics in the garbage. I've never worn make-up since that day. And then," I continued, "I calculated all the hours I spent putting my hair in rollers and sitting under the hair dryer. It totalled two weeks of my life every year. I got my hair cut short the next day and I never curled it again."

You turned to look at me, your eyeliner pencil poised in your hand. "Well," you said dryly, "I hope you never figure out how long it takes you to get dressed in the morning."

Sadly, tragedy and loss did shape your adult life. In October of 1952, when you and Gordon were engaged and your wedding date was fast approaching, in fact the wedding invitations had been mailed, Gordon became very ill. In that epidemic year, he, as well as many others, had contracted polio. You followed him to Regina, promptly got a job as a stenographer, and stayed by his side through the many months of recovery and physiotherapy.

You were incredulous when you learned there were people in Churchbridge who assumed you would be calling off the wedding because of Gordon's disability. It never occurred to any of us in your immediate family either. We knew you were in love, and we had not been raised to abandon someone in a time of need. Quitters we were not.

Gordon was released from the hospital in the summer of 1953 and you were married that September. Gordon could walk a bit with the help of leg braces and crutches and managed to stand for your wedding photos.

At first, you hoped Gordon would be able to farm with his brother, but with his physical limitations, it was proving difficult. Like a drowning man reaching for a straw, when the two of you heard of a "faith healer" in Humboldt, you made the move. You found a secretarial position, while Gordon attended daily "therapy" sessions. Unfortunately, this self-professed healer ended up being as much help as the drowning man's straw.

It was a difficult year for you. You hated your dingy crowded living accommodations. You didn't like your job either. And you lived with the daily concern that you might end up being the sole family wage earner. A secretary for life was not what you had envisioned.

Then, in 1956, a door to a more promising future opened. The grocery store owner in Churchbridge was retiring and looking for a buyer. Gordie's Groceteria became a fixture in the town till you retired many years later. It was a perfect fit for the two of you, with living quarters attached at the back of the store. Gordon could wait on customers from behind the counter, and even restock shelves, from the wheelchair he ended up in for most of his life. A physically strong woman, you did the heavy lifting of bags of flour and boxes of goods. I never heard you complain about the hard work. I know you preferred it to sitting behind a typewriter all day. And you could move freely back and forth between house and store as needed.

You did sometimes complain about the lack of privacy. The store was on a busy street corner and folks on the sidewalk were right outside your kitchen and living room windows. And your evenings could be interrupted by someone knocking on your backdoor wanting to pick up some "necessity" from the store, even though you were officially closed.

In 1958 your daughter, Kathy, was born. She was followed three years later by your son Blaine. Your children were the centre of your life. One of your great pleasures was sewing outfits for the two of them. Your life was all that you had hoped for. And then tragedy—at 18 months of age your adored Blaine developed bronchitis and died in hospital. The family grieved with you, but it was not enough. For many, many months you were a human zombie, living each minute thinking of what you would be doing with Blaine at that moment: bathing, dressing, feeding, playing on the floor with him, and on and on all day. You said Mum finally helped to bring you back to reality by reminding you that you still had a daughter and she needed you.

But it was a life-altering loss. You turned to religion to help fill the aching hole in your life. And you became over-protective, maybe even controlling at times, of your daughter, and later, your grandchildren. Also, you gained a lot of weight, I think unconsciously trying to find solace in food. Over the years you tried many diets, always gaining back the weight you had lost, and more. Fortunately, you were tall, had good posture, and a great sense of style, so you carried your weight well, and when you dressed for a special occasion, you looked smart and stately.

All that weight did wreak havoc on your joints, resulting in multiple hip and knee replacements over the years. After your last hip surgery you complained of great pain when you sat in a wheelchair. You experienced weight discrimination in the hospital when they dismissed your complaints, saying that was the largest wheelchair they had. Finally, an x-ray revealed a crack in your hip joint, which eventually led to the diagnosis of bone cancer. This was your second encounter with cancer, having had surgery for breast cancer years before. To be closer to the Cancer Clinic in Regina, you now moved in with your daughter and family.

Sadly, shortly after the move, you fell in the hallway, striking your head on the wall and breaking your neck. You died three days after being admitted to the hospital. Lorna, who lived in the Regina area, was the only one of us, your sisters and brothers, to see you to say goodbye.

This letter is the goodbye I never got to say. I apologize for all the times I annoyed you and forgive all the times you annoyed me. I am so glad we finally learned to appreciate one another and realize our mutual love.

The unexpected suddenness of your death was a shock to all of us. We tried to find comfort in the nurse's comment that your accident and speedy death, saved you from a long and painful death from bone cancer.

Your death came only a year after Gordon's death. As you faced death you looked forward to a reunion in heaven with Gordon and Blaine.

We were not ready to let you go. You were only 75, the first rent in our sibling group.

In loving memory,
your sister Jean

Mary Elizabeth (Putland) Yanke

December 8, 1933 – January 28, 2008

Dear Denis:

I want you to know how much pleasure I get from displaying and using all the pieces of your wood art that I own—what you humbly called your "wood stuff." You were a craftsman with the eye of an artist. Every graceful vase, bowl, and dish is unique in design, influenced by the grain of the wood. A part of you is in every room in my house – a vase with a seasonal arrangement welcomes visitors in the entry hall, display shelves in the kitchen and living room conveniently hold many bowls and dishes ready for use, a lidded dish on the coffee table offers nuts, a "catch-all" tray on a bedroom dresser waits for pocket keys and coins, an ornamental jug sits on the floor in the study, and so on, from room to room. You always said I was your best customer. Everyone in my family has some of your work, given as gifts, as do many friends. Each piece is a special treasure, because now there will never be any more.

I wept tears of sorrow and outrage at your funeral. The timing of your death, though not unexpected, seemed so unfair. Yes, you had an incurable type of cancer–chronic myelomonocytic leukemia (CMML) aggressive type two. However, your chemotherapy regime of seven consecutive days a month was doing its job and keeping your blood count stable. You and Diann had adapted to spending the week of your treatments at the cancer clinic's hostel in Regina. The two of you made the best of the situation, using any free time between treatment sessions to visit Lorna and her family in nearby Avonlea, and to make brief car trips, exploring the surrounding countryside. As the many needles used to administer the chemo left your tummy area bruised and sore, you bought loose pants and held them up with braces, appearances be damned.

Almost immediately after receiving your diagnosis, you began preparing for the day when Diann would be left alone. In 2012, you sold the farmland that you had taken over from Mum and Dad when they retired, retaining the 40 acres with house, barn, your woodworking shop, and Diann's extensive lily garden. As you surpassed the most optimistic time estimate of survival after diagnosis, your sense of urgency increased. Not wanting Diann to be isolated on the farm in winter, you decided to move to Churchbridge, buying a house with a double lot so Diann could continue to grow her prize-winning lilies. You bought the house in spring, and then sold the farm acreage, stipulating a possession date in fall, so that Diann would have the summer to transfer her most treasured plants to the yard in town. In fact, tending the large farm yard, which she was determined to leave in good shape for the new owners, and developing the yard in town, kept Diann so busy that you went to two of the week-long chemo sessions that summer by yourself.

July 19, 2014, you had your auction sale, the final step in ending your life on the farm. What mixed emotions you must have had that day as you watched your household goods, farm machinery, and woodworking equipment go, piece by piece, under the auctioneer's gavel.

I know that as I walked the grounds, taking some last pictures, I felt gut-wrenching nostalgia. The old bush had given way to a rose garden, but here was the spot where we once had our playhouses. The veranda was now closed in, but this was the side of the house where we fed our stick horses their sand "oats." The hill was now a gravel driveway, but I remembered the grassy slope we rolled down in summer, and the snow-covered incline we skied down in winter.

And I realized you knew, as I did, this farm had been the culmination of our parents' dream of owning their own farm, and when they bought it they envisioned it being passed down through the generations, just like the Baimbridge/Putland homestead where Dad had grown up. But it was not to be. Your daughter Roslyn was married and living in Calgary, and your son Ross had allergies that precluded farming as a career. Strangers would be making their memories here.

In the week after the sale you moved into your house in town. Life was progressing according to plan, but with a more optimistic prognosis than you had dared hope for. You were being given a new drug for which they had little data, but your doctors were happy and hopeful as it was keeping your blood count stable.

Then in November your plans went off the rails. Diann began to experience numbness in her feet, progressing to her arms. In December, almost two years after your diagnosis, you were told she had an inoperable brain tumour. By the time we visited her in the hospital in January, her entire right side was paralyzed. You and Roslyn, who had flown in from Calgary, were taking turns at her bedside. You, doing what you did so well, could still make Diann laugh by finding humour in everyday situations.

In late February Diann's final struggle ended and yours began. At her funeral you looked bewildered and lost. "I was supposed to go first," you said. You went to one chemo treatment after her death and said you couldn't go to another. You had begun to have problems swallowing in the last weeks before Diann's death. Now the problem became much worse, so you were eating and drinking very little. In a phone call you told me tests could find nothing wrong and you knew "it's in my mind." You were seeing a grief counsellor who suggested it would help to go back to doing the things you used to enjoy, like playing online chess with your chess buddies around the world. But you said you were too weak and slow to play, and of course you were from lack of nourishment. In your weakened state you developed pneumonia, refused treatment, and within a few days that was the end. Your last words were, "The job is done." Yes, it was. A gentle, loving man, you had lived a good life.

"The job is done." Yes, four short months of grief, more efficient than cancer, had done its work. It seemed so sad and unfair that you and Diann had never had a chance to enjoy your new home.

And now I am left with memories.

You were the shyest kid I had ever known, clinging to our mother's leg whenever we were away from home. Whether we were visiting friends or relatives, or shopping in town, Mum was your bulwark, your safety net. To the deep embarrassment of us four older siblings you spent the first two weeks of school sitting at your desk, head down, refusing to say a word.

There was still a trace of that shy and quiet kid in the adult you became. A self-taught computer afficionado, you enjoyed playing chess with about 25 people around the globe. You and Diann did become personal friends with some of the players and their families, exchanging visits on a regular basis with folks in the Netherlands and the U.S.A. You had friends close to home too.

Though an inveterate teaser, you were a kind-hearted man. There was your warm hug whenever we came for a visit. There was your teasing at breakfast when you laughed at me eating cereal with skim milk. "You might as well use water," you said. In the years when I resisted buying a computer, you said I was the illiterate one in the family, even if I was the only one with a university degree. You had a gift for finding humour in everyday situations, with a joke presented in such a deadpan manner it took a minute to realize you had just said something very funny. When you were undergoing treatment for your cancer, you wrote that you were scheduled for "more cat and dog scans." I heard your acceptance of the reality of the diagnosis when you said, "It does not sound that great, but it is what it is." And then you mused, "If it had not been for the blood tests, we would be holidaying in sunny Arizona right now, happy as can be. In the end maybe it would have been for the best." But you were only 73, too young to give up without clinging to hope, no matter how ethereal.

Yes, I have many good memories. And I have more – I have your "wood stuff" – a tangible connection to you that lives in my house and my heart.

With my love,
your sister Jean

Denis Gordon Putland

December 27, 1939 – June 16, 2015

361

Dear Lorna:

I am writing this letter to thank you for being a special sister. Kind, fun-loving, and a stunner in the looks department, you never lacked for friends—girls and boys. Though I had to share you with others, you were always my best friend.

For years, until as adults Mary and I learned to accommodate one another, you were the peacemaker between us. Never judgmental, you would patiently listen as we each privately unloaded our grievances. Usually that was all we needed—a sympathetic sounding board. However, if necessary, you were adept at helping us find a common middle ground between our opposing views.

I spent a lonely Grade 11 year in high school in Yorkton till Mary and you joined me the next year. The three of us hung out together and shared a few guilty pleasures—crispy wafer cookies, Eatmore chocolate bars, and those creamy chocolate éclairs. You were always more dexterous with your hands than me and I convinced you to set my hair in pin curls every night, though that deal was equally advantageous as you charged me 25 cents a night.

When I had the table and floor in our shared room strewn with papers as I worked on an essay, you shielded me from Mary's disgust. Years later you would joke about how I worked too hard at school—how I never won a medal when I graduated, but you did—for being the most improved student.

Another high school era story you liked to tell was to describe the dismayed look on the Home Ec. teacher's face when she learned you were my sister. That look said, "Oh no, not another one!" as it was no secret I did not like Home Ec. classes and the result of my sewing assignment did not even rate the rag bin, going straight to the garbage. You would conclude your story with how you became the teacher's favourite student when she discovered you could understand a pattern and sew a straight seam.

As I said, you were more dexterous with your hands than me. In fact, when I was expecting my first baby you patiently taught me how to use a pattern and helped make gowns that I was proud to have my infant wear. Over the years your sewing skills kept your growing family well dressed, and combined with your artistic flair, created costumes for special days and community events. Also, for many years you augmented your family income by upholstering furniture—a self-taught skill I viewed with awe.

You looked for laughter in life and opportunities to share your sense of fun, often laughing at yourself. Two plaques that hung on your kitchen wall attested to your attitude toward cooking and cleaning. One read, "The only reason I have a kitchen is because it came with the house." The other said, "I can't clean house and save the world at the same time."

Your "pork chop" story, which you liked to tell, made fun of your lack of interest in cooking meals. You were widowed and living alone in a senior's apartment when your daughter Susan invited you for supper and asked what you would like her to cook. "Pork chops with mushroom sauce," you said.

"But Mum, you make that all the time," Susan said.

"Susan, you can't cook pork chops in a toaster," you said.

You liked other people's stories too. You had a hearty laugh when Lloyd told you about his ridiculous mother calling him up and asking him to take a pinch of a spice and measure it, so she could compare his pinch to how much her pinch measured, and how frustrated I got because he wouldn't do it. On my next birthday I was surprised to receive a parcel from you as we never exchanged birthday gifts. As I reached into the padded envelope I felt nothing. "Would you spend that much on postage to send me nothing as a joke?" I wondered. It was possible. On a second try, reaching down into the depths of the envelope my fingers felt–something. Out came three small measuring spoons joined by a ring. When I saw they were for a dash, a pinch, and a smidgen I collapsed in uproarious laughter. Then it now became your story to tell!

On one of your weight loss kicks you were keeping track of how many miles you were riding on your indoor bike. I congratulated you when you phoned to say, "I want to make it from Avonlea to Winnipeg and I'll soon be there." A few days later when I heard my doorbell ring and opened the door to see you standing there below the steps, a regular bike by your side, I stared stunned and speechless. "I told you I was biking to Winnipeg," you said.

"You couldn't have," I sputtered.

"Yes, I did," you said, laughing at my incredulous expression. Finally, you gave a wave and Merv pulled up the driveway in your car. We shared many a laugh over the years recalling that trick.

You delighted in describing the fun you had dressing up for Halloween or April Fools' Day and assuming a different persona to mystify the students on the school bus you drove. Even your young grandchildren and great-grandchildren thought you were Lorna's weird sister, Mabel. I do believe you had a latent actress lurking within.

You used creativity to compensate for lack of money. Your patchwork beach blankets were practical wedding gifts that kept on giving year after year. Frames from the Dollar Store became personalized birthday gifts for children and grandchildren when they encased the original poems you created, each line beginning with a letter of his or her name. At Christmas time your grandchildren looked forward to their very own bag of frozen lefse, a Norwegian potato pancake that was a family tradition. When we moved back to Winnipeg after 22 years at the "Bog 'n Bush" we received, encased in one of those frames, a collage of pictures you had taken on your visits.

You took a child-like pleasure in your collections: salt and pepper shakers, silver spoons, stuffed animals, and cookie jars. When the stuffed animals threatened to overtake your small apartment, you tied strings to them. Each great-grandchild was invited to pull a string and take his/her chosen toy home. As for those cookie jars—the grandchildren and great-grandchildren knew any sitting on your kitchen counter would be holding some of their favourite cookies. And, fittingly, at the end of the celebration of your life, each grandchild got to choose a cookie jar to take home.

You never did things by half. Throughout your life, you gave your many enthusiasms your all. Your oil paintings hung on every available wall space. A big bookcase was needed to house your many scrapbooking photo albums that chronicled family activities. You took great pride in how you decorated each page in a style appropriate to the photos. Your wicker basket, stuffed with balls of yarn and big knitting needles, went with you wherever you went—even to the local hockey rink where your knitting needles seemed to move on autopilot as you watched your grandchildren's and great-grandchildren's games.

You began knitting afghans many years ago. I was a fortunate recipient of your handiwork, as were your children and some good friends. Your needles had to work faster as you began producing your cozy throws for the grandchildren, then their spouses and finally for the great-grandchildren. Each addition to your family was heralded with a happy phone call and the announcement, "Now I have to get to work on another afghan."

Above all else you loved your family and that love flowed back to you, multiplied many times. The nurse that cared for you the last days of your life said that you could feel the love in the room as your family gathered to say goodbye to you, but she couldn't understand why they toasted you with whipped cream. There were two food items you were never without: one was the bottle of Diet Pepsi always by your side, the other was the Dream Whip in your fridge. Your family could have toasted you with Diet Pepsi, but by using whipped cream they were paying tribute to your quirky sense of humour.

The celebration of your life your children organized was–so Lorna. Tables about the room displayed your interests and handiwork: cookie jars, copies of your cookie recipes for the taking, and plates of the cookies for dessert; photo albums including ones for each of your brothers' and sisters' families, which we were given to take home; and colourful table after table displaying your knitted afghans. Another "take-away" was copies of *Lorna's Cuppa Tea*, a personalized version of a coffee tabloid. Your family made it in memory of the delight you got from picking up the coffee tabloids at various places and reading the jokes to anyone who would sit and listen.

And, at this last party for you, you were there with us all afternoon in rotating pictures on the big screen at the front of the room. There were very few pictures of you alone. Usually you were engaged in family activities or holding a new addition to your family on your lap. Invariably you were smiling. I know there were times when you smiled despite one of the bouts of depression that began in your middle years. I like to think your great sense of humour helped you during those times more than any prescribed medication. You never stopped seeing the "funny" in life and sharing it with others. And when we laughed at your jokes and stories, you laughed too.

Now that you are gone, we have lost so many stories, so much laughter that could have been, but know I will always be smiling when I remember you.

Thank you, dear sister.

Love,

Jean

Lorna Velma May (Putland) Phillips

May 8, 1935 – January 15, 2017

Dear Bill:

You were the last one left in the family to share my childhood memories. I was a teenager by the time Leila and Leslie were old enough to form memories, and family dynamics were much different then. Now you are gone, and I am left alone with my memories of those long-ago days.

You were a good-natured, happy-go-lucky kid, a willing participant in all your older sisters' childhood activities—except our playhouses—that was "girl's stuff." We knew how to make up our own fun games. Sloughs were for stone skipping and wading contests, sticks became steeds we rode, snow was for making snow angels, snow forts and friendly snowball fights. We took advantage of the hill our house was built on—rolling down the grassy slope in summer, then in winter sailing to the bottom on our toboggan, and later, feeling very grownup, on our skis. You loved Roughie, our dog, and spent hours playing with him, training him to run beside you with your mitten-protected hand in his mouth, and to pull you on the toboggan.

You were always a bit of a tease. Your nickname for Mary was "Mare-zee-dotes," which she hated. I was "Jean, Jean, the big fat threshing machine." I was neither big, fat, nor a threshing machine, and knew you were just looking for a rhyming word.

From the time you were young you liked making things by hand, using a leather stencilling kit you got for Christmas to produce decorated belts. Then, with information gleaned from books, you learned to tan hides and sew leather mitts and other apparel. By the time you were a teenager, you were a skilled, self-taught taxidermist, being paid for your work by area hunters.

You did have a stubborn streak and did not react well to being ordered to do something, especially if it did not make sense to you. You were an enthusiastic baseball and hockey player, but detested track-and-field events,

367

especially races. There was a day when practicing for a field meet, you did not run a race fast enough to please our teacher, who then had you repeat the run, alone, to the far fence and back again, with an angry, "Speed up this time." You made the run, but certainly no faster, and probably, a little slower than the first time. The teacher grabbed you in anger, shook you so violently he popped the buttons off your shirt, and ordered you to do the run again. This time you did a slow jog! Defeated, the teacher called an end to outdoor practice that day.

I know your recollections of life on the farm were not as happy as mine. As soon as you were old enough to help with outside work, you lived with Dad's demands, criticism, and sometimes, harsh discipline. You told me that when you were 12, and he had you operate the road grader he was pulling with the tractor, you were sick with fear of his wrath if you did not lift the grader blade at exactly the right time. When it came to the difficult relationship between you and Dad it was, no doubt, partly a case of two stubborn heads butting together, and as yours was the smaller head you were the one who got a licking. That you were tough enough to hold back the tears when he used his belt, just made Dad angrier. However, despite your toughness, you had a relaxed, carefree attitude to life that, also, did not sit well with Dad. Fortunately, your strength of will and independent spirit served you well. You learned to use humour to deal with difficult situations, keeping your innate sense of self, and under the tough exterior you developed, matured into a caring adult. Although you did not express emotion easily, often using humour to cover your feelings, we all knew you loved us. And after your first cancer diagnosis, I found your brotherly hugs warmer and more frequent.

It was a combination of your tough spirit, sense of humour, and zest for life that helped you survive the 13 years of successive surgeries and chemo treatments as the cancers moved through your body. Every setback was faced with humour. I still laugh when I recall your zany email inviting us to a funeral for your penis. Only you!

You kept your will to live to the end. As your ravaged body lay close to death, you tore the oxygen mask from your face, but then replaced it, saying, "I'm going to live one more day." Those were your last words.

You would have enjoyed the celebration of your life. Your family arrived in the three vintage automobiles you had restored. We shed tears, but there was also lots of laughter. You were a "napper" and there were several pictures of you sound asleep, many in unorthodox and uncomfortable looking spots: hardwood floor, rough ground, wooden dock, anywhere you could lay your head. On every table there was a stand-up card with one of your "Billisms" (a favourite saying) and a picture of you involved in one of your varied activities.

You were a man with many interests and talents. Joining the Air Cadets was the beginning of a lifelong love of planes and flying. One of your great pleasures was taking family members and friends for a ride in one of your planes, taking off from the runway you had built at the edge of a field. Always one to look for new challenges, you bought an amphibious plane, taking lessons to learn to take off and land on water. Selling your planes when you decided to retire and move to the city, must have been a difficult decision. However, you took on a new challenge in your retirement–restoring the vintage automobiles you owned.

You were an avid sportsman, enjoying trap shooting, fishing, hunting and trapping, ironically, the only son who shared Dad's love of these sports. You continued to play both baseball and hockey as an adult, as well as golf. In winter you enjoyed snowmobiling, and in summer riding your quad in rough wilderness areas.

While a successful farmer, you also became a self-taught precision machinist, doing much work for the potash mine. That same attention to detail was evident in your work with wood, whether making furniture or smaller pieces–bowls and boxes with perfectly fitted lids. One of your last creations–the fireplace frame and mantle you created for your new house in the city when you retired from the farm, is a testament to your skill.

Over the years we have shared many happy times together. When we visited you on your farm, there were invariably hot dogs roasted over a fire in summer and after-supper games of cards in the winter. And you were always willing to take us for a ride in one of your planes to view familiar landscapes from above.

The trip we made to Armit Lake many years ago, when the only access was by hiking in with backpack, and then canoeing, ended up being a memorable battle with nature. You wanted to camp for the night on an island in the lake. Great idea—except for the armies of attacking over-sized mosquitoes that led to a miserable, sleepless night of frantic slapping. When we crawled out of our sleeping bags in the morning, eager to return to the mainland, we were faced with violent, surging, wind-blown waves. Not knowing how to swim, and not having much trust in lifejackets, I was a leery boater. When you suggested I sit at the end of the boat, I assumed it was because it was the position where I would feel the safest. I should have known better. Tease that you were, I swear you then proceeded to hit every wave at an angle designed to drench me in as much water as possible. As I held on for dear life, I ended up having the most exuberantly "fun" boat ride of my life. Who could be afraid after surviving that ride!

You and Vel, and John and I, made many trips together with our two RVs, visiting Dad in BC. Things did not always go as planned, but the trips were always fun because of your talent for finding humour in any situation.

There was the year we took John's sister, Doris, with us so that she could visit her sister, Blanche, in Vancouver. We were looking forward to showing Doris how great it was to holiday with an RV. So of course it ended up being a trip with a litany of mishaps, beginning with our auxiliary battery inexplicably dying on the first night, leaving us with no lights and forcing an early bedtime. When you and Vel drove into the campground where we had agreed to meet, you were mystified to see we had retired so early in the evening.

You usually led the way with your vehicle, while we stayed far enough behind to avoid breathing your diesel fumes. One day, driving on a winding road through the mountains, with me at the wheel, we lost sight of you around a curve. Driving as fast as I dared, I tried to catch up with you, to no avail. Finally, the road straightened out as we drove through a town, and there was still no sign of you. Puzzled, we kept on going, hoping to spy you around the next bend. And then—horrors—our vehicle began a dreadful loud shuddering. I barely managed to pull over onto the shoulder of the road before our motor died. I felt sick—how long would it be before you realized we were not following you. I put on our flashers, hoping a passing motorist would stop to check on our predicament, but as car after car whizzed by, I felt sicker.

"Finally!" I said, as a vehicle pulled up behind us and stopped. I could not quite believe my eyes when, opening my door, I caught sight of the motor home behind us. It was yours! How could that have happened? Later you loved to tease me about my driving, telling the story of how you had stopped off in the town for an ice cream cone, and I had driven, looking fixedly ahead, right by your parked vehicle without seeing it.

We soon learned our "blown" motor could not be repaired. The garage had to order a new one, which would take a week, so we left our vehicle behind to pick up on the way home, as you and Vel generously made room for the three of us.

Your vehicle was not immune to problems on that trip either. There was the miserable rainy day you got a flat tire, and as you and John were replacing it with the spare tire, every passing car sprayed the two of you with muddy water. Job completed, you drove around the curve just ahead–and there was a service station with a big parking lot where you could have done the job and stayed dry. Instead of being upset, you made a good-humoured joke about it. Doris' lasting memory of that trip was, "Your brother! Always joking!" So, we did show her how nice it was to travel in a motor home, just not how we anticipated it would be.

You did like to tease your older sister. On another trip we were sitting in a restaurant waiting for our breakfast to be served when you said, "I must have left the lights on in the motor home." I looked out the window, and sure enough there were lights shining in your vehicle. When you asked me if I would go turn them off, I should have realized that was completely out of character for independent you, and I was being set up. I was confused when, upon entering the motor home, I could find no lights on, as I had clearly seen from the restaurant. After a thorough search, including peering under the bulwark above the dash, I returned to the restaurant to find everyone at the table doubled over in laughter at my gullibility. The "lights" you had asked me to turn off were the reflection of lights in the restaurant. That was another story you liked to tell!

The longest trip we made together with our RVs was our three-week trek to the Yukon and Alaska in 1999. Of course, as on every trip we made together, we had vehicle problems, though none as serious as a blown motor this time. However, travelling with you was like having our own personal mechanic on call. When we had to get a new relay switch for our auxiliary batteries, you wired it in for us. Then there was the day we were shocked by a loud bang that sounded like we had hit something. A strip of corner trim on our vehicle had broken loose, and the wind had caught the edge of the unprotected metal siding and blown it right back against the wall. As John and I stood there assessing the damage, you came with your tool kit, and within an hour had everything screwed back in place with scarcely a sign of the damage.

We had two personal goals for the trip. You wanted to travel the Dempster Highway north from Dawson City to Inuvik, above the Arctic Circle in the Northwest Territories. And I wanted to explore the glacier fields at Valdez in Alaska. However, when we were in Dawson City, we were advised not to tackle the Dempster Highway due to forest fires and dense smoke. So, instead of going north we drove west, heading for Alaska.

You had never been outside of Canada, and we knew you were nervous about going through U.S. Customs at the border. You needn't have worried– a few straightforward questions and we were on U.S. soil. We didn't realize how worried you were till later, when we saw you had put your T-shirt on inside out that morning!

It was a short stay in Alaska. Discovering we needed a new driveshaft, and not wanting to pay for major repairs in American dollars, we decided to abort our goal of reaching Valdez, and returned to the Yukon. The Ford dealership that was recommended to us was fully booked for several days, so you convinced them to sell us a driveshaft and allow us to park on their lot to install it. You and John got our motor home up on blocks and you crawled under to make the repair. I was inside when I felt the vehicle start moving–coming off the blocks and rolling backwards till it came to a gentle stop against your motor home parked behind us. I was horrified, imagining you being crushed to death beneath my feet. Vel, who was witnessing this spectacle from outside, had a similar vision. What a relief when you emerged from under the machine, laughing at our fright. You said when you felt the vehicle start to move as soon as you removed the old driveshaft, you grabbed hold of the undercarriage and simply went for a ride.

So, neither of us achieved our personal goal for the trip. You never experienced Inuvik and I never saw the glaciers at Valdez. We quickly put those disappointments behind us and focused on enjoying all the other experiences the Yukon offered.

I discovered you were a "people person," interested in the many stories folks had to tell. Whether it was in a park where we camped, or a town where we stopped, I was intrigued to see how easily you engaged strangers in conversation, drawing them out about themselves, while revealing little or nothing about yourself. It was a talent that could have made you a great interviewer for newspaper, radio or TV.

You made inquiries to get contact information for two of our Putland cousins, Daryl and Gary, who lived in Whitehorse, and we spent several evenings around our campfire with them and their families, chatting and learning how to make jam-jams. With practice we became experts at making these camping confections – wrapping a triangle of croissant dough around the end of a peeled stick about the size of a broomstick, making sure the tip of the stick was enclosed by the dough. We then cooked our dough slowly over campfire coals, turning it frequently so it browned evenly. When cooked we slipped the pastry tube off the stick and filled the cavity with jam. It became one of our favourite camping treats for the rest of that trip.

You also convinced us to make a side-trip to Atlin to search for our estranged Uncle Bob. Although we never did get to see our uncle, as he was now living in a seniors' home in Dawson City, we did learn he was a well-known character in the town: a hard-drinking "old-time" gold prospector, a frequent photographic attraction for tourists with his bushy white beard and floppy felt hat.

We shopped and went on "tourist tours" in Whitehorse and Dawson City, exploring restored beached riverboats, museums, and old log buildings, as well as natural wonders. Miles Canyon, a deep gorge cut through rock walls by the Yukon River, was a testament to the power of water. When we visited the historic gold fields around Dawson City, you were our personal tour guide as you shared stories gleaned from your reading about the Klondike Gold Rush.

We embraced exploring an unfamiliar landscape. As we drove through a huge area that had been devastated by fire four years earlier, we enjoyed the spectacular displays of brilliant, purplish-pink fireweed covering the ground beneath the fire-blackened tree skeletons. We camped beside mountain-rimmed lakes and dipped our feet in icy glacier-fed streams. We hiked winding wilderness trails and clambered down steep banks leading to rivers–some swiftly rushing torrents, others slow moving, broad, and rock-studded. We waded in crystal-clear creeks, gathering smooth water-washed stones. We sat around campfires, roasting hot dogs and smokies, making smores and jam-jams, and playing countless games of Kaiser, our favourite card game–simple family-bonding activities.

Thank you, dear brother, for all those memory-making hours we shared as adults. They are very special treasures that will keep you close forever.

Your loving sister,

Jean

William Edward Putland

June 1, 1937 – August 15, 2018

Dear Jordan:

You were so many "firsts" in our family: your parent's first child, your grandparent's first grandchild, and our first great-grandchild. And you were the only child, grandchild, and great-grandchild for 11 years, which gave you a special place in our lives and our hearts.

Although your teenage parents, Laura and Curtis, never married, they remained friends and your dad was always present in your life. So, in fact, you were a member of two extended families. As her only child for so many years, you had an especially close relationship with your mother, continuing through your teenage years. Because you spent so much time with your maternal grandparents, Darryl and Janis, you had a very special bond with them as well, almost more like a late-in-life child than a grandchild.

You were a sturdy, active, happy toddler and soon introduced to the family's love of the outdoors, winter and summer. Camping holidays began when you were still a babe-in-arms. From the time you could walk you were "at home" in ice arenas where your mother was playing ringette, or your Uncle Jason had a hockey game. Camping, hiking, boating, fishing, and later, water skiing, knee boarding, and "quading," riding your all-terrain vehicle (ATV), became your favourite summer activities. When quading you were never happier than when you were covered in mud from head to toe! In winter you loved to go sledding with your snowmobile. Your relationship with sport machines began at an early age, with your own child-sized machines, a quad and a snowmobile, gifts from your grandparents.

As your great-grandfather and I were both retired by the time you were born, we were free to make frequent trips to Saskatoon and share in many of your childhood activities. One of my favourite memories comes from a ringette tournament in Edmonton when we were sharing a hotel suite. You were probably not more than two or three years old, and you and your mother were having an early morning, giggling "play" pillow fight. You were both having so much fun!

When you were older, maybe five or six, and out in the yard with your grandfather, I watched as you dragged some boards over to where your "papa" was working, and then struggled, over and over again, to make a ramp for your quad. Your first attempt, from the ground to a trailer bed, was too steep, so you had to devise a lower support. The problem was when you got to the top of your ramp there was no place to go except to fly off into the air for a hard landing on the ground. You managed that once before your papa intervened and helped you lower your ramp to a few inches off the ground.

Every Christmas was a family holiday celebrated at our Bog 'n Bush. When you were too young to trudge through the snow on our hiking trails, your mother pulled you on a toboggan. When you were older, you walked with us, and eventually explored the trails on your own, always on the lookout for a "climbing" tree with stout low branches. You played in the snow in the front yard, skated on the ice on the pond, and helped your great-grandfather fill the bird feeders. Later you graduated to traveling the hiking trails on a snowmobile, and finally, you were able to exuberantly join the adult family snowmobilers in the wilderness area north of our property.

When you visited with your family in the summer, our whole 20 acres was your playground. You could race around the trails and call down to us from the hidden depths of now leafy trees. You liked to fish tadpoles out of the pond, put them in a jar, watch for their legs to begin to develop, and reluctantly return them to their natural home before leaving for your home.

Age 11, cradling newborn Connor in your arms, you welcomed him with a tearful, "Thank you Mummy for giving me a brother." You looked forward to teaching him how to play soccer, and I saw the bemused expression on your face when you realized you would be 22 when he was your age. You gained another brother and a sister when twins, Zachery and Emilee, were born the next year. Now you became a much-loved older brother.

When your grandparents bought a cottage, weekends at the lake, both winter and summer, were fun-filled family times as you enjoyed all the sporting activities you loved. One of my favourite pictures of you was taken on your grandparents' boat. It was a chilly day as you are wearing a warm hooded jacket, a toque and mittens, but your joyous smile makes me smile every time I look at the picture.

After high school you joined the workforce, becoming a skilled sheet metal roofing installer. And you marked your entry to the adult world by growing a dark and bushy beard. Gone was the fresh-faced teenager. You were making a statement—you were now a working man. In your spare time you began retrofitting cars with your dad, installing stereos with subwoofers that emphasized the bass in music. Aiming to be the loudest Bass Head, became a passion. You also became a father with the birth of Xavier, your mother's first grandchild, your grandparent's first great-grandchild, and our first great-great-grandchild.

There was to be another "first" however, sadly one we didn't anticipate. You hear about fatal traffic accidents every day, but you think it can't happen to you or your family, but it can. On April 18, 2017, a month before your 21st birthday, the unbelievable happened, and we lost you in a tragic traffic accident.

At the celebration of your young life we released blue balloons that floated off into the ether to signify your passing. And everyone in the family, including your brothers, sister and son, added hand-painted stones to a memorial wall. It is an act of love and remembrance repeated each year on the anniversary of your death.

When we moved back to the city, we brought with us some stones from the Bog 'n Bush. It was one of those stones I placed on the wall, in memory of your fun-filled childhood visits. Now, on a shelf in the front entry, one of Uncle Denis' wooden bowls holds more of the stones, my personal memorial to you, and whenever I go to Saskatoon I take another stone with me to add to that memorial wall.

You are still a part of family holidays as we share memories of happy times together. And this Christmas you watched over the family gift opening and the board and card games from the picture your mother placed on a shelf, with a memorial candle and some sweetgrass.

We miss you deeply, but we will be forever grateful for the years we had with you and the joy you brought to our lives.

With my love,
Great-Grandma Jean

Jordan Lee Baptist-Kenney

May 18, 1996 – April 18, 2017

My Dear John:

The kids once asked me how two people so different ended up getting married. And I said you were the first person who made me feel I could dance.

They laughed and said, "That's a pretty flimsy reason." But maybe it wasn't. Maybe it wasn't just that you loved to dance and were a good dancer. Maybe it said something about the kind of person you were–the most non-judgmental person I have known. To criticism of someone or something, your response invariably was, "Well, they must like it."

After a long marriage, our last years together were not what we had planned, as over a nine-year period, dementia gradually destroyed your sense of direction, your ability to perform everyday activities, your sense of reality, and finally, much of your memory. Although you no longer knew how many children we had, or their names, you knew they were your kids when you saw them–someone you loved and who loved you. And you still knew I was your wife and remembered my name, for which I was thankful.

I thought I had already mourned the loss of the person you were, so I was not prepared for the debilitating grief I suffered at your death. Many years before, because we had no church affiliation, I had prepared a guidebook with memorial options for the family to consider. Now I found I couldn't control my weeping and felt unable to face a formal celebration of your life. All I wanted was our children and grandchildren and great-grandchildren around me. So, instead, we toasted your memory with a family dinner around our dining table with your favourite meal–barbecued ribs and fries. It was a fitting tribute as you had liked nothing more than having the family all together for a meal. You would tell them how much you loved them and how wonderful it was to have them all together.

We interred your ashes in the Carol Shields Memorial Labyrinth located in King's Park–the park where we went for our daily walk for so many years, after the supper dishes were done when we lived on the university campus, and first thing in the morning after we moved back to Winnipeg. We continued those daily jaunts even after we both used walkers to be mobile. It seemed the perfect spot for your final resting place, the location marked with an engraved commemorative stone. The family gathered around as I read a piece by Henry Scott Holland that spoke to how I was feeling. It began, "I am I, and you are you. Whatever we were to each other, that we still are." As we were preparing to leave the park, great-granddaughters Emilee and Rowyn each spontaneously plucked a small bloom from one of the flowering shrubs bordering the path through the maze. They then placed the tiny flowers gently on your stone. It was a sweet and tender expression of their love for you.

In addition, Lynn honored your memory on Facebook, writing:

> *I have been putting together a photo collage of my Dad and his life from 1929 to 2017. I have been agonizing over how to show off this tribute to my Dad. I have decided to do 365 days of Dad. So, for the next year, I will post a photo or combination of photos each day of the most remarkable man I have known – a dad who would be willing to drop everything to rescue, help or just come for a visit. His family was the most important thing in his life. He has taught me so much and never once said I couldn't do something because I was a girl, which in my era was more typical than you know. I know how to use both power tools and knit because of my Dad. I hope some memories will pop to the surface for the family as you see the pictures.*

> *I love you Pop.*

For the next 365 days she posted a picture of you–you alone, or the two of us, and sometimes, family pictures. We soon learned that one of the first things many members of our extended family did every morning was check Facebook to see what picture Lynn had posted. For me, each picture brought back a memory of happier times together and helped heal the pain of those last years.

I remember the young husband eager to show off his horsemanship. You were going to "break" June, the two-year-old you had raised from a colt, getting her to accept a rider on her back. Grabbing the reins, you leapt onto June's back, expecting to be astride a bucking dynamo. Instead June just stood there, turned her head and looked at you as if to say, "What do you want me to do now?" I had to laugh at your crestfallen expression, while assuring you that instead of being disappointed, you could be proud of the bond you had built with your colt—with all that petting and grooming and those carrot treats.

I also remember the young husband who teased me about my "not quite straight" garden rows, but came to my rescue later, after I learned, to my dismay, I had planted far too many peas. When I was faced with several tubs of pods to shell, you willingly set aside your farm work and helped shell peas all day.

However, I was puzzled the day you insisted on carrying the tub of corn I was husking to the shed where you were busy doing tractor repairs. "I like company while I'm working," you said. Indeed, you were a very social person. When you walked over to visit our neighbor Bob Glass, I often watched as the two of you stood in his barn doorway, leaning on forks, and talking for half an hour. I wouldn't be idly watching, but busy with some household task, simply amazed to see you standing in the same spot 30 minutes later. Such a laid-back attitude was foreign to me!

Freed from other eyes, we were absolute gluttons the first year of our marriage. Did I cook a sensible half dozen cobs of corn for the two of us? No, I cooked two dozen—and we ate every cob, their plump kernels deliciously dripping homemade butter! We could make a couple pounds of crisp bacon disappear, no problem. And there was the time you, your cousin, and a friend assured me you could each eat a whole chicken—not broilers, but full-grown hens. Taking you up on your bet, I roasted three birds and you did manage to eat them, but all three of you ended up lying on the floor groaning with over-stuffed stomach pain.

We both liked desserts, especially anything chocolate. The first time I made a chocolate fudge pudding recipe for six, the two of us ate it all, and would have liked more. So, the next time I doubled the recipe. Big mistake! We didn't end up groaning on the floor, but we were feeling just a tad sick before we were very far into the second half of that rich pudding. It was a good thing we were young and active and worked off all those calories. And we did learn to moderate ourselves.

In another memory of our first summer together, we were walking in a field with your nephew, Lorne, when we came to a huge patch of Canada thistle. I was wearing a dress because women were still not wearing pants in the early 50s. It took the immodest mini-skirt fashion to make trousers acceptable for women. I came to an abrupt halt in front of the thistles. "I can't go through that," I said, looking down at my bare legs. You immediately crouched down and said, "Get on my back." I wrapped my arms around your neck, and you grabbed my legs and carried me piggyback through the prickly patch, while I alternately giggled and screamed when you pretended I was slipping from your grasp. Teenager Lorne was not amused. "You two should grow up and start acting like a married couple," he said.

We had no car that first year, but we managed. In winter we used the heated horse-drawn van to go to town and to visit our neighbour friends. Once the snow was gone you would "hitch" a ride with a neighbour to go to town for groceries. When we wanted to visit our friends, we climbed on the tractor and away we went—not elegant, but it got us there.

When Darryl was born, to be followed by Lloyd and Lynn, we became a family, with all the joys and worries that entails. For each baby there was the excitement of the first tooth, the first step, the first word—and all the other "firsts" that came after. There were scary trips to the hospital emergency department: with Darryl, when coming down with measles, he ran such a high fever he had a convulsion, and with Lloyd, when he ventured to put an inquisitive finger on a moving auger belt, and another time, when he was swinging on a wire gate and a protruding bit of wire got caught in his eye.

The first years of our marriage were difficult financially with uncooperative weather and disastrous crop failures. As a result, I took a teaching position in our local school for two years while you became the boys' primary caregiver. It was a good "fit" as you always were a doting father.

Although we were monetarily poor, we were rich in the friendship of our neighbours, Leonard and Beattie, Verner and Elaine, and Bob and Lizzie, with all those fun-filled evening card games. After we moved to Winnipeg you had your friends from work, bowling, and curling, while I had my work friends, but we never shared the same friends, till our kids married and gave us an extended family of in-laws. However, whenever we went back to Saskatchewan to visit our farming friends, it was like we had never left–friends of your youth are friends for life.

Our life took a different direction when we could not reach an agreement with your family to buy the farm, and we made the difficult decision to move to Winnipeg. It took a lot of courage for you to take that leap as you had never lived anywhere but on the farm and had no specialized training other than a six-week course in diesel mechanics.

Our timing was right. Your job at the University of Manitoba used your skills in animal care as you tended students' test animals, making sure all guidelines were precisely followed. You worked closely with the university veterinarian, identifying ill animals and assisting in surgeries. As you were working with others, the job also suited the social side of your personality. You especially enjoyed learning about other countries through your interactions with professors and students from around the world.

You had a lifelong love of baseball, in your youth playing back catcher on several teams in the area around Rhein, your hometown. In Winnipeg, you became an active member of the community, coaching the boys' baseball and hockey teams for many years. You were not a coach that focused solely on winning, instead ensuring that weak players got fair game time. It was not a stance that sat well with the most competitive parents, but you held your ground, influencing other coaches to follow your example. You were very pleased and proud that son Darryl, and grandson Jason, followed in your baseball footsteps, playing back catcher. Both eventually became community club coaches as well. Your love of sports has trickled down to the third generation with our great-grandchildren now playing baseball, soccer, hockey, and ringette.

Curling was another sport you began playing in your youth, and you liked to remind us that your team once won the championship in the Yorkton bonspiel. You continued to curl in Winnipeg, even participating in the big city bonspiel one year. You sometimes recruited son Darryl, and future daughter-in-law Janis, to play on your team.

You also enjoyed bowling and wanted the two of us to join a bowling league. The idea was abhorrent to me. I had bowled a few times with the family and was a terrible player–my lowest score was 11 and my highest not much better! You didn't understand my refusal to join with you, insisting I would improve with practice. Finally, in desperation, I asked you to imagine how you would feel if I pressured you to enroll in a university course I was taking. Then you understood and went bowling alone without complaint.

I think the kids were right, we were very different in both personality and interests, so maybe it was a case of opposites attract. You were an outgoing "people person" while I was more restrained and private, so you made friends more easily than I did. I did things "by the book," while you never opened an instruction manual, relying on what you called "common sense." We did many projects together over our almost 64 years together, but coming from two very different perspectives, I don't think we managed one without an argument–sometimes rather heated. It just became the normal way we interacted. But things did get done–not always to my complete satisfaction, I admit.

Negotiation and compromise helped us accommodate our differences and understand the other person's point of view. For example, our attitude to money was very different. I was a "saver" and you were a "spender," inheriting your father's distrust of banks. Friction over money was finally eliminated when we each put the same amount into an account to pay all household, food, and family bills, with the rest of our paycheques being ours to use as we pleased. You did come to see the rewards in saving, and in later years were generous in praise of my money management.

When I returned to teaching in 1965, two years after our move to Winnipeg, you were a man ahead of the times, voluntarily becoming an equal partner in household tasks, both cooking and cleaning. You simply shrugged off any teasing about being a "house husband." Without your help I could not have managed my job and family responsibilities while taking evening and summer courses at the university to get my education degree.

And we did have other shared interests, none more important than our three kids. They were the centre of our life. We attended all their sport games–you as coach and me as spectator. In winter, Sunday afternoons were family time at the university skating rink, while in summer we made day trips to one of the many lakes around Winnipeg, sometimes taking our boat. Then the kids would practice water skiing, or you and the kids would fish while I relaxed on board with a book.

We experienced Canada from coast to coast on our annual family camping vacations. We "tented" for years, including memorable trips west to British Columbia, east to Newfoundland, and north to Alaska. The Alaska trip has become almost a family legend with its litany of vehicle mishaps with the tent trailer we had at that time. Despite all the broken axles and cracked wheel hubs you never lost your patience. Over the years we have slept beside waves splashing on lakeshores, cooked countless meals over campfires, and explored the countryside on hikes. We have clambered over tangled deadfall, struggled to the top of huge boulders, and walked beside deep gorges cut through rock cliffs by the river below. We have watched otters slicing through water, beavers slapping water with their tails to warn of danger, moose browsing, knee-deep in water, bears climbing trees, elk grazing beside a road, and mountain goats perched on a lofty narrow ledge. And then in the evenings there were invariably family card games and campfire popcorn.

As adults, the kids became campers and nature lovers too, while we moved up from a tent to a motor home. The RV was large enough that we could take family with us on trips to BC to visit your sister Blanche in Vancouver and my dad in Qualicum Beach. And when my brother Bill also got a motor home, our families made several trips together with our two RVs to Qualicum Beach to see Dad. Our last trip with Bill and Vel was our second trip to Alaska. It was a great adult-only trip, but very different from our family trip many years before when every experience was viewed through the exuberant eyes of our young kids. After that last Alaskan trip we downsized, replacing our motor home with a camper van, dubbed our "hobbit house" by Lynn, but it was a perfect fit for the two of us. We still enjoyed family camping trips, with the kids now having their own camping outfits.

We were both country folks at heart, however, and when all the kids had left home and married, we made another life-changing move, buying an acreage–our "Bog 'n Bush"–and building our "dream house." For the first time in our married life we were no longer renters, at last owning a home of our own. We worked together enclosing our 20 acres with a rustic rail fence. We cut a network of hiking trails through our bush, while a nearby wilderness area provided opportunities for hiking, fishing, and snowmobiling. Family members joined us on regular weekend visits and for Christmas and birthday celebrations. There were countless games of cards in the screen porch in summer and by the wood-burning stove in winter.

Gardening became another common interest as we built a raised-bed vegetable garden on our property and developed a perennial flower bed bordering the pond. Every year I planted 50 to 60 pots of flowers, adding colour and life to our large deck and patio areas. And you realized your dream of building a greenhouse, growing giant tomato plants that pushed their way out of any open window they could find. We ate thick slices of sun-ripened tomatoes every day, gave away as many tomatoes as we could, and then spent many hours working together cooking and freezing spaghetti sauce for winter months.

Time marched on, and, after 22 happy family years at the Bog 'n Bush, we moved back to Winnipeg due to health issues. We bought a house on a secluded bay near the university, in the area where we used to live. Soon after the move we began to see the first signs of your dementia as you were becoming lost in a part of the city you used to know so well. We had nine years together in this house, making new family memories–many happy ones despite your illness.

Now I live here alone. I still miss you my love, but I no longer grieve for you. I have come to realize you can't live that closely with someone for all those years without them becoming a part of you in a way. I still make pancakes every Sunday morning the way we used to. At every meal, before I sit down to eat, I turn on the radio just as you did. When I go for my morning walk, you walk with me as I remember all the walks we made together. The painting of the Bog 'n Bush at the foot of my bed reminds me of the happy years we shared there. I think of you when I watch curling on TV and when I look across the room to the corner of the sofa where you always sat.

And I see you every day when I turn on my computer. There on my desktop is my favourite picture of the two of us. We were visiting Darryl and Janis in Saskatoon and they had a photographer out to their acreage to take some family pictures. When the photographer was finished with us oldies, she suggested we go for a walk on the meadow while she took more shots of the young ones. While we were wandering around you bent down, picked a dandelion and handed it to me, saying, "A flower for you my love." The alert photographer caught the moment on camera. We are looking into each other's eyes. I have a quizzical little smile, holding the dandelion to my nose as if smelling a rose, while you have a face-splitting grin, delighting in your joke.

You always had a gentle sense of fun. And you never lost your love of dancing, not even when you were in your wheelchair at the seniors' care home. Listening to dance music, you would wiggle your feet, hands, and body to the music. If someone tried to interrupt what you were doing, you would say, "Can't you see I'm dancing?"

And you are dancing forever in my heart. I can feel your arms around me. I can feel our bodies moving in unison to the rhythm of the music. Forever. Always.

Thank you for all the years of shared love.

Your Jean

John David Baptist

August 16, 1929 – September 18, 2017

PART 7
To The Future

.

A Letter to My Great-Great-Great-Grandchildren

As I sit here, age 88, in 2020, I am trying to imagine your life. To gain some perspective, I have calculated that my great-great-great-grandparents would have been born in Great Britain in approximately 1780.

How has life changed in the intervening 240 years? What will your world be like in 2172, 240 years after my birth, when you, my great-great-great grandchildren, are 88?

Life expectancy in Great Britain in 1780 was 36 years. Today, worldwide average life expectancy is 71.5 years, while here in Canada it is 82 years. In 1780, few lived to see their grandchildren. At age 88, I have five grandchildren, nine great-grandchildren and one great-great-grandchild. However, I am young to be a great-great grandmother. The average generation gap between me and my great-great-grandchild is only 21 years, while it is 30-35 years with my youngest great-grandchildren.

In Great Britain in the 1700s, the relationship between germs and disease was not understood, and smallpox, measles, diphtheria, whooping cough, and polio spread rapidly, causing many deaths. Due to immunization programs these diseases are now rare or eradicated. Today antibiotics are used to fight germs and infections. Major surgeries are performed routinely: joint replacement, heart valve replacement, heart bypass surgery and heart, kidney, liver, and lung transplants.

A farmer walking behind a horse-drawn plow in 1780 could not have imagined today's 1000+ acre farms with their huge gas-powered machines for seeding and harvesting, equipped with air-conditioned cabs and GPS systems.

By 1780, the Industrial Revolution had precipitated migration from farms to the city, a societal shift that continues today. However, city life was much different in the 1700s. Everyone in the family worked, including children as young as six years of age. Very few children went to school and few people could read or write. Today in Canada there is compulsory education for children from age five or six continuing until age 15 to 18, depending on the province in which you live. Many continue their education after high school at vocational schools, college, or university.

My ancestors would have travelled by foot, horseback, or horse-drawn coach on bumpy dirt roads. Longer trips became possible when inns were built at intervals along roads, providing a place to rest for horses, drivers, and passengers. The Industrial Revolution led to the construction of canals for the transport of heavy goods until the first railways were built in the 1830s. Wooden ships with sails were used for ocean travel, trading, and exploration. Today we have automobiles, buses, and transport trucks speeding along a network of multi-lane paved highways crossing the country, rapid-transit systems in cities, cruise ships the size of a town, jet planes, and rocket-propelled flights into outer space.

Communication in the 1700s was in person or by written word, delivered by hand or a mail carrier on horseback, or by coach. Radio, television, communication satellites, computers, Skype, smart phones, iPads, and eBooks are all part of my world, and all beyond the scope of my great-great-great-grandparents' imagination in 1780.

So how can I envision your life? The predicted life expectancy for someone born in 2000 is 100 years. I estimate that you will have been born around the year 2084. What will be the life expectancy in 2084? I wonder, is there a human threshold?

I wonder, when you are 88, if you still live on earth. If so, is it a parched desert, or have you successfully stopped global warming, or created ideal microclimates underground? Has earth been abandoned as you moved into outer space, building space stations, or discovering other habitable planets? Are you controlled by robots who have outsmarted their creators? Have you discovered other forms of intelligent life, perhaps more intelligent than you, or with a different kind of intelligence? If so, did you colonize them or herd them onto reservations? Or did they enslave you? Or did you treat each other with respect as equals?

Can you mind-travel by visualizing where you want to go? Can you read others' thoughts so you can communicate without the need for spoken language? Do you have hospitals with Parts Departments, where you go for regularly scheduled warranty check-ups and receive arm, leg, kidney, heart, or brain replacements as required? Have diseases been eliminated with targeted drugs or gene therapy? If so, how do you decide when or how to die? Do you produce your offspring by cloning? Due to genetic engineering and superior nutrition are you giants? Or...or...or?

You are probably smiling, or perhaps chortling at my wild musings, which will seem as naïve to you as the predictions of my forebears in 1780 would seem to me today.

Thinking about the world from 1780 to the present, the year 2020, I have been smacked in the face with a sad reality. Regardless of the differences in living conditions or technical knowledge, there is one common thread that runs through human history from century to century—and that is war. In the 240 years from 1780 to today, Great Britain, the country of my ancestors, has been involved in 86 wars! Since 1870, when my great-grandparents immigrated to Canada from England or Scotland, Canada has been involved, with other countries, including Great Britain and the United States, in six major wars, four of them in my lifetime. Casualties from all these armed conflicts have numbered in the hundreds of thousands dead and wounded. It is a human tragedy.

While war is a constant in our history, how it is fought has changed through the years with changes in technology. In the 1700s, soldiers met in face-to-face combat, armed with bayonets or rifles. Later, machine guns and armoured tanks were more efficient killing machines. Airplanes made it possible to drop bombs on cities. Then the casualties of war became civilians as well as soldiers. Today, with guided missiles and unmanned drone planes dropping bombs, civilian casualties far outnumber the soldiers killed or maimed. With more and more countries developing the potential to build nuclear bombs, the world is in increasing danger of a catastrophe of unprecedented dimensions.

Poorer countries, lacking the technologic weaponry of more powerful nations, have learned the effectiveness of terrorist attacks. Remote-controlled bombs placed in cars, buses and public gathering places, suicide bombers, explosives hidden beneath roads and hi-jacked planes flown into multi-story office buildings strike fear into the hearts of adversaries.

Wars are fought not only country against country, but by opposing groups within a country. In some cases, the object is to eliminate another ethnic group. The term that has come into common use to describe this barbarism is *ethnic cleansing*. What a sickening misnomer.

After World War II, the United Nations (U.N.) was formed to prevent future wars. It is failing in this lofty aim although it has, over the years, organized several peacekeeping missions to try and defuse hostilities. Canada participated in every U.N. peacekeeping effort from 1956 to 1989. However, since 1995 our participation in peacekeeping has declined, and from 2001 to 2011 our resources were redirected to waging war.

Why do countries go to war? It seems to me there are three main reasons: fear, greed, and revenge. There is a fear of others who are different in beliefs, customs, or system of government. They are viewed as a threat to our way of life. Greed is the motivation in a struggle for power or when access is wanted to others' resources, whether it is oil, gold, diamonds, water, or any other coveted substance. Revenge for an actual or perceived injury often leads to war. Of course, none of these factors are the official reasons stated by a government when it declares war.

The United States-led war on Afghanistan was essentially a war of revenge in retaliation for the terrorist attacks on the World Trade Centre and the Pentagon in 2001. None of the terrorists who took control of the planes came from Afghanistan, but it was believed they got their training in Afghanistan. Canada, out of loyalty to its closest neighbour, was persuaded to join in the war, finally withdrawing its troops in 2011.

The U.S. war on Iraq in 2003 was even more problematic. The American people were assured by their government that Iraq had chemical and biological weapons, though an international inspection committee found absolutely no evidence to support this claim. The U.S later admitted that Iraq had no such weapons, but the war destroyed the country's infrastructure and created sectarian animosities. What led to the war? I suspect the underlying cause was greed as the U.S. wanted to assure access to Iraq's oil, and false fear was used to gain their citizens' support.

There were many marches held across Canada to protest our joining in this war. My family and I participated in the march organized in Winnipeg. I am happy to say that our government, despite strong pressure from the U.S., did not join in this war.

Today, as I write this, a civil war rages in Syria, where a dictator is slaughtering civilians to retain his power. And Israel and Iran are making threatening noises, each convinced the other is going to attack them with nuclear weapons. Will this madness ever stop?

When I look at what is happening in the world today, I feel fortunate my ancestors chose to come to Canada. Our country has not been a theatre of war since 1814 in the War of 1812. We are a democracy, so if we do not approve of our government, we can simply vote them out of power. We have a Charter of Rights and Freedoms that guarantees fundamental freedoms such as freedom of religion, thought, belief, expression, press, and peaceful assembly as well as equality rights, language rights, and legal rights in dealing with the justice system and law enforcement.

We value multiculturalism and celebrate our diversity in many ways. We believe in the equality of the sexes and equal pay for work of equal value. A woman has the right of choice regarding anything that affects her body, including abortion. Our society is more humane and inclusive than many others, including the United States. We do not have capital punishment and homosexuals have equal rights, including the right to marry. We have several social programs designed to prevent financial hardship: Medicare, Old Age Security Pensions, Unemployment Insurance, and Social Assistance for those in need. But more needs to be done. We still have people living in poverty and homeless people living on the street, dependent on foodbanks, soup kitchens, and emergency shelters.

Our past treatment of our Indigenous peoples is a national disgrace and it will take several generations to erase the harm done by residential schools, which deprived a whole generation of family support and love and exposed some students to physical and sexual assault. In 2008 our government issued an official apology for this misguided policy. In 2015, the *Report of the Truth and Reconciliation Commission of Canada* on the residential school system and its legacy was published. Five years later, many of its calls to action have not been implemented. In 2019, the *National*

Inquiry into Missing and Murdered Indigenous Women and Girls released its final report. One year later no national action plan has been announced. Systemic racism still exists in our society, including in our child welfare and justice systems.

Our federal government, regardless of the party in power, seems content to tinker with a system that needs radical change. The Indian Act, which treats Indigenous peoples like second-class citizens, needs to be abolished, allowing reserves to establish their own system of local self-government. Funding for education for schools on reserves should be increased to at least on a par with the rest of the country. Reserves should be encouraged and helped to become economically independent. However, First Nations still find attempts to expand their land base by securing land owed to them through treaties or by purchasing from a willing seller, thwarted by a cumbersome process that takes decades and prevents good land from getting into Indigenous hands. I live with the hope that my compassionate grandchildren and their generation will do a better job of reconciliation than my generation has.

Overall, I am optimistic about the future. I think my Canada is a much more open and inclusive society than it was in my parents' time.

My fervent wish for you is that with each generation between me and you the world will have become a kinder, more trusting and sharing society, that negotiation is now used to settle differences, and wherever you are, you are living in a world free of the butchery of war.

Your great-great-great- grandmother,

Margaret Jean (Putland) Baptist

APPENDIX

Uncle Henry's stories about his father Amos

Excerpts from: *The First Hundred Years Around Churchbridge 1880-1980*
Amos Putland Family
(1888-1979)
By son Henry Putland

My father. Amos Putland, often reminisced about coming west from Thorold, Ontario. He had been a stone mason by trade, having a tombstone business of his own in Thorold. He also worked in the limestone quarries. They mined limestone for use in construction of the Welland Canal, which was continuously being improved. The industry was booming, money flowed freely. However, at the age of twenty-six, he began suffering from the rock-dust which was affecting his lungs. Advice from his doctor was to find some type of work in the open, free from dust, if he wanted to live.

On this advice, Amos, and brother Edward and two acquaintances, John Riddall Sr., and Walter Park Sr., all of the same area, decided to come out west, to what was then Assiniboia, Northwest Territories. This was the autumn of 1887 or 1888. The records that I have show that the railroad unloaded all immigrants at Langenburg in the year 1888. A few settlers did receive rail transportation closer to their destination, depending on whether or not they had a friend on the work train. These four men, on leaving Ontario, took along equipment which was recommended for getting established as homesteaders.

Amos filed on SW ¼ 18-20-32 W1st, Brother Edward on the NW ¼, J. Riddall on the SE ¼ and W. Park on the NE ¼, all on the same section. These pioneers had their first sod shanties situated as close together as possible. Communication was by walking only during the stormy winter weather.

Some rather frustrating events happened to them on their trip by railroad. The places for overnight lodging were called stopping houses. Some of these did get badly infested with bedbugs and fleas. On the stopover at Winnipeg, Amos and Edward spent most of the night killing bedbugs on the walls with their nail hammers. Mr. Riddall and Mr. Park had the same experience. They remarked at the breakfast table, "Those beggars of bugs walked away with our blankets during the night!"

On arrival at the homestead site, construction of sod houses was begun and continued late into cold weather. Sod was in some cases the only material available. Prairie fires had practically destroyed all tree growth except in the valleys. Firewood was therefore hard to obtain. These fires were sometimes deliberately set by Indians to drive the white man out of their lands. The Indians also used fire to chase buffalo into these valleys, making it easier to kill them. In some areas of' the southwest there are cut-banks where large kills were made. In these places many arrows have been found, some stuck in the rib bones, proving that the meat was not always used and that the animals were sometimes slaughtered for their hides.

Amos Putland, on coming west, had brought his driving horse and light democrat. However, they were of little use because there were no trails and no bridges across the streams. Oxen were the main power until heavy horses started to come into use.

For two years, during the winter 1889-1890, Amos and Edward travelled to the town called "Pile of Bones," which is today the city of Regina. The name had come about from the bones of the buffalo–the prairie being literally white with bones from buffalo hunting days. These two pioneers worked as carpenters in "Pile of Bones." The Royal North West Mounted Police were stationed at this location with a large number of horses. The second winter a large number of Indians had fled from the U.S.A., approximately five hundred in number. They were part of Sitting Bull's tribe which had been involved in the Massacre of General Custer's army. The U.S. soldiers had, at times, harassed these Indians and they fled to Canada, begging to be ruled by the Great White Mother, our Queen Victoria. The Canadian government would not agree to this, but the Indians stayed the winter, camping on the open plains, literally starving to death. As there was little wild game left and the Canadian government would not supply any food, these Indians were in a very sad plight, sneaking down back alleys to try to find food.

The rooming house where Amos and Edward boarded, was owned by people who took care of a number of horses. One day a horse died and the stable boy had been told to bury it. He was asked by the boss at supper time, "Did you get the horse buried?" The young man answered, "Just dragged it to the outskirts of town, will bury it tomorrow." Then he said very quietly to Amos and Edward, "I won't have to tomorrow." Sure enough, the dead carcass had gone for food to the Indian camp!

In the spring of the second year, Amos travelled to his homestead by horse and cart, taking six full days to travel from what is now Regina to one mile north-east of Yarbo. He camped out on the open prairie, making fires with dry grass and "buffalo chips" (the dry manure of buffalo of a few years past). On being asked, "Were there no stopping houses?" his answer was, "Yes, but most were overrun with bugs and fleas and too costly when money is scarce." So, the alternative was camping out under the stars, horse tethered out and he sleeping under his cart.

The original homestead was given up. and a second homestead was filed two miles west of' Dovedale school site on the NE¼ 14-21-33W1st., being one-and-a-half miles west from grandfather George Baimbridge's homestead. In 1893, Amos Putland and Mary Baimbridge were married. Mary came with her parents from England in 1888. They farmed this new quarter and rented NE¼ of section 12 until the year 1900, at which time they made an arrangement to take over the Baimbridge farm. Grandfather Baimbridge, elderly and in failing health, needed help with his farm work.

However, times were becoming very tough for Amos and Mary. Amos had been seriously burned in 1872 as a boy of twelve, which had left him with a partially crippled leg that was now giving him great pain. This had been a lifelong problem, but the leg had been bruised while building with logs and had turned into an open sore. (His only sister had been burned to death in the above-mentioned fire.) In the winter of 1905-06, he had his leg amputated at the hip joint. This was the first operation of its kind in the west, done in the old Victoria hospital in Yorkton by Dr. Patrick. Amos just barely pulled through. However, he did fully recover and continued farming for the rest of his life.

Amos had taken the contract to have the Riversdale (later, Dovedale) post office. He also contracted to deliver mail from Churchbridge to Esterhazy, and to four country post offices. Kinbrae, Clumber, Sumner and Riversdale. This contract carried on from 1900-1915 at which time the Dovedale post office was closed. This post office venture was done for about $500 a year, travelling well over one hundred miles each week with horse and buggy in summer and a team of horses and cutter in winter. Horses were always changed at the home post office.

During the years of Amos Putland's mail route, many frightening experiences came about. One such event happened at Esterhazy when the first automobiles came to town. A car drove down the street just as Amos was untying his team of horses. The team bolted. With his one leg hooked around the buggy pole, Amos hung onto the bridle as the team ran a full half mile east to the creek. Eventually, Amos managed to bring them under control. He was a very capable horseman, fearless, even with his handicap. Some old settlers said that he was the best horseman they had ever seen. One lady who operated the Kinbrae post office, remarked that he was the bravest man she had ever known. When a person considers the prairie trails and winter storms it is noteworthy that in all the years of his mail deliveries not one trip was missed.

The first Model T was purchased in 1918. It was the first Ford in the district equipped with a self-starter to make it easy for Amos to operate. However, he did not really learn to drive a car because of his leg complication. Son George had the privilege of being his chauffeur.

During the years of ox and horse power, any land to be plowed had to be cleared of trees. This tree growth developed very fast after the first settlers began controlling the prairie fires. Sons and daughters all took their full share of the heavy work such as land clearing, cutting wood for winter fuel, haying, harvesting, and doing the winter chores. Amos, himself, cut wood and scrub while sitting on a bag of hay. Yes, just sit down and try swinging an axe for many hours at a time! It has been said that this man did more work with one leg than the average man with two!

In 1926, Amos and his family witnessed a very tough year. A hail storm in July caused about 75 percent loss of the crop. No insurance had been carried, this being the first hail in forty years of farming. The same year, on October 15th, a terrific thunderstorm came up late in the fall. Monday morning the disaster was found! Five horses had been killed by lightning and three more crippled.

In 1929, the two older sons. George and Edward, took over the farming. Amos, now semi-retired, took up gardening, having a half-acre of garden and fruit trees. He and his wife did all weeding with hand hoes for ten years.

Amos passed away at the age of 79. Mary died in 1947 at the age of 78.

Nine children were born to Amos and Mary. Rose Ellenor (Nellie) married Herman Karstad and had six children. Herman passed away in the 1960s and\Nellie married Harry Martin, now living at Qualicum Beach, BC.

Mary Hannah (May) married Jack Galbraith. She is widowed and now living at Qualicum Beach.

Sarah Sophie (Sadie) married Harry Banks. Both are deceased with no living children.

Violet Baimbridge married Archie Taylor and lives on a farm south of Bredenbury. They have three children.

Winnifred Edith married George Malcom. She is widowed and living in Fort Qu'apple. They have one son, David.

George Amos married Lucille Swanson and they are now retired in Churchbridge. They had a family of nine.

Dorothy Bertha married Eugene Sinclair and lives in Fort Qu'apple. They have two sons.

Edward John married Vera Fraser and had a family of seven. Vera passed away and Ed married Mary Hay. They live in Qualicum Beach.

Henry August married Doris Boreen and is living on the original 1888 homestead of Grandfather George Bainbridge. They have a family of fourteen. All but two are married and have families of their own.

Other Homesteading Experiences of Amos Putland by son Henry

The house of A. Putland was situated southwest of a hill. The barn was on the east side of the hill.

In March 1904, a tremendous blizzard of three days occurred. The only way out of the house on the third day was from the upstairs window. The barn was completely covered. The only way the livestock could be fed was through a hole in the roof by passing the water down by bucket. This went on for one whole week. The only way to remove the snow was by shovel, and during the storm shoveling just piled the snow up deeper.

One winter's day after travelling to Langenburg on business, Amos, brother Edward and John Riddall, returning to their homesteads, were interrupted by a storm. A short distance southwest of Langenburg they had become lost and saw a house with a light shining in the window. Keeping a light in the window was a normal practice of all early settlers when a storm occurred.

The three men decided to call in at this house. They were invited to partake of a meal and stay overnight until the storm abated.

The meal was of very black bread and some strong meat in a stew. However, these men ate, thinking that the meat possibly was strong mutton or goat meat. They left the following morning as the storm had subsided. A week later John Riddall said to Edward and Amos, "I found out what kind of meat we had last week. It was dog meat." Amos answered him by saying, "Well it's too late to tell us. l can't bring it up now."

Many times the food consumed was not very appetizing. Salt pork was quite often kept for long periods of time by storing it in a bin or barrel of grain and sometimes this would be quite tainted.

Some of the bachelor homesteaders were very uncouth in their preparation of food. One such homesteader in the area had his barn connected to his sod house. This was done by quite a number of homesteaders who stabled their oxen under the same roof with just a wall separating the living quarters from the hogs and oxen. However, one day Amos, on walking to Churchbridge, called in at a homesteader and he said, "How about a cup of tea?" Amos accepted the invitation. At this point, this bachelor decided to make some bannock. Without washing his hands, he mixed some batter, slapped it on a very soiled table, went to the door leading into his barn and came back with a hay fork. He used the handle for a rolling pin to roll out the bannock. At this point Amos suddenly was not hungry and excused himself, saying that he could not spend any more time on the way. He left the house with a feeling of relief.

It has been said that sometimes some of the early-day butter ended up as axle grease because it had been kept for long periods of time without proper cooling methods and became rancid. It did not take early settlers long to find cooling methods, such as water or hanging containers down a water well. Some used ice cut during the winter and stored in insulated buildings. In some cases, this ice lasted a good part of the sunnier.

The early days of raising hogs was at times hilarious and at times a disaster. One early homesteader had one sow and raised a few pigs. His barn was attached to his house. On one occasion. a neighbour called in. The door of the house was partly open, so the neighbour rapped on the partly open door. All of a sudden a terrible commotion seemed to break loose. The sow was in the kitchen and made a mad rush for the door with the kitchen table on her back. She deposited the table against the door jamb and took off for the wide-open spaces! The owner being away, the neighbour just went on his way with a very hilarious story.

There was one young farmer who had become quite a large hog raiser. His hogs were allowed to roam at will. He did have his wife's garden well fenced, but the hogs had the run of the farm, being fed twice a day in troughs situated in the barnyards.

This young family also milked a few cows, getting a five-gallon can of cream in four or five milkings. This cream was always allowed to become sour making it a No. 1 grade, whereas sweet cream would be graded "table" or "special." However, they had no cooling facilities set up so they left the five-gallon can at the cream spout of the separator for two days and then shipped or hauled it to the creamery. This cream separator was set up in a lean-to kitchen.

During this particular night the cream can was nearly full of cream. The hogs roaming around the yard had somehow got the door open and had taken over the kitchen, upsetting the five-gallon cream can. This kitchen was about 16 x 24, a rather large room with about twenty hogs and five gallons of cream!

In the morning on coming downstairs from the main part of the house, this young wife just took one look and burst into tears. It took many pails of hot water and hours of work to bring that kitchen back into living shape, and I imagine that the husband would be in the doghouse for some length of time and possibly advised to fence the hogs.

Amos' Experience With His Leg Amputation

After many years of much suffering from a severe burn on his leg, and on consulting his doctor at Saltcoats, Amos decided in 1905 to have his leg amputated. After a week in Yorkton Hospital, the date for the operation had arrived. His doctor came in with another doctor, a drug addict, who was to give the anesthetic. Amos was too nervous to notice that both doctors were obviously drunk, but the head surgeon did notice and succeeded in having the operation postponed. Two weeks later the doctor came in, this time sober, and began the operation. He made long cuts to sever the leg, ignoring the uncontrolled bleeding, until the head surgeon, standing by, insisted that the operation be halted to allow the main artery to be tied off. By this time a large amount of blood had already been lost. The doctor then proceeded with the operation, hitting a bone above the joint and breaking the end off his knife. At this point the head surgeon took over and soon the operation was complete. The loss of blood during the operation was very serious indeed, and Amos was given up for dead after extensive pounding on his chest by the attendants. This was the method used at that time to bring a patient's heart back to functioning. His wife, Mary, who had been standing by in the waiting room, was called into the operating room. She clasped her husband's hand and called him by name. His eyes flickered and he showed the first sign of life.

Two days later, when Dr. Patrick was dressing the wound, he had given the patient terrific pain. On being asked what is going on as he was pulling out yards of gauze bandage, the doctor said, "Amos, we had given up on you, and in haste we used anything available to take care of the blood, so I am taking care of that right now. This all has to come out. Sorry about the pain." Amos was black and blue across the chest and shoulders from the pounding to bring his heart back to work on what little blood there was left.

Teacher of Riversdale, Charles Durnin
Letter to H. Putland

On April 2nd, 1898 I arrived at Churchbridge station and a bewhiskered man came into the coach and asked, "Is the teacher for Riversdale School here?" I stood up and replied, "Present."

"Well," Mr. Piercy said. "Come with me, I have a fur coat for you." Mr. Piercy had come to meet his daughter who was a student at Birtle High school.

Although it was April 2nd, outdoors it looked like midwinter. It was 20 degrees below zero and the sleigh runners screeched like 40 degrees below. On our journey to the Amos Putland home, I saw a herd of horses out on the prairie pawing in the snow to get to the grass. I said to Mr. Piercy, "Someone has left his horses out last night." He replied, "Oh, these horses are out all winter." In Ontario where I was raised, horses were always in a nice warm stable in winter.

We arrived at the Putland home about 2 a.m. and Mr. Piercy said, "This is to be where you will stay." I knocked and Amos Putland opened the door and greeted me with me with, "Are you hungry?" I said, "No Sir." "Then I shall show you to your room." And lo and behold seven steps up and I was in my room and very soon asleep. Eleven o'clock the next morning we had breakfast and I met all the family. It was Sunday and, in the afternoon, Mr. Rowland, the secretary-treasurer of the school, came over to call on what he said was the new "Master."

The next morning, I went over to the school and we all started in to work and for the next five months and a week that I was there, we never took a holiday except Saturday and Sunday.

Seeding on the farm did not start until May 1st and soon Mr. Putland, who had a bad leg, began to suffer considerably. He would plough as long as he could, then put the team in the stable. When I got home after 4 o'clock, I would take the team out and plough for another three hours. Then sometimes in the morning, I would be up early and would take the team and wagon and two water barrels to the creek two or three miles west, fill the barrels with water and return home before breakfast. Soon, Mr. Putland got a hired man to do the work. At that time the ulcer on his leg was so bad he had to call the doctor. A woman with some medical training who was the teacher in a school a few miles west also came. Soon the rest and the formalin powder on the ulcer did the work and he was up again.

Reprinted with permission from Barbara-eldest daughter on behalf of the Henry Putland family, and Ruth Swanson editor of the First Hundred Years Around Churchbridge.

EPILOGUE

COVID-19 – the Global Pandemic

The year 2020 will go down in history as the year of the global pandemic – COVID-19.

As a senior living in my own home, I live a quiet life, but the winter of 2020 began quieter than usual with Lynn and Neville on a holiday in Australia and British Columbia from January 28 to March 10. I missed the Wednesday evening Scrabble games and Saturday shopping excursions with Lynn.

Canada had its first case of the COVID-19 virus in January, so Lynn and Neville took the precaution of wearing masks on the airplane for each leg of their trip. Though the number of cases of the virus in Canada, and the death toll, had risen sharply while they were away, particularly in Quebec and Ontario, Manitoba still did not have a confirmed case when they returned home. So they organized a "We're home!" family supper for Sunday, March 15, and I looked forward to life returning to normal.

Then the COVID dominoes began to fall. March 12 Manitoba reported its first case of the virus. The next day my last water exercise class before spring break was cancelled, as well as registrations for the spring and summer sessions. My housecleaner cancelled all visits till further notice. The nurse that cuts my toe nails cancelled all visits except emergencies. My appointment for a haircut was cancelled. I had tickets to fly to Saskatoon for a grandson's 40th birthday celebration. The party was cancelled.

More troubling, Kyle informed us on March 12 that Charity and Forrest were ill with cold-like symptoms. We wondered, "Could it be the virus?" Lynn and Neville had just spent 10 days with them in Coquitlam, B.C. after returning from Australia, as at that time those travelling from outside the country were not required to self-isolate. Now they debated if they should cancel their planned Sunday family supper. As neither they, nor any of the Winnipeg families, had any symptoms associated with the virus, and they were anxious to see the family after being away for seven weeks, they decided to go ahead as planned.

Forrest recovered from the suspected cold quickly. As Charity continued to feel ill she was tested for COVID-19 on March 18, receiving a presumptive positive diagnosis that day, requiring their family to immediately self-isolate. As soon as Lynn and Neville learned of Charity's positive test, they self-isolated for two weeks. It was a worrisome two weeks as Kyle also became ill, Charity's positive test result was confirmed on March 26, and Lynn and Neville wondered if they could have spread the virus at their family supper. All turned out well. Charity and Kyle were symptom-free after 17 days and Lynn and Neville did not get sick or infect anyone.

It was a good thing Lynn and Neville did decide to go ahead with their family gathering on March 15, as within days the Manitoba government asked everyone to restrict contact to their own household group, except for work or essential shopping such as groceries.

My household consisted of me, myself, and I. I could not go out, no one could come in. I felt like a marooned Robinson Crusoe. And then something weird happened to my psyche.

The day my housecleaner cancelled, the sheets on my bed were due to be changed, so I had to do the job myself, for the first time in five years. Then, for the next two weeks I never made my bed, not once, simply leaving the covers thrown back. It was completely out of character for me as I have always made my bed first thing in the morning – always! If I was pushed to the edge with a university essay due, I might let dishes pile up in the sink, but my bed was always made. Also, I normally keep all toiletries out of sight in a cupboard in the bathroom. Now I left toothbrush, toothpaste, denture cup, hairbrush, and mirror sitting on the vanity counter. And I did none of the cleaning my housecleaner wasn't here to do: no dusting, no sweeping, no vacuuming, no mopping.

However, I did maintain most of my usual routine. I still did leg and arm exercises every morning before breakfast. I still did my morning and afternoon 30 minute "gerbil walks" around and around in the house. I made meals and put the dishes in the dishwasher and did the laundry. I also continued my regular morning writing sessions.

At the end of two weeks, when I changed the sheets on my bed again, I admired my neatly made bed and realized I did not like looking at an unmade bed every day. That was the turning point. I snapped back into my regular self. My bed was made every morning. All my grooming aids were kept out of sight once more. I gave the house a thorough cleaning, admittingly awkward with my walker, but found it very satisfying to be doing it myself, without outside help. I still cannot explain those odd two weeks in limbo, but they did happen.

As the weeks of isolation stretched into months, I began to see a positive side to all this aloneness. I was getting more writing done than I had in months – the completion of my memoir was within sight. Also, it was almost five months since I had been in a store or a restaurant and my credit card bills for those months were negligible. I was finding when household or clothing items I thought I needed sat on a list for months, they no longer seemed so necessary.

I considered myself a careful grocery shopper, not prone to impulse purchases. However, after months with a family member getting my groceries from a list I emailed, I realized my monthly grocery bills were also lower. I now recognize I often picked up items not on my list: luscious looking strawberries or raspberries on sale, a package of crisp peapods as I walked by them, an extra red pepper, a cluster of vine-ripened tomatoes when I only needed one, and so on. I am too thrifty to let food go to waste, so extras that were getting past their "best before" date ended up in the freezer. Now I am working on getting rid of the backlog in the freezer – no potatoes go on a list till I eat all the servings of frozen mashed! I don't know when I will feel comfortable going into a grocery store again, but when I do, I will be a more aware shopper.

Boredom was never a problem despite all the alone time. There was always something to do: writing, reading, crosswords, cooking, and cleaning—but I missed the family. Our online family channel, where we could all send and view messages and videos, as well as our FaceTime phone calls, helped me feel connected. Outside of family, the two things I found the most difficult to live without were the twice weekly water exercise classes and getting a haircut every five weeks.

When the snow finally melted and the streets dried, it was wonderful to be able to do my daily walks outside, instead of in the house. However, as I use a walker, I felt restricted to walking on our bay as I cannot keep two metres from others on the sidewalk. I would have to depend on folks I met stepping off onto the grass to keep a two-metre physical distance between us.

Manitoba is one of three provinces in the country with the lowest number of per capita cases of the virus and resulting deaths, and as I write this, near the end of June, we are in Phase 3 of a gradual relaxing of restrictions. Retail businesses and restaurants no longer have occupancy limits, provided they can ensure physical distancing. Restrictions have been eased for child care, day camps, golf courses, and some inter-provincial travel. While outdoor pools are being allowed to open, indoor ones remain closed, so there will be no water exercise classes this summer, if not longer. However, after 14 weeks, it was a relief to get rid of my sheepdog look with a haircut, though it was a strange experience with everyone required to wear a mask.

And finally, family life is gradually returning to normal. By mid-May, our "bubble" was expanded from a single household to all our immediate family. On Mother's Day the family picked up barbecued ribs, fries, and coleslaw for supper at my house. Since then, there have been two family gatherings at Lynn and Neville's. I have enjoyed my first "dining out" experience in months–a relaxing meal with Lloyd and Karen under the trees on a restaurant patio, with tables spaced far enough apart to maintain the required physical distancing.

Our family has suffered less than many from the virus. No one has lost their job and no one's business is on the verge of economic collapse, two personal financial stresses faced by thousands in the country. As it was soon obvious that existing social supports could not prevent personal tragedy nor a country-wide economic collapse, the federal and provincial governments have rolled out billions in financial aid. However, these various programs do not cover everyone, and they will eventually have to end. There has been discussion in the media of the need for revamping unemployment insurance or instituting a national guaranteed basic income to replace all existing social aid programs. This would eliminate the need for a host of special support programs in the event of another pandemic.

The future is uncertain. How long will it take the economy to recover? Will it ever fully recover? Has our behaviour been permanently changed, and if so, how? Will shopping online continue to increase, replacing the need for many retail buildings? Will those now working from home decide to continue the practice, reducing required office space. Will we ever book flights to other countries, or holiday on cruise ships, as frequently as we once did? Will we ever again feel comfortable in crowded sports arenas or music concert venues – cheering, yelling, or singing?

Will life ever return to normal, or will there be a new normal? Will we measure time as "before COVID-19" and "after COVID-19?" Probably, till the next global event.

THE OBAMAS AND ME

I am sure Barack and Michelle Obama would be dismayed if they knew how much trouble they caused me as I was deciding on a title for my book.

After I wrote the piece "Yes I Can," I told granddaughter Marlo, I was going to call my book *Yes I Can* as I felt it really symbolized the way I have lived my life. "But Grandma," Marlo said, "that is almost exactly like Barack Obama's election slogan, *Yes we can*."

"Okay," I thought, "that's out." So, I decided on *Becoming Me* as a title, made a folder with that heading, and dropped notes into it as thoughts occurred to me. The first draft of the piece "Osteomyelitis and Me" was titled "Becoming Me." When Michelle Obama's memoir *Becoming* was published, I almost choked!

When I bewailed being foiled a second time by an Obama, Marlo said, "Well Grandma, it's a long time since Barack Obama was campaigning. I think you can go back to using *Yes I Can*." Just in case, I decided to check Google to see if Barack had written a book with that title, and he had – *Yes We Can – a Salute to Children*.

I flailed around for months trying to come up with a meaningful title. Then one day I came across the quote that now appears at the end of "Osteomyelitis and Me" and I had my title! Indeed, looking back on my long life *I Smile Because It Happened*.

ACKNOWLEDGEMENTS

My everlasting gratitude to Diane Kristjansson whose classes on "Writing Your Memoir" rekindled my determination to do just that, and who read and gave perceptive feedback on early versions of several pieces in this book. And thank you to the members of our writing group that evolved from those classes – Anne Marie, Henry, Herbert (who we mourn), Libby, Lil' Jean, Lillian, and Norma – for your constructive insights and the lively discussions at our monthly meetings.

Thank you to the family members who read and responded to first drafts of some of these pieces. Your comments and reactions were invaluable. Sometimes you found inconsistencies: "Grandpa wouldn't have said it like that." But when you said a piece moved you to laughter or tears, I knew I was on the right track.

There are several people whose work contributed to this book in some way:

- Uncle Henry, whose tales about his father are reprinted in the Appendix
- my sister, Leila, whose genealogy research was the foundation on which I built the pieces, "Our Fraser Ancestral Roots" and "The Two Uncle Bobs"
- Carolyn Moore, who posted Leila's request for information about Uncle Bob on her Discover Atlin Facebook page, all the folks in Atlin who so generously shared their memories of our uncle, and especially, John Nesgaard, who replied with a two-page letter, and Terry Milos, who shared a chapter on Uncle Bob that would appear in her memoir, *North of Familiar: A Woman's Story of Homesteading and Adventure in the Canadian Wilderness*, Caitlin Press, 2017

- my son-in-law, Neville, who provided historical information and perspective for the piece on South Africa.

My daughter Lynn repeatedly bailed me out of the morass of computer confusion and did the initial page layout for the book. My Granddaughter Marlo contributed to the cover design. A loving "thank you" to both of you.

A bucket, a barrel of thanks to my editor, Barb Farwell, who walked with me every step of this 9-year journey. Your thoughtful response to each piece as it was written has made this a better book, and me a better writer.

My appreciation to the folks at Friesen Press for their manuscript evaluation, technical support, and copy editing as they made my dream a reality.

Lastly, a heartfelt thank you to all the family and friends who have been a part of my life, past and present. Without you, there would be no story.

ABOUT THE AUTHOR

Margaret Jean (Putland) Baptist, Jean to family, was born and raised on a farm in Saskatchewan during the depression of the 1930s and the years of the Second World War.

Contracting osteomyelitis at the age of eight was a life-threatening event that she survived to live a long and fulfilling life.

Now 88 years young, she continues to live independently in her own home in Winnipeg.

CPSIA information can be obtained
at www.ICGtesting.com
Printed in the USA
BVHW090514271221
624439BV00003B/3